A STEVE LANSFORD LEGAL THRILLER

THE COURT FOR LAST CHANCES

TEE FERGUSON

Yellow Leaf Publishing

ISBN: 979-8994774304

Produced by Publish Pros | publishpros.com

This is a work of fiction. Names, characters, businesses, places, events and incidents are either the products of the author's imagination or used in a fictitious manner. Any resemblance to actual persons, living or dead, or actual events is purely coincidental.

For Mom

Thank you for your lifetime of love and support.
You were the greatest mom,
and I have always tried to be a parent like you.
Thanks for everything.
While I know that you were always proud of me,
I still wish you could have read this.

My love always.
Tee

STEVE

CHAPTER 1

Steve Lansford sat in the chair awaiting his fate. Steve was a young, third-year law student from the University of Connecticut on the cusp of his graduation. As he sat in the semi-comfortable leather chair in the fancy waiting room of Rockingham & Myers, Attorneys and Counselors of Law—the most prestigious law firm in all of New England—Steve reflected on his years of hard work.

He was a business major in college. While Steve loved the study of law, he loved business more. He relished business concepts and dreamed of doing mergers and acquisitions for Fortune 500 companies across America. He wanted to find small corporations and take them public. Rockingham & Myers was the largest firm on the East Coast that specialized in mergers and acquisitions. Steve had targeted this firm since he was a freshman in high school. Being a senior partner of Rockingham & Myers would put his finger on the pulse of the business world.

He did it right. Steve studied hard as an undergraduate at Penn State University. He got straight A's, and he graduated with honors. Instead of going to frat parties and getting poor grades for a full semester, so that he could pass the initiation into a frat, he chose to do community service. He spent at least ten hours a week working with underprivileged children with his church group. Steve worked two jobs for part of the summer so he could spend several weeks working with Habitat for Humanity and build homes for the poor in Los Angeles, all at his expense.

Steve dated casually in college and law school but refused to get serious with anyone. His priority was to be in this position at this moment. He chose the University of Connecticut's law school because his college advisor told him he would be the "big fish in the little pond." If he went to one of the Ivy League schools, he would have difficulty standing out amongst all the other brilliant minds. Instead, he decided to go to a good law school where he was editor of the law journal, Moot Court champion, Mock Trial champion, and class valedictorian. Very few people had one of these accomplishments, let alone having all of them.

While at law school, Steve spent his summers as an intern for Rockingham & Myers. He was a workhorse, spending sixteen to twenty hours a day, at least six days a week, cranking out billable hours for the firm. During his second summer, his legal skills and knowledge clicked with his job. Steve handled all the paperwork, pleadings, and motions for his boss, Frank "Big Frank" Rockingham, the senior partner. Big Frank loved him. This job, he thought, was a sure thing.

The interview process was grueling. It began with what his classmates call "speed dating." First, you signed up for a series of ten-minute interviews with recruiters from several law firms. Speed dating happened at a large hotel in downtown Hartford. Some students had only a few dates with different law firms. Steve and a few others had a speed date with every firm, putting them there all day.

After speed dating, a few of the speed daters were called back to the firm for second interviews. A dater would interview with four or five partners and then have lunch with two or three other partners. This process lasted at least half a day. If daters were called back for a third time, it was usually to receive an offer and be welcomed aboard.

Steve Lansford had completed all the groundwork. He was now waiting to meet with the partners for his coveted third interview, which should be a job offer. Steve knew that the hours would be brutal, and he would probably work seven days a week. He also knew that first-year associates made a six-figure salary and were given a company car—usually a low-end Mercedes or BMW. Fancy, but not overly expensive.

On the other side of the room was his friend David. Steve knew David from speed dating. They were among the coveted few who had interviews with every single recruiter. David was from a wealthy family in Greenwich. His father was the CEO of a small computer software company in the process of absorbing other small software companies. David was both a party boy and a frat boy; while he did have good grades and went to an Ivy League law school, he spent the majority of his time socializing with his fellow Ivy Leaguers instead of trying to distinguish himself from his peers.

David acknowledged Steve's presence with a head bob and a, "S'up." Steve walked over and congratulated David on his accomplishment of attaining the infamous third callback. David thanked him, and they both began to grin that giddy grin, the one that starts when you know that something great is about to happen and you can't wait. They were like children on Christmas Eve, knowing that soon they would be showered with gifts they had wanted all year long. This was possibly the greatest feeling in the world, and they sat in the leather chairs, taking in every minute.

Magda, the receptionist, walked over to them both and said, "The partners will see you now. Please follow me."

"Which one of us is going first?" asked Steve.

"The partners are going to see *both* of you now," explained Magda.

What the hell is this? Steve thought. Why are we going together?

Steve, David, and Magda walked through the large, frosted glass doors that separated the lobby from the offices. They walked down the corridor that divided a sea of office cubicles, filled with junior partners, paralegals, and legal secretaries. They continued down the corridors and past the partners' offices. The partners' offices were aligned by seniority; the farther you walked down the hall, the more senior a partner you were and the nicer your office was.

At the end of the corridor was the Senior Partner Conference Room. Magda held open one of the glass double doors. David and Steve walked in and stopped to take in the room's magnitude. While Steve had worked at Rockingham for two summers, he had never been in this room. The rear wall of the conference room was lined with law journals and fancy bound books; these were standard in every lawyer's conference room. The irony was that nobody uses books anymore, as all this information was now online. The purpose of the library was to impress clients who didn't know that the books were for show. The remaining three walls were adorned with various awards and pictures of partners greeting and shaking hands with presidents of the United States, as well as other famous politicians and international figures. Most of all, Steve was impressed with pictures of the partners meeting with CEOs and CFOs of many Fortune 500 corporations. The walls also featured personal letters of gratitude written by the likes of Lee Iacocca, Thomas Edison, Henry Ford, Steve Jobs, Bill Gates, and Mark Zuckerberg.

"Are you humbled?" asked Big Frank to Steve and David, snapping them out of their daze.

"This room is amazing," said David. "It's impressive to see how many corporations and political figures this firm has influenced."

"That's the idea. Nobody can help but come into this room and be humbled by its presence. When you see that this firm has influenced the political, legal, and economic realms of this country for many generations, you can't help but feel as if you are in the presence of greatness," said Big Frank. "This room gives us a home-field advantage. Every deposition I take and every settlement conference I have with opposing counsel takes place in this room. This room has helped me resolve a lot of cases in my client's favor."

Steve and David were escorted to the conference table. On one side sat the four most senior partners: Big Frank Rockingham; Don

Myers, son of Fred Myers, the founding partner; James Fracaccio; and Audrey Lodge, daughter of Fred Myers.

Big Frank cleared his throat and started the meeting. "Okay. We all know each other here. We met during the second interview, or in Steve's case, we know you from your summer internship. This is the third interview for each of you. The two of you are our two final candidates for the two positions we are trying to fill. None of us were math majors, but we can all do the math… both of you will be offered positions with the firm."

Steve and David looked at each other with giddy grins and shook each other's hands. They then gave their undivided attention back to the partners.

Big Frank continued. "Let's start with you, David. We are offering you the position of first-year associate. You will work directly with Attorney Lodge. As you know, Attorney Lodge does mergers and acquisitions for our computer technology clients. Your salary as a first-year associate will be $260,000 per year. You will begin work after you take the bar exam in August. Enclosed in your employment package is a bonus of $20,000 for you to live on while you study this summer for the August bar exam. Are you going to accept this position today?"

"Of course," stated David. David stood up and shook the hands of all four partners. "Thank you for this opportunity."

Attorney Lodge stood and said, "David, you are going to be a great addition to our firm, and I look forward to showing you the ropes."

Big Frank said, "Attorney Lodge is going to show you around her office and introduce you to your new team. Here's your employment package, which includes your choice of health insurance and explains the structured raise increase schedule. Attorney Lodge will review the process of ordering your company car." Big Frank handed David the large envelope that held his benefits. "Congratulations again, David. Welcome to the firm."

David and Attorney Lodge left the room. Steve watched them leave. Steve then turned his attention back to the Big Frank and the remaining partners. Steve attempted to maintain his composure, but a large smile kept shining through his serious posture.

Big Frank continued. "Steve… I've known you for two summers, and we have worked closely together. You are going to be a phenomenal attorney, and you will make a great addition to our firm. There is no doubt in my mind that you will be successful no matter what you do. Unfortunately, we are not able to offer you a first-year associate position at this time."

Steve's heart sank into his stomach. He knew that he had to keep his composure under all this pressure and fight off the desire to let his anger speak for him. Steve took a deep breath and asked, "Why am I here?"

Big Frank explained. "We know that you have received every possible honor at your law school. You have a junior partner's understanding of the law, and you produced more billable hours than our other associates during each summer you were here. We don't want to lose you, but we can't offer you a first-year associate position. Instead, we have created a position just for you. We are offering you the position of contract associate attorney, where you will work in our habeas corpus division."

"You want me to be a criminal lawyer?" questioned Steve. "I have no idea what any of this is about. What is a contract associate?"

James Fracaccio and Don Myers stood up. Attorney Myers said, "Steve, I know you are surprised, and this is not what you are expecting. Why don't you and Frank go downstairs and talk about it over lunch? He can give you all the details. Maybe you can meet the habeas team. I hope you choose to take our offer… but if you don't, I understand and wish you nothing but the best." Steve shook the partners' hands as they left the room.

Steve looked back at Big Frank when they were alone in the conference room. Big Frank stood up and said, "Follow me, kid. I don't think you need lunch. I think you need a drink."

CHAPTER 2

Big Frank avoided taking Steve to Marty's, the restaurant and bar located in the same building as the firm. He knew that Audrey would be taking David to lunch at Marty's because that is where every partner takes their new servant. The third callback is the beginning of what Big Frank called the "brainwashing technique." First, you overwhelm the starving law student with a large salary. Then, you hit them with the bonus paid to study for the bar. Next, you introduce them to the team of other lawyers and paralegals they will be working with, so they get excited about the job. Finally, you close the sale with a lunch solely between the senior partner and the new associate; the partner assures the associate that they will guide them through their journey from newly licensed lawyer to seasoned attorney. The sale is completed when the associate orders their new custom car, which will be waiting for them on their first day of work after taking the bar.

The reality was that being an associate in a large firm is like working in a sweatshop. The hours are long, and the odds are good that new associates will work seven days a week. Any relationship that a new associate has with a spouse or significant other will be strained. Marriages will end in divorce, couples will spit-up, and children will hardly know their parent. Family members get used to not seeing that particular relative on holidays, and eventually they become like that cousin you only see at funerals.

Drinking tends to be the favorite pastime of partners in the firm, and Big Frank is no exception. Big Frank has four ex-wives, three of whom still receive alimony. Big Frank, however, does have a relationship with his son, Little Frank. Although Big Frank was hardly around for Little Frank's teenage years, he built a closer relationship with his son when he hired him as an associate and eventually made him a junior partner.

Big Frank walked Steve a few blocks away to The Gas Chamber, a small, hole-in-the-wall bar frequented by low-end attorneys and court employees. This was Big Frank's favorite watering hole because the drinks were cheap, and none of his clients, partners, or associates knew of this place.

"Well, congratulations," said Big Frank. "You are the first person to not fall for the whole 'humbling conference room bit.' I have seen seasoned attorneys fall apart and give me everything I want in that room because they feel intimidated. But you, well, you just have that look in your eye that says, 'Why are you screwing me?' I knew you were tough, but I thought you would agree to anything in that room. I was wrong."

"What happened? Why did you give David the position I wanted?" Steve asked. "More to the point, why did you give David the position that I earned?"

"Well, kid, like most things… it comes down to money. I get it. You worked your tail off. You achieved great success in school. You proved that you are going to be a great lawyer. You showed that you will generate all the billable hours we ask you to bill. We both know that David does not perform like you. We have no idea what kind of lawyer David will become. What we do know is that David brings money into this firm. David's father will give us all of his merger and acquisition work for his company, and he'll also bring along work from other software and IT firms on the East Coast. By hiring David, this firm has assured itself of millions of dollars of work for the foreseeable future. As long as David continues to bring in millions of dollars in work to this law firm, he will be on the fast track to make partner."

Steve was speechless. He understood the need for firms to continue to generate business, but he still felt that his hard work should amount to something more. "So what is my offer?"

"You've met Don and Audrey Myers. They are the children of my original partner, Fred Myers. They have a brother named Sam. Sam is also a partner in the firm. Don and Audrey embraced the firm; they are involved in the community and are social butterflies in elite circles. Like David, they bring money into the firm. Sam, on the other hand, is more of a loner. He never fell in love with the family business, but he chose to go to law school and become an attorney anyway. Sam's father hired him as a lawyer for the firm, where he worked as an associate for most of the partners. He was not a great lawyer, but he was not a bad one either. Sam's problem was that he had a wife and chose his marriage over work. This did not go well with the other partners, but Sam knew that his father would never fire him. Sam's wife died of cancer about ten years ago. Sam was devastated, and his work suffered. Sam's dad didn't want to fire him, but he did not want to keep taking the heat from all the partners, including his son and daughter, for keeping his slacker son at the firm. Fred and I came here to The Gas Chamber to drink and solve the problem.

"We decided to open a satellite office on the other side of town that Sam would run. I had connections with the governor's office and the public defender. With a few phone calls, we picked up some contract work."

"With all the work the firm already has, why did you need a state contract?" Steve asked.

"We got the contract for Sam because we wanted him to do something that he couldn't screw-up," Big Frank said. "What do you know about habeas cases?"

"Nothing. It is a passing area of criminal law, which I briefly studied, preparing for the bar exam. I spent most of my career in civil litigation."

Big Frank explained. "A habeas case is a prisoner's last chance to get his conviction overturned. Most lawyers will hate you because you are claiming they screwed up when they tried the prisoner's case. In the end, nobody likes you, including your client, because you will lose between 99% and 100% of your cases."

"What does this have to do with Sam?"

"Well, we needed work for Sam that he couldn't mess up. So, we got a government contract to represent incarcerated inmates on their habeas matters. The firm owns a few buildings on the other side of town, and we gave Sam an office. We call it our satellite office, but we don't put it on the letterhead, nor do we advertise it. This is not the kind of work that we want our other clients to know about. The contract covers the cost of Sam's salary and the overhead for his satellite office. Occasionally, Sam even makes a positive cash flow from the contract, which gets distributed to the partners. Sam works with almost no supervision from the managing partners."

"Why do you need me?"

"Over the past few years, Sam has started to slip. Deadlines are being missed. Clients are complaining. I've received a few phone calls from the governor, registering his concern. In a nutshell, Sam's office is now a rat's nest. We need someone to go in and wade through the mess and get the office back on track."

"What does Sam say about this?"

"Not much. He says he can use a hand as things are piling up, but at the same time, he doesn't seem all that concerned either. I think he lacks focus."

"And you want me to walk in and straighten out this mess?"

"Exactly."

"So, tell me about the contract."

"Well… your contract is for a year. The contract may be renewed by the firm. You will make $60,000 a year. You will get medical and dental insurance during the contract period. You will not get a company car, but you will get paid for your mileage to and from court. You will have your own office in the satellite office. You will share a secretary and paralegal with Sam. You will answer to Sam, but that doesn't matter because Sam probably won't care what you do and will act more as an advisor and mentor than as a boss. You will answer to me and give me a weekly report as to the problems that exist and the steps you are taking to rectify these problems. So kid… whaddya say?"

"Well… on the one hand, I have several offers from firms all over New England. All of these offers include salaries and perks comparable to David's. I have not responded, as this firm was my first choice. On the other hand, you are offering me a job that I have no interest in for a salary that sucks and absolutely no perks, other than medical and dental. Why would I possibly take your offer?"

"Because I'm Willy Wonka."

"Yeah… I'm going to need a ruling on that. What exactly does that mean?"

"It means that I have the golden ticket. You and I both know that you want to work in business law. You want to do mergers and acquisitions. You want to take some small companies public. As Gordon Gecko would say, 'You want to be a player.' You want to be one of the people making the deals."

"Right. That's not a secret."

"Well… I can make that happen for you. You and I know the extent of this firm's influence in the business, legal, and political worlds. I can make a phone call right now and get you a chief financial officer position at a Fortune 500 company without even having an interview. I can get you an associate or junior partnership job with any major law firm in America. I can get you a six-figure government job, even during a major financial crisis, hiring freeze, or government shutdown. I have that much influence because this firm has been the dominant law firm in business for several decades. When I give advice, people listen, and people take my advice. No one questions my authority or my expertise. So here's what I'm saying. I know that this habeas situation is about to become a serious mess, and the firm would be embarrassed if we were fired from this contract. If you clean up this mess and right the ship, then the firm will be very grateful. I hope we will be in a position to offer you an associate's job here at the firm next year. But, either way, after you complete this contract, if you are offered a job, or if you are not offered a job with this firm, I will make a phone call on your behalf and get you one of these jobs, if that is your wish. Which of your offers have that as a perk?"

"None."

"That's what I thought. Let's go, kid. Roll the dice, and move your mice. What do you want to do? I'll give you the time it takes to finish your beer to give me an answer."

Steve simmered. There was nothing he hated more than being forced to make a snap decision. He was a half a glass away from making a decision that would have a major impact on his life. He was silent as Big Frank sat next to him, staring out the window, waiting to close the deal. Big Frank had closed hundreds, if not thousands, of deals; he knew when to stop selling and let the buyer put all the pieces together on his own and come to the same conclusion Big Frank had suggested an hour earlier.

Steve saw the writing on the wall. He could make more money at another firm and keep his dignity, but he would not have the opportunities that Big Frank was offering. Nobody could offer these opportunities except Big Frank. There was no way around it. He had to accept the offer, clean up the mess, and rely on Big Frank to keep his word.

Steve drank the last of his beer in one swallow, looked Big Frank in the eye, and said, "You got a deal."

Big Frank let out one of his huge belly laughs that sounded like an old man trying to clear his throat. Big Frank shook his hand and said, "Fucking kid's gonna help us out. Thank you. The bar exam is at the beginning of August this year. Take the exam. Take a week off and review the law for habeas cases. Then report to me on August 10. I'll drive you over to the satellite office and get you set up. And I'll introduce you to Sam. Here's your contract and benefit package."

Steve and Big Frank stood up. Big Frank handed Steve his benefit envelope. They walked out of The Gas Chamber and said their goodbyes. Steve was parked a few blocks away next to the park. He had a few minutes left on the parking meter, so Steve sat down on a park bench and took stock of what had happened over the past few hours.

He went over the past seven years of his life. What did he do wrong? What could he have done to put himself in an even better position? It seemed unfair that David was able to use his father's business to essentially guarantee a full partnership in a law firm without having to put in the same amount of hard work as Steve. And he wondered: could he trust Big Frank to keep his word?

It was clear that one of two things happened today: he either made the best decision for his career or the worst. Only time would tell.

CHAPTER 3

A month had passed since Steve's third callback at Rockingham & Myers. Steve finished his final exams and officially graduated first in his class at law school. Still, he skipped the graduation ceremony. Everyone knew that you don't receive your diploma at the graduation ceremony, only a diploma holder; the real diploma is mailed to you six months later.

Graduation ceremonies were for the families, not the graduates. Steve's remaining family was his dog, Buddy. Steve's dad left when he was an infant. He ended up dying five years ago from a massive heart attack, but his body wasn't found in his trailer for several weeks after his death. Steve's mom passed away when Steve was in his second year of college at Penn State. She was in a nursing home with dementia for six months prior to her death, before she died of heart failure. Steve inherited the house and a few dollars from his mom's savings and checking accounts. He sold her home and used the money to pay for college and law school. Steve was one the few people to walk out of law school with a law degree and no debt.

His apartment was not expensive. It fulfilled Steve's major requirements: cheap, clean, and near the firm and school. It was a five-minute walk to school and a five-minute drive to the firm, but it was now a fifteen-minute drive across town to the satellite office. Steve had few tangible objects. He used his money sparingly. He didn't date much, so he didn't spend much money on women or going out. The one-bedroom apartment was decorated with a desk, a computer, a couch, a coffee table that doubled as a dining table, a television, a mattress on the floor, and a few lamps. He did not entertain much, nor did he have friends drop by. There were no pictures in the apartment. The walls were decorated with books stacked against them, the spines facing outward so he could easily read the title of the law book he needed.

The kitchen was not used much because Steve wasn't much of a cook. His cooking consisted of frozen pizza, toast, cereal, peanut butter sandwiches, and whatever restaurants delivered in his neighborhood and sent coupons in the mail. He didn't waste his time on cooking or doing dishes, as this took time away from his studies and goals. Fitness was important to him, and Steve spent time every day at the school's gym staying in shape. While he was not a fan of physical fitness, he believed law firms preferred to hire attorneys who appeared to be physically fit.

Buddy was grateful that he got to spend a lot of time with Steve over the past few weeks. When school ended, days after the third interview, Steve regimented himself to studying for the bar exam sixteen hours a day, seven days a week. Buddy would spend his days lying in Steve's lap as Steve reviewed subject outlines and practiced taking old bar exams. Steve was now scoring well above the score needed to pass the exam.

Steve decided to change gears. This was early June, and the bar exam wasn't until the beginning of August. He was ahead of schedule, so he decided he could get started on learning about his new job. He asked Buddy, "How do I go about this? How do I learn this small niche area of law that very few people practice? I can learn the law by reading the statutes and court decisions. But law is more than what you read about in books."

Buddy gave him a puzzled look but never gave him an answer. Instead, Buddy rolled over on his back, requesting his hourly belly rub. Steve began his ritual of rubbing Buddy's stomach as he thought about who could give him advice on habeas and criminal law.

Professor Kent, he thought, was a step in the right direction. An appellate attorney, Kent knew and understood criminal law better than anyone. But he had never actually tried a case, negotiated a plea bargain, or picked a jury. Still, Steve decided, Kent could give the overall view of habeas law and recommend some books.

Steve grabbed his backpack and Buddy and went out the door. Buddy wagged his tail profusely because he knew that he was going to Mom's house. Mom was actually a 24-year-old neighbor of Steve's named Jenny. She was home most of the time because she worked out of her apartment doing medical billing for her own business. She loved having Buddy visit her during the day because he kept her company. Buddy would spend his days getting pampered by his mom and eating an assortment of snacks she would feed him.

Jenny was attracted to Steve. Not only was he a handsome and kind young man, he could also be very funny and outgoing, if you were able to pull him away from his studies. Jenny didn't leave her apartment much, except to buy groceries or go to the gym. That meant her only choice of available bachelors was from the building: Steve and two older men in their seventies who shared an apartment. As far as Jenny was concerned, Steve was the proverbial last man on earth.

Jenny was a tall and slender brunette. She was quite an athlete as a child and eventually settled on lacrosse as her sport of choice in high school. Jenny earned a scholarship to the University of Connecticut, but during her senior year, she got a career-ending injury when she tripped over another player and landed on her shoulder. She had surgery and six months of physical therapy. Her physical therapist told Jenny about the growing demand in the field of medical billing and volunteered to give Jenny all the medical billing from her office and all of her fellow therapists. It was an offer Jenny couldn't refuse. And shortly after completing her therapy, she was up to her eyeballs in medical billing work.

Steve walked down to the apartment at the end of the hall and knocked on the door. Jenny answered the door with a smile. "Hey, guys. What are you up to?"

Buddy yipped and began to wave his paw at her, his usual habit when he was excited.

"Hi, Jenny", said Steve. "I need to talk to a professor on campus. Any chance you could babysit Buddy for a couple of hours? As you can see, he misses his Mommy."

Jennifer smiled and gladly accepted. "When are you gonna come by and pick him up? If you want, I can order a pizza and we can chat... just the three of us."

Steve thought for a minute. Jenny is awesome, but she could easily distract him from his studies. On the other hand, his dream job was recently put on hold, and he was already passing the bar. Also, Buddy loved her, and he was a good judge of character. "Sounds good he said, but I can pick up a pizza from Sergio's on the way back. My treat. It's the least I can do for you seeing as how you've been the responsible parent to Buddy the past year."

"It's a date."

CHAPTER 4

Steve cautiously knocked on the door of Professor Kent's office. During his first year, Steve went to visit one of his professors during office hours and spent forty-five minutes hearing how rude it was to knock on someone's door. This professor was having a major epiphany and lost his train of thought when Steve knocked on his door. Apparently, nobody told this professor that students have a right to knock on doors and ask questions during office hours, as students are the major source of money that pays their salary. Nevertheless, as a precaution, Steve got in the habit of delicately knocking on a professor's door and waiting for a response.

"Come in," said Professor Kent. Professor Kent was a true scholar of the law. He read every Supreme Court decision on every subject of criminal law in the state of Connecticut and the federal system. Kent could tell you the volume, year, and page number of almost any case he had read.

He had worked his way through college and law school as a law librarian. After law school, he clerked in the Connecticut Supreme Court. He was then offered a position as a professor of law, where he would study and research to his heart's content. As part of his professorship, Kent ran the appellate clinic, where he helped third-year students work on real appeals in court.

"Steve, good to see you. What brings you by?"

"Well… how much time do you have?" replied Steve. Steve explained what happened at the third interview and how he had accepted a position as a habeas attorney.

Professor Kent stared at Steve in disbelief. "It's just such an unusual turn of events. I can understand if you didn't get the job. I can also understand if they offered you a position in the business law section of the firm, but in a lesser role than you applied for. But applying for a junior associate position in the business law section and being offered a smaller position in what is essentially a small area of criminal law is just bizarre." He paused, then added, "Well, what can I do to help?"

"I want to hit the ground running. I need to learn everything about habeas law, both the law and the reality of practicing it."

"I can refer you to some great books on the subject. I can send you a list of cases that have defined this area of law. As for what really happens in the world of habeas law, I can't tell you from experience. As you know, I have never tried a case. What I can do is tell you what habeas attorneys tell me."

"Do you know someone who does this?"

"Yup. My former brother-in-law, Abraham, was a habeas attorney for about ten years. I would see him at family functions, and he would bore the shit out of me for an hour or two, telling me how his life sucked because he hated being a habeas attorney. Eventually, he divorced my sister and became a real estate agent."

"What was his experience like?"

"The good thing about being a habeas attorney is that you get a lot of trial experience. Abe started habeas work right out of law school and had never done a trial. Ten years later, when he left, he had easily more than 200 trials. A lot of beginning lawyers start in this field and then move on to other things, once they get enough trial experience."

"Doesn't sound bad."

"The problem with habeas law is that you represent a convicted criminal. You are blaming their previous attorney for butchering their original trial. At the trial, you have to call the former attorney as a witness in your case and have him explain why he screwed up the case. While the court almost always finds that the attorney was competent and didn't make a mistake, the original trial attorney hates you for bringing the claim."

"But isn't that a part of practicing criminal law, knowing that this claim will be made if your client gets convicted?"

"Absolutely. It's the *practice* of law, not the perfection of law. Lawyers are like anyone else; they can make mistakes. However, a lawyer hates to go to court to have to explain the decisions they made in defending their case. Lawyers will rarely cooperate with you. They will not give you a copy of your client's file. They will try to avoid being called to the stand. I've even heard of them threatening their former clients not to call them to testify. Lawyers are not paid to testify in these cases, so they are losing money while being scrutinized and criticized about their actions. And here's the best part: if you lose the habeas case, the prisoner can file another habeas saying you did a lousy job as his habeas attorney. Then you get called into court and explain what you did on the habeas case. Some prisoners have filed seven and eight petitions."

"I guess I understand why Abe hated it," Steve said.

"In general, it's tough being a lawyer. Society doesn't like us too much. Everyone thinks you're a millionaire, yet the pay is usually not that great, considering the commitment. You hear from distant friends and relatives when they want free legal advice," said Professor Kent. "When you're a criminal lawyer, society likes you less. The state attorneys are the good guys; they represent all things good. They represent the people. The public defender represents murderers, rapists, and child molesters. The question a defense lawyer always hears is, 'How can you defend someone who you know is guilty?' The judicial system only works if both the defendant and the state are represented by attorneys, but a lot of people don't understand that. Some think that defendants should not be represented. Top that with the fact that only one in several thousand habeas petitions is ever granted each year, which means you lose all the time. Abe never won a case in his entire career. Aside from that, your client usually hates you because he thinks you were so incompetent that you lost his case."

"Well… that sounds pretty grim. Why would anyone want to do this?"

"Did you ever wonder why anyone wants to be a proctologist? It's the study of asses, crap, and intestines. As the joke goes… you start at the bottom, and you stay there. Some people pick proctology because they are fascinated by the study of germs; after all, they're studying the spot where most germs live in the human body. Likewise, I believe that in order to survive practicing as a habeas attorney, you need to appreciate the study of criminal law. You also need to avoid looking at the practice in terms of wins and losses but instead focus on doing your best to zealously advocate for your client, no matter the circumstances."

"I don't get that at all. In law school, we were taught that winning is what makes the client happy. So, winning is not just anything; it's the only thing. What are you trying to say?"

"What I'm saying is that you should strive to win every case. That's what your client wants. But, if you measure success as a habeas attorney—or really as any kind of attorney— by the number of cases you win, then you will always be depressed. A successful lawyer is one who represents his client as best as he can, regardless of the circumstances. It doesn't take a lot of guts or skill to fight a battle that you can easily win. It does take a lot of character, skill, and strength to fight a battle to the best of your ability, all while knowing you will most likely lose."

Steve sat quietly for a minute, trying to absorb all the professor had said. Finally, he stood.

"Thank you, Professor Kent. I really appreciate this talk. I need to wrap my head around all this. Can I follow up with you later with questions that I may have?"

"Absolutely. Even if you have no questions, you can always come over here and chat. It's important to keep your spirits up. Especially in this line of work."

CHAPTER 5

Thoughts ran through Steve's head. Was this a date, or was it not a date? Is Jenny interested in me, or are we just friends? Do I bring flowers? Or is that too much of a romantic gesture, and she'll think I am taking this way too seriously? Do I want to start a romantic relationship at this time in my life? Shouldn't I focus on my career? What's the point of focusing on your career when you are spending at least a year pulling this coveted career out of the crapper? Maybe this is the perfect time to start a relationship because I am not going to be spending the coming year working seven days a week… or am I? Then, he came to a resolution. He liked Jenny. He decided to take things one step at a time and see how it goes.

Steve ordered a pepperoni pizza from Sergio's. He did not know what kind of pizza Jenny liked; he figured pepperoni was a safe bet because you could always pick off the pepperoni if you wanted just cheese pizza.

Sergio's is a small pizzeria in Hartford, known for its romantic atmosphere and great food. Steve usually ordered take-out or delivery at least once a week and had become friends with Sergio.

"Mr. Lansford… what you doing getting a pepperoni pizza?" Sergio asked in a heavy Italian accent. "You usually get the special with all the meat. Are you a vegetarian now? What's wrong?"

"I have a date," Steve explained.

"You have a date? Really?" Sergio was shocked. "It's about time," he added, with a smile. "What kind of impression are you making with pepperoni pizza? How romantic is that? You need to be romantic." Sergio went to one of the empty tables and grabbed the candle and candle holder. Sergio then went into the kitchen and came back with a grocery bag. "Here, clearly you need a little help with romance. I gave you some warm bread, a bottle of wine, and a candle."

"What do you know about romance?" Steve asked.

"I have five kids. I know more than you will ever know about romance. I also gave you a couple of salads. One salad and she will get the impression that you think she's fat, but two salads tell her that you are health conscious."

Steve left with his "Romance Kit" compliments of Sergio, the Red Hot Lover himself. Steve knew that Sergio had been married for more than thirty years and still had a romantic relationship with his wife, Gina. They worked together in the restaurant. The reason the restaurant is so romantic is because Sergio and Gina created this atmosphere and the restaurant's menu based on romantic dates that they have had.

Steve walked up the three flights of stairs to Jenny's apartment. Jenny answered the door and asked, "What's all this?"

"Sorry… I got a little carried away with the idea of having dinner with another human. No offense, Buddy." Buddy barked approvingly. "Why don't you finish your work, and I will set the table for us." He then prepared the table as the romance expert taught him: a single candle stuck in a small wine bottle, two plates, two place settings, two salad bowls with salad in them, two glasses of wine, one wine bottle on the table, one pizza box on the kitchen counter, and dim lighting. Where was Sergio when he was sixteen and dating for the first time?

"This is nice. Everything looks wonderful," Jenny said approvingly. A rush of relief came over Steve as he realized she was on the same page as him; this was an actual date, not a dinner as "friends." They both sat down and talked while enjoying dinner. Buddy watched from the background as his parents enjoyed their romantic dinner.

Jenny was a good listener and was able to get Steve to talk about the recent events in his career. "Do you see this as a good opportunity?" Jenny asked.

"Absolutely. If I do well, Big Frank could get me almost any job in America, if he keeps his word."

"No. I'm talking about the opportunity you have to slow down a little and enjoy life. You've worked so hard and sacrificed having a personal life in order to have a job where you will work harder and continue to have no personal life. Maybe this is nature's way of saying there is more to life than work. Maybe it's time to live a little."

"I enjoy life. I have a great dog, and Buddy and I have a wonderful relationship," he said kiddingly.

"What's your hobby? And don't tell me it's studying law."

"Uhmmm."

"That's what I thought. We need to get you a hobby."

"Well... what do you do? You are in your apartment almost every minute of every day working."

"That's true, but I actually love to hike. Every Saturday, regardless of the weather, regardless of how much work I have to do, I get up early, grab my hiking boots and my backpack, and I go hiking. I have hiked every trail in Connecticut and almost every trail in New England. Someday, I hope to be able to take three months off from work and hike the Appalachian Trail."

"That's fantastic!" Steve exclaimed. He was surprised that she was a hiker, but then he realized that she was an athlete, so he shouldn't be shocked. "What do you know about the Appalachian Trail?"

"It's about 2,200 miles long. It starts at the top of Georgia and ends in Maine. It's considered to be the Mount Everest of hiking trails. Every year, I say that this is the year that I will hike the Appalachian Trail. And every summer seems to come and go without me hiking the trail."

"Why is that?"

"Well, business is booming, and I need to be here to get the work done. It's just me. I go out and get the work, and then I do all the work. It's hard to fit in a three-month vacation without losing all my clients. It's hard and time-consuming to be the entrepreneur, the manager, and the employee in the business."

"Growing pains of a growing business. That's a good thing."

"Yeah, but it's a tiring thing."

"I can help you with that. You just need to hire a few employees and then train them to do the billing the way you want them to do it. Then you train one of these people to manage the other employees. Once that is up and running, you can focus on being the visionary who plans the future of your company. You may even be able to take time off and hike the Appalachian Trail."

"Won't that cause me to make less money as my overhead increases?"

"At first, but it could free you up to go out and get more business, and then you'll be in a position to make more money because your business is doing more work than you could do all by yourself. It's a classic problem for growing businesses, but once you cross that bridge and hire people, you will be able to grow your business rapidly and make even more profit."

"You would help me do all that… " Her voice dangled the question.

"Yeah. It would be fun," he said with a smile. "Tell you what. I'll help you develop your business if you introduce me and Buddy to hiking."

"That's an offer I can't refuse."

They continued to talk for hours and into the early morning hours. As some would say, they had *the night*—that date where two people sit and talk all night about their lives, hopes, and dreams, which eventually leads to falling in love. For the first time in a long while, Steve put away his laser focus on his career and goals and got lost in learning about Jenny and the world she lives in.

It was time to say good night. He picked up a sleeping Buddy and held him in his arms. Jenny walked him to the door. She lovingly petted a snoring Buddy. Steve then leaned in and kissed Jenny. They said good night. And it was a good night for Steve.

CHAPTER 6

The first half of summer flew by. Steve studied for the bar exam, but he also learned all the law that was applicable to habeas cases. He took the bar exam and felt confident that he passed, but he still worried because you never really know until you get your score. Both Steve and Jenny kept their promises: Steve went hiking every Saturday with Jenny, and Jenny and Steve worked to develop and apply new business strategies for Jenny's medical billing company. Buddy was spoiled because he spent lots of time with his mommy and daddy and got lots of belly rubs.

Today was the day. Steve had his meeting with Big Frank. He went to the main office of Rockingham & Myers, where he found himself waiting again in the semi-comfortable leather chairs. Steve stared at the walls of the lobby and pondered how different the situation was today than three months ago when he last sat in the same seat. While he felt sorry for himself, he had to look at the silver lining that Big Frank promised: the opportunity to work almost anywhere that he wanted. All he had to do was straighten out the mess, and he was on his way. He became eager to start right away; after all, the sooner you start, the sooner you finish.

Magda came up to him and said, "Attorney Rockingham will see you now." He followed Magda through the frosted glass doors and down the corridor that separated cubicles for offices. Big Frank's office was at the end of the corridor. Since Big Frank was a senior partner and the only living founding partner of the firm, he had the largest and most coveted office in the firm. Frank's office was the corner one with a beautiful view of the Park River, which runs through the City of Hartford. Magda held the door open for Steve as he entered the office.

Big Frank's office was different than Steve expected. While the conference room was meant to intimidate outsiders, Big Frank's office was decorated to make him happy. His office walls were covered with football memorabilia. There was a television on the wall so he could listen to all the college and professional football games while he worked on weekends and late at night. Steve was amazed at all the memorabilia Big Frank had collected, in part thanks to his professional and personal contacts in the legal, business, and political worlds.

Big Frank got out of his chair and walked to the door of his office. "Fuckin' kid! Good to see you. How was your summer?"

"Great. I got a lot done. I feel confident that I passed the bar, and I have a very good understanding of habeas law. I'm excited to start, and I'm ready to go."

"Good. Glad to hear it. Have a seat. Let's talk about your new position. I don't have time to take you there and introduce you to Sam, but he is expecting you this morning."

"Excellent. I look forward to meeting him and getting started."

"First and foremost, you are *not* an attorney yet. You can't go into court by yourself. You can't argue anything before the court. You can't give legal advice. Draft motions, prepare cases, watch Sam in court, and learn the trade. Any questions?"

"Any restrictions in two months when I get my bar results?"

"No. Then you'll be a full-fledged attorney. Habeas is a great area to practice in for beginning attorneys. You have cases that you can't win and are not expected to win. Therefore, use this opportunity to learn litigation and hone your trial skills. Within this year, you will probably try more cases than most attorneys will try in their lifetime."

"What else?"

"I want you to send me a list of all the cases that are pending. Then I want you to give me the status of each case and tell me how far along the case is, as well as any and all trial dates that each case may have. After that, I want weekly updates on the status of each case. By the end of your contract, your goals are to be a seasoned trial lawyer and to have all pending cases up to date and ready for trial. Any questions?"

"No."

"Remember… I'm a man of my word. You pull the firm out of this jam, and I will do what I said. One last thing… if you have any problems or concerns with Sam, you need to let me, and only me, know what's going on. If I need to have a sit-down with him, then I will. Sam is technically your boss, but he is more of an advisor than anything else. Sam has valuable knowledge that he can share with you, but he may not be up to the task of being the leader at this point. That's why you need to tell me what's going on with Sam and why these cases are all screwed up. Good luck. kid."

Big Frank got out of his chair and walked over to Steve and hugged him. "Thanks again for doing this."

"No problem, Frank. Thanks for believing in me."

Steve left the office and walked to his car and then began the fifteen-minute drive across town to his new office. He drove down Asylum Street in the center of the business district downtown, on his way to the south side of town. The locals called the area D.M.Z., short for Demilitarized Zone, because of the large amount of crime and gang activity. As he drove further south, he saw the neighborhood change from high-rise office buildings to two- and three-story office buildings; eventually, the business district was made up of laundromats, fast food restaurants, and small, family-owned convenience stores. The business offices tended to be converted brownstones.

As Steve approached his new office, he realized that the firm had purchased a three-story brownstone directly across the street from the city jail and the police station. From a business standpoint, it was the perfect location for a criminal law practice and a habeas law firm.

He drove around to the back of the building, where only three cars were parked.

Like most brownstones, the satellite office had a stairway that led from the street to the first floor of the office. There was also a stairway to an office in the basement. There was no sign or any indication that this was the Rockingham & Myers Law Firm. Steve walked up the stairs to the first floor and walked through the entry door. The front door opened to a small lobby area that was surrounded by office doors and a stairway to the second floor. The lobby had a musty smell, as if it had a mold problem. There was a directory on the wall indicating the office numbers, but only one door had a name next to it. Apparently, Sam M. was in office number 5. Clearly, this office gets no walk-in traffic; nobody is trying to locate the Rockingham & Myers Law Firm on this side of town.

Steve knocked on the door of office number 5 and waited for a response. "Door's open," he heard from the other side. Steve turned the knob and slowly opened the door to find a large, heavy-set man wearing green New York Jets sweatpants and a matching t-shirt. The office looked more like a college dorm room than a law office. The office walls were covered in wood paneling, like a scene from *The Brady Bunch.* In the corner was a life-sized cardboard cutout of the Joker from Batman movies, asking, "Why so serious?" On the walls were a series of framed posters similar to the trend of inspirational posters. But instead of the traditional inspirational content, Sam's posters were mocking. They featured sinking ships or a tree branch falling in quicksand with inspirations such as failure or laziness. Instead of an aspirational saying, they featured phrases like, "Maybe your purpose in life is to be an example of what not to do."

Sam got up from his chair. "You must be Steve. Welcome to the firm." Steve reached out and shook his hand.

Steve inquired, "Is there a dress code here?"

"Absolutely, suits need to be worn at all times. You never know when a $1 million case is going to walk in here. You need to be prepared."

"Okay," Steve said seriously.

"Just kidding, kid. Nobody comes in here. Either your client is in jail and can't come in here to talk to you, or he is out of jail, and he forgot he has a pending case because he's out of jail. Wear what you want but keep a suit here in case you are called to court in an emergency.

Sam looked at the clock on the wall. "It's twelve o'clock. Let's go to the Italian restaurant next door and talk over lunch. Then, we can come back to the office and go through all the files and plan a strategy for resolving these cases."

Steve left his briefcase in Sam's office and followed Sam next door. Rico's was a small restaurant and bar, frequented by the police and prison guards who wanted a drink after work. The food was less known for excellent quality and taste and more for the quantity received at a low price.

They sat in a booth and ordered from the five-dollar lunch menu. The firm had a strict no-alcohol policy, but that did not stop Sam from ordering a beer with his lunch.

Sam looked at Steve and said, "So what's your story? Nobody does this kind of work unless you are desperate. Why does a young man with your qualifications take a job like this? You must have had six-digit offers from all over town. Hell, from all over the county, but you chose this. You have to be sitting on a great story? Let's hear it."

"Why do you care?"

"Well, let's call it a test. I've done a ton of trials. I can tell you that being a lawyer is essentially being a good storyteller. Jurors and judges love to hear a good story. If you can sell them on a good story, they want to provide your story with a happy ending. So, tell me your story."

So, Steve explained how he had worked hard to get the coveted junior associate position, only to lose out to David, the son of a tech company CEO. He was now doing this in hopes of getting an even better offer next year.

"So, what did Big Frank say about why you are needed over here in habeas land?"

"He said you were swamped and can use a hand."

"Did he tell you that I am an alcoholic and not committed to the firm?"

"No. Just that you are falling behind and need help."

"Here's my story, kid. I was the chosen one. I was the smart kid of the family. Dad sent me to prep school, and I did well. I got into the Ivy Leagues and was set to go off to college as an architecture major. I loved to design buildings. I would spend hours everyday planning dream homes or office buildings. I would show my plans to my teacher, who would constantly challenge me to continue to work harder and learn more. So, on the day when I leave for college, my old man pulls me aside and tells me that I need to do a double major; he wants me to major in pre-law as a backup to architecture. You know… just in case something happens that I would have something to fall back on. So, I agree. I do well in college, and my dad approaches me in my junior year and tells me to take the LSATs, just in case I later want to go to law school. He keeps riding me about it for months, so I take the exam just to get him off my back. I do well on the exam, and my dad is happy again.

"Over the summer, before my senior year, I get a job in a large architecture and construction firm. I do great, and they tell me to apply for a full-time job when I finish school. I'm excited. I'm living my wildest dreams. Before I leave for school, my old man comes to me and says he wants me to apply to law school. I say no, my career is going to be in architecture. He tells me that that is great, but I should go to law school, just in case architecture doesn't work out. I tell him that I have no interest in being a lawyer. He tells me that he will support me in whatever I do, and we have an agreement. When I graduate, I will apply to law school. If I don't get a job as an architect in the first year after graduation, then I will go to law school."

Sam stopped for a minute to take a swig of his beer.

"So, I apply and get into all the prestigious law schools. But I don't want to go; I want to be an architect. So I apply to the architecture firm that I worked at over the summer. They deny my application. I continue to call, but there are no openings, even though I know they hired three of my classmates, who were less talented by the way. I apply to architecture firms all over New England and no offers. My dad comes to me and says, 'Why don't you go to law school and work for my firm? We need you. You can continue to try and get a job in the architecture world, but if you don't, you can be a lawyer in my firm.' I agreed."

"So, I go to law school, but I still continue to apply for architecture jobs, but I don't even get an interview. Finally, I give up and work for my dad as an attorney. He's thrilled. He brings me in, and I work as a lawyer for all these architecture firms and construction companies. And then it dawns on me. My dad is the legal consultant to almost every architecture firm in the New England, and he knows every CEO of every architecture firm in the country. He could have gotten me a job with any of these firms, but he could also have told them not to hire me."

"Ten years go by, and I have stewed and festered for almost a decade. I have not been involved in architecture for so long that my knowledge is no longer current in the architecture field. I finally get up the nerve to confront my father. He looks at me and then hugs me and says, 'That is exactly what I did.' My old man explains that being a lawyer was in my best interest and in the family's best interest. He needed me, and this was the best way to get me to be a lawyer." Sam stopped again and stared out the window for a moment.

"I decided that I needed to do what is in my best interest, even if that was not in the firm's best interest. I committed the mortal sin. I fell in love with my wife, who was an architect. We started spending as much time as we could together. We still worked full-time jobs, but I refused to work weekends, and I would only work ten-hour days. I took a lot of heat from my family. My dad, my brother, and my sister were furious that I did not dedicate my life to the firm as they had. But my wife, Desiree, was worth it. She made my job bearable. She made life worth living."

"I don't regret my decision when it comes to Desiree. I don't regret giving up my career as a senior partner in a law firm, making millions per year. I don't regret taking a massive pay cut because I don't produce as much income as other partners. I don't regret using all my vacation days and taking a leave of absence when she got sick. I don't regret being there for her when she was bedridden with cancer. I don't regret taking care of her in her final days instead of putting her in hospice. I don't regret any of it, and I would give up everything I have to spend one more day with her." He stopped and looked Steve dead in the eyes.

"One thing about this law firm, kid… you will eventually sacrifice everything about you for the firm if you want to stay here. You will sacrifice relationships with family and loved ones, and you will sacrifice things that are important to you. As for me, I still get a modest salary, not nearly as big as my siblings, but I continue to get it because the firm owes it to me. They owe it to me for all the damages I have suffered. They can't take it away from me."

The conversation stunned Steve. It reminded him of the old Wild Kingdom television show, where Marlon Perkins would grab a poisonous snake and milk all the venom out of it into a glass. Sam's hatred for the firm spilled out in his speech like the venom Marlon Perkins milked out of a cobra.

Sam's speech laid a damper on the conversation. They sat there for a moment in silence; Sam still feeling the anger from his father's betrayal and Steve wondering how he could (or should) change the subject. He took a page from Big Frank's playbook and decided to remain quiet. Eventually, Sam would come back to the main reason why they were having lunch, which was to train Steve on what he needed to do.

"You have any questions for me?" Sam asked.

"What do I need to know? I mean, I've read all the statutes and case law. I've read several books. But I know that there is more to practicing law than what is in the books or in forms. What do I need to know that is not in the law?"

Sam thought for a moment and said, "Let me phrase this right." He then thought for a moment. "You need to understand that in order to do this job and to best represent your client, you need to be dead inside."

"Umm, yeah. I'm gonna need a bigger explanation of that."

"You deal with some of the worst things that can ever happen to a person. I have seen autopsy photos. I've listened to tape recordings of victims being tortured and eventually murdered. Just last month, I sat down with a pedophile who told me play-by-play about how he molested children. You represent these people, so you have to be able to separate your personal feelings from the case. If these people and their acts disgust you, then you will not be able to represent them in the manner that they need to be represented. You need to be able to talk to a rapist and fight to the best of your ability to get him a new trial, even though he told you that he did it and will do it again. Everyone wants to represent the good guy, but you are not in that line of work."

"I get it. How do you do it?"

"It's like getting into a pool. Some people jump in and get out quickly because the water is too cold. Others gradually enter by putting their feet in and eventually walking all the way in and getting used to it. I would say start slowly. Maybe represent a few drug dealers at first and then work your way up through the violent crimes until you reach the levels of rape, molestation, and murder."

"It's hard because you need to keep an emotional distance from your client. You don't want the distance to be so great that they don't trust you or feel that they can't talk to you about their case. On the other hand, if you become too emotionally involved, this job will make you depressed and ruin your career. I've had clients lie to me, and I believed them. Then, when their lies came out at trial, I felt betrayed. The flip side of that is when you believe your client is truly innocent, and you are unable to get them a new trial. You can't help but feel depressed because you let them down."

"It's a tough job," Sam conceded. "On top of all of that is that the rest of society has the luxury of not knowing what you know. You have to keep your client's secrets, no matter what. If your daughter starts dating a former client of yours who is a rapist, you can't warn your child. Knowing this information can be a huge burden on you."

"How do you survive this? Are you surviving this?"

"I am a survivor. I am still alive. I still practice in the field. The trick is that the world is not black and white, but it is made up of shades of gray. There are honest thieves, crooked priests, murderers with moral standards, doctors who intentionally hurt others, and sex offenders who help people. Nobody is perfect. I once met an attorney who told me that he doesn't practice criminal law anymore because he doesn't like representing bad guys. I laughed my ass off. No client is perfect. I see lawyers represent pharmaceutical companies that make drugs, knowing their patients will become addicted. I've seen banking lawyers defend banks that intentionally stole money from their clients. I've seen corporate lawyers represent auto manufacturers who chose not to make a minor change in a car design to save lives because it was more cost-effective to pay the lawsuits than recall the cars. We all represent good and bad. You will eventually see that your clients are all just people. It's easier for society to categorize them as 'bad' because it makes it easier for us to ignore the fact that they are not that different from us."

Sam and Steve walked back to the office. Sam explained that the firm bought the office several decades ago. They planned for it to be a rental property investment until they had a hard time getting good renters. The building sat vacant for a long time until they started this branch of the firm, which Sam called the firm's dirty secret. He explained that the firm doesn't advertise this branch because they don't want anyone to know it exists. While some view that as an insult, Sam admitted that he enjoys the fact that nobody from the office wants to come over here and check up on him. He can wear sweats to the office, drink beer on the job, and work any hours he wants. It was hard for Steve to imagine such freedom in a law firm.

Sam pointed out that the basement office belongs to Leon. Leon was the maintenance man. He cleaned the building in exchange for room and board in the basement office and a small wage. Leon also did some investigation work for the firm on occasion. Leon was a former client of Sam's. Leon had a serious drug problem and had to do ten years for possession with intent to sell. Sam tried to get him a new trial but lost his case. Sam spoke with the parole board to be a sponsor for Leon and agreed to house and employ him if they released him from prison. It had been three years, and Leon had stayed out of trouble.

Steve and Sam entered the building and went upstairs to Sam's office. "Let's spend the rest of the day going through the files," Sam said. They walked across the hallway to office number 8. "This is your office," said Sam. The office was similar to Sam's, with the wood paneling and musty smell. There was a desk with a computer and a conference table with hundreds of file folders on it. "These are all the files. Let's go through each file and see what has been done and what we need to do."

"Hey!" a voice shouted from the hallway. Steve looked through the doorway and saw a tall red-haired woman looking at him as if she was trying to get his attention.

"Hi," Steve said, which sounded more like a question.

"Did you get your ticket?" she asked.

"Ticket to what?" Steve inquired.

She then flexed both of her arms in front of her body, like a bodybuilder and said, "To the gun show." She then laughed and snorted while laughing some more. Steve could see that she was in great shape and clearly spent a lot of time lifting weights.

"This is Roxy. She's our paralegal. She trains as a semi-professional mountain bike racer. Roxy, this is Steve. He's the new guy I told you about."

Roxy walked over to Steve and held out her hand. Steve shook her hand. Roxy had the grip of a young man trying to impress his girlfriend's father. "You guys need any help?" she asked.

"We got it," said Sam. Roxy left and went back downstairs to her office.

"She seems nice."

"Yeah. She's weird, but she works hard, and she works for cheap."

"Where did you find her?"

"Prison. She's a former client like Leon. Her boyfriend was cheating on her with her best friend. She got drunk and decided to beat the crap out of both of them. The jury didn't buy her self-defense claim or the fact that she was too drunk to form the intent to commit assault. She told the judge to go fuck himself at her sentencing, so he gave the maximum sentence. I tried to get her a new trial, but you already know the outcome of that. Anyway, when she was released, she came to me looking for a job. She's been here for more than five years. She's a little nutty, but she means well."

Sam and Steve finished reviewing all the files and Steve took detailed notes on each file, so that he could update Big Frank. "It's

4:30," said Sam. "Let's call it a day. Tomorrow, we'll go across the street and meet some clients."

CARLOS

CHAPTER 7

Carlos sat in the alley during the rainstorm, with his back propped up against the wall. His body was wrapped in plastic garbage bags to keep his clothes dry and to keep his body heat in. It was late fall, and the cold weather was upon the city of Hartford. Five a.m. seemed to be years away. The pain was increasing along with the itchiness and the uncontrollable shaking. Carlos was between fixes, and the withdrawal had been hurting for hours. He needed relief now, but his only chance to beat the pain and get some sleep was at least another hour away. There were very few options left. His usual dealers had extended him some credit, but he could not get any more. There was always the option to give blood for a few bucks, but he did that a few days ago and would have to wait a few more days. The local bottle and can hound had gone through each trash can in this neighborhood already, so there weren't even any bottles or cans around for Carlos to recycle and get some change.

The last hope was Julito. Julito owned the corner bodega. Carlos did the occasional odd jobs for Julito around the store. In exchange, Julito gave Carlos some money when he needed it. Unlike other people, Julito never lectured Carlos or pointed out the obvious fact that Carlos had a drug problem; instead, Julito said that he had been there because he was a recovering addict himself. When Carlos was ready to quit, Julito offered to help him. In the meantime, Julito helped out Carlos when he needed a couple of bucks, needed to come in out of the cold, or just wanted to talk. Carlos reciprocated by taking out the trash or cleaning the loading dock. The only problem was that Julito did not open the bodega until 6.

Carlos had time to reflect on his life, and this was not a good thing. *How the hell did I get here?* He asked himself. *I'm sitting in an alley in the rain, waiting to borrow money for my next fix.* He chuckled because his situation was so ridiculous that he had to laugh. *It could be worse,* he thought. It could be snowing outside. He chuckled again. Maybe this was his moment of clarity that he heard about in all the AA and NA meetings he occasionally attended when attempting to get back on the sobriety train. Maybe this was the rock bottom he had to hit before he finally committed to sobriety and changed his life. Maybe it was, but then again, this was not the first time he had been in this position; he had been in this same alley in a snowstorm waiting to get his next fix before, and he probably would be again.

This alley had been Carlos's home for the past two years. There was an Italian restaurant that threw out its leftover food into a dumpster in the alley at the same time every night. The long roof tops between the two buildings provided more shelter from the rain and snow than the other alleys in the neighborhood.

Before the alley, Carlos lived with his mom on the other side of town. She knew he was using drugs but hadn't known how much the addiction controlled him. At first, Carlos borrowed money from his mother; then items around the house went missing. While mom knew that Carlos was pawning these items, she was trying to gently convince him to get into rehab. The last straw came when Carlos broke into his mother's bedroom and took her wedding ring off her nightstand while she slept. Carlos and a fellow junkie drove to Bridgeport and hawked it for $500. His father had worked nights at a gas station for more than a year to save the money to buy the ring. Since his father had passed away, the ring carried priceless memories and sentimental value for his mom. But Carlos's addiction won out. Five hundred dollars could get him high for several weeks, and his addiction needed to be fed.

That was the end. When Carlos came home, his mom attempted to confront him about the ring. He simply looked at her and said, "I'm sorry. I did a terrible thing, and I will leave now." Carlos grabbed his jacket and left, never to return.

Looking back on the past few years of his life did nothing but increase his pain. Yes, he could vow to get clean. Maybe he could go cold turkey; if he made it through the withdrawals over the next few days, he might be able to maintain sobriety. He imagined himself getting his one-year chip for sobriety. But he dismissed the dream just as quickly. He didn't care. He didn't want to feel the pain anymore. The physical pain was excruciating; the emotional pain of knowing that he ruined his life was even worse. He just wanted to feel nothing.

Get up and move, he thought to himself. *Maybe if I move and get the blood flowing, it will relieve some of the pain. I can take a brisk walk down the street to the bodega. Maybe Julito got there early and will help me out.* Carolos looked up at the clock on the bank building. It was a quarter to six in the morning. Time to get going. Carlos picked himself up and pulled the garbage bags off him. He stretched his back and his legs for what seemed like the first time since he was a wide receiver on the high school football team. It felt good. *Let's get our fix on.*

Carlos walked down the street to the bodega. The sunlight was trying to come out, but it was blocked by all the rainclouds. The rain continued to fall, but it did not matter because Carlos was going to get high. He would get $20 from Julito and then immediately see Rico and get an eight ball. Then he could go to McDonalds and get an Egg McMuffin, two hash browns, and an orange juice to go so that he could eat breakfast and then shoot up his eight ball in the alley and pass out until nightfall. He was feeling better just thinking about it.

The bodega was now a block away. Suddenly, two gunshots rang out; they sounded close. Carlos stopped in his tracks and looked around. He did not see anyone on the streets. Carlos ran to the bodega at the end of the block to avoid being caught up in the gunfire. The front door was unlocked so he quickly moved inside. "Julito. Hey man, I'm really in need of a favor," he said. Julito was not behind the counter. Carlos looked over the counter and down the grocery aisle. Still no sign of him. As he walked down the aisle, he noticed that the door to the back room was slightly ajar, and the light was on. "Julito?" he called out. Still no answer. Carlos slowly pushed open the back-room door.

Julito's body was lying face down on the floor in front of an open safe. It was obvious that Julito was dead as he appeared to have been shot in the back of the head from close range. Also, from the blood stain on the back of his sweater, it looked like Julito was also shot in the center of his back. The safe was open, and money was still inside. Blood was everywhere.

Carlos stood in horror and shock. His only friend was dead. It was surreal. Just yesterday, they talked about their hopes for the future. Now, he was standing in a crime scene with Julito as the victim. All he could think was run. *Run,* he said to himself. *If anyone sees you, they will think that you killed him. Get out now.*

Carlos turned around and ran down the grocery aisle and through the front door. He turned left out the door and bumped shoulders with a woman walking in the opposite direction. Carlos continued to run until he could run no more.

CHAPTER 8

Detective Bynes had been with the Hartford Police Department for more than twenty years, with fifteen of those years investigating homicides. Bynes's nickname on the street was "Stallion" because he could outrun anyone. He used to warn people that he arrested not to run because he would catch them and charge them with interfering with an officer. Even though Bynes was in his early forties, he could still catch the young hoodlum on the street.

Bynes received a call at 7 a.m. to go downtown to the corner bodega to investigate a murder. He was already awake and dressed for work, so he quickly got in his car and drove to the scene of the crime, after making a brief detour to 7-11 to get his usual morning Pepsi. Bynes hated coffee but wanted caffeine; Pepsi became his morning ritual.

Bynes got out of his car and lifted the yellow police tape that covered the entrance to the bodega. He was met by Miggs, the officer in charge of the crime scene. "What do we got?" Bynes asked the officer.

"We have a Hispanic male, shot two times. One in the center of the back, and the second in the back of the head. Safe was open and emptied. The medical examiner, the forensic guys, and the photographer are all here fighting over who goes first. The photographer is having a hissy fit because he doesn't want to miss his dental appointment at 9 a.m. Apparently, his dentist books way in advance."

"The photographer goes first, forensics second, medical examiner third. Any witnesses?"

"Yeah, a woman said that she witnessed the whole thing. Walked in to buy some coffee and a donut before work. Said she heard gunshots and then saw the perp walking out the door with a gun in his hand; he ran into her on the way out. She said she could probably pick him out of a line-up."

"What did he look like?"

"Hispanic male, light-skinned, 130 pounds, about five feet, five inches tall, just a bit taller than her. He also had an eagle tattoo on his right hand, the hand he used to carry the gun."

"Maybe he's a local kid. The local high school mascot is an Eagle. Maybe he played on the football team," Bynes said. "I'll manage the crime scene. Leave three officers outside to manage the crowd. Take everyone else and canvass the neighborhood for two blocks in each direction. See if anyone saw anything."

"Will do."

"Hey, Bynes, check this out!" a voice from the back room yelled. Bynes walked into the back room and saw Art from forensics standing over the dead body and looking into the safe with a flashlight."

"What's up, Artie?"

"Looks like they had the victim open the safe, get on his knees, shot him in the back of the head, and then took what was on the shelf in the safe. Looks like there were stacks of cash in the safe and some assorted boxes on the bottom."

"How do you know this?"

"Blood splatter. If they shot him in the head while standing, the blood from his head would be sprayed over the walls and not in the safe. So, he had to be down lower, probably on his knees, when he was shot. The blood coated everything in the safe, so anything they took out had to be covered, too. If you look on the shelves, you can get an idea of what was taken by the shapes that were left. These rectangles on top are consistent with dollar bills. Down below are assorted boxes. I would guess that someone stole boxes of rolled coins. You can see that the boxes of rolled pennies were left behind."

"Anything else?"

"There is an alarm system but no camera system. I called the alarm company. The alarm was turned off at the back door at 5:15 this morning. A code was punched in again at the back door at 5:45 to turn off the alarm. I asked the company to send me a list of every time the alarm was turned on and off. They just emailed it to me. The alarm is consistently turned off at 5:45 at the back door in the morning seven days a week. And the alarm is turned on again at around 9:20 in every evening."

"You're saying the killer knew the code, opened the back door, waited for the victim, had him open the safe, shot him twice, took the money from the safe, and left out the front door? Why wouldn't he leave out the back door to the alley?"

"That's what it seems like. Unless the victim came to work early and then went outside again and then forgot he had turned off the alarm and then attempted to turn off the alarm again. Then, he opened the front door and was robbed."

"Was there a cash drawer in the register?"

"No," Art said.

"Why would he open the store, but have no money in the register for when his customers bought something?"

"Maybe he knew the killer," Art offered.

"Where's the witness?"

"Outside in the police car, waiting to talk to you."

Bynes walked outside and saw a police car that was about thirty feet from the store. He saw the bleached blonde curly hair and knew it was 'Krystal with a K'. 'Krystal with a K' was a drug addict who supported her habit any way she could, which was usually prostitution. She had a lengthy criminal record and was well known by Hartford police and local criminals. If it came down to a trial, Krystal with a K was not a strong witness because of her criminal history and her side career of snitching on local criminals for money. Any criminal defense lawyer fresh out of law school would be able to discredit her testimony.

Bynes opened the door to the back seat of the police car and sat next to Krystal. She was wearing a red sweater and a short black skirt and was soaked to the bone from the rain. She was probably walking home in the rain after a night of street walking, Bynes thought to himself. "Let's turn on the heater. It looks like you are freezing to death."

"Thanks." Krystal said. "I got a cup of coffee to keep warm, but I'm still cold."

"Where's your jacket?"

"It wasn't raining when I went out last night. I didn't think it would rain."

"I know this is difficult, but can you tell me what you saw?"

"Sure," Krystal said as she snapped her gum. "I was walking home from work at about 6 a.m. I was going into the bodega to get a cup of coffee and a donut for breakfast. I heard gunshots, and I stopped to look around. A guy came running out of the bodega holding a gun. He came out of the door and ran into me. He didn't stop. He kept on running. I know Julito, and I went in to see if he was okay. I walked into the store, and I didn't see him. I saw the door of the back room open. I walked back there and saw Julito." She started to cry. Bynes gave her a tissue from his pocket.

"I have a few questions."

"Okay"

"When you were walking to the bodega, which way were you walking?"

"Toward Ashland Street."

"So, the Bodega was on your right?"

"Yes."

"So, when this guy came out of the store, he ran out of the store and ran to his left and ran into you?"

"Exactly."

"How did he run into you? Did he run into the side of you and knock you down, or did he run into you head-on, knocking you down?"

Krystal thought about it for a moment and said, "He hit my left shoulder and I kinda spun around and fell to the ground."

"Was he carrying anything?"

"Oh yeah, I forgot. He had a bag under his arm."

"Which arm?

"Uhmmm... his left arm."

"Do you think you can identify this man?"

"Yes. I had a good look at his face."

"Alright. I'm gonna have an officer take you downtown to look at some mug shots and see if you can identify this man."

"I wanna run home real quick and feed my cat and change my clothes."

"No problem. I'll have the officer take you there first."

"I only live a couple of blocks from here. I can take a cab to the station."

"Sure. I'll let the desk sergeant know that you will be there in about an hour."

"I will be there," Krystal said. She began to cry again. "Julito was such a sweet man. There was no reason to kill him. He would have willingly given the robber his money. Julito gave money to a lot of people like me, because he knew we were hurting. There was no reason for him to be killed."

Krystal got out of the car and walked down the street. Bynes sat in the car and watched her walk away. None of this makes sense, he thought to himself. Why would a robber find a way to get the code to unlock the back door, rob, and kill the victim, and then leave through the front door for everyone to see? Why would somebody rob and kill someone who would probably lend the money if they asked? He also got the distinct feeling that Krystal with a K was lying to him. How did she get such a good look at the killer when she was thrown to the ground? She could only have seen him for a split second. Let's see if she makes an identification, he thought to himself.

CHAPTER 9

Bynes wrapped up the crime scene. The bodega would remain closed for a few weeks, with crime scene tape covering the entrances in case Art and the lab guys need to come back and check something. The body was taken to the coroner's office to await an autopsy; Bynes would have the results in a few days.

Now it was time for the worst part of the job, telling the victim's wife that her husband had been murdered. Detectives are trained on how to deliver this news. One theory was to place your hand on the person, maybe on the shoulder, or hold their hand between both of yours. This human touch was supposed to make the detective more personable and somehow soften the blow yet not cross the line of sexual harassment. Hugging the victim's family would go too far. Bynes took all the classes and had delivered the bad news more than most in the department. Bynes' approach was to just drop the bad news, wait for them to react, and then get a hold of themselves. Bynes knew that this was a sterile and impersonal approach, but he believed that if he tried to make it personal, he might miss the reaction.

The reaction in itself could be very telling. There was the traditional crying and wailing. With that as a guide, he could judge the reaction and maybe tell if someone was faking. While this wasn't proof for a jury to hear, it could give him a sense of whether the spouse or family members were involved.

Bynes drove to West Hartford, the city next to Hartford. Julito lived in a nice home in a nice neighborhood. It was less than five miles from the bodega. Bynes parked his car on the street and walked up to the front door. A young woman in her late twenties answered the door. "May I help you?" she asked with concern.

"Ma'am, are you Carmen Hernaiz? Is your husband Julito Hernaiz?"

"Yes. What.. what's wrong? What happened?" she asked, starting to panic.

"There's no easy way to say this, so I am just going to say it. There was a murder in your husband's bodega. Someone identified the body as your husband's." Carmen covered her mouth, fell back against the wall, and slowly slid to the floor as she began to cry. She covered her face and whimpered. Bynes stood silent for a moment, observing. He knew this would come across as impersonal and cold, but he was a detective first, and nothing he could do would ease her pain at this time. After a few moments, she got herself together and stood up.

"Is there anything I can get you?" he asked.

"I'm sorry. I'm fine. I'm sorry." She apologized.

"No problem, ma'am. I'm sorry to tell you such bad news, but there is no other way to tell it. I have some questions for you, if you think you can answer them now." Bynes spoke in a low, soft tone, trying to show sympathy and concern, as he was trained.

"I'll try."

"Do you know if there was anyone who would want to kill Julito?"

"No. Everyone loved Julito. He grew up in that neighborhood. He had problems as a drug addict and got into some trouble here and there, but he got his life together. He worked hard, and he saved his money. He opened the store, and he invested in some rental properties. I met him when he was becoming successful. We saved our money and bought this home. Julito always gave back to the community.

He gave people money if they were in need. If his renters needed extra time to pay, he was okay with that. Everyone loved him. I don't know why anyone would hurt him."

"Does Julito have any other relatives?"

"Yes. Julito has an ex-wife who lives in New York. They have two children from that marriage, but the kids are adults themselves."

"Do you and Julito have any children?"

"No. But we were trying."

"Any employees at the store?"

"He hired a few people from the neighborhood from time to time, but he was always in the store, running the register and talking to the customers. He loved it. He spent the whole day talking to his friends. The store was closed on Saturday nights and all day Sunday. That was our time to spend together."

"Did anyone else have the code to the back door of the bodega?"

"I don't know. Maybe one of the people who worked for him from time to time."

"Did you work in the store?"

"Sometimes. If he received a delivery, or he knew it was going to be a busy day and needed extra help, he would ask me for help."

There was a pause. Carmen covered her face and began to cry and whimper. Bynes put his hand on her shoulder and said, "I'm sorry for your loss."

"How did he die?" she asked.

"It looks like he was murdered as part of a robbery, but it's our protocol that we have to rule out other motives for the murder. It appears that the killer went into the store and had him open the safe and then murdered him. We have a lead that we are pursuing. That's all I can tell you at this point."

"Thank you," she murmured.

"Someone from forensics will come by, probably tomorrow. We want to look through Mr. Hernaiz's financial information. It's a formality, but mainly we check to see if he was being blackmailed or involved in unusual activity that could be a clue to his murder."

"Okay," she said. "I will gather his financial information that is here. He does have an accountant across town who managed his books and investments; I don't have that information."

"Thank you for the help. Again, I am very sorry for your loss."

Bynes locked eyes with Carmen for a second. He smiled gently and then walked out the door. He heard the door lock behind him.

She's faking it, he thought to himself. She was wearing mascara and cried twice for a few minutes, but when he left, her makeup was perfect. Women usually cry so much that their mascara runs to the point that when Bynes is done telling them the terrible news, they look like Alice Cooper.

CHAPTER 10

Bynes returned to the station. It was late in the afternoon. He walked into the office and approached the desk sergeant. "Hey, Sarge. Did Krystal with a K drop by today?"

"Yup. She nailed it in twenty minutes."

"You're kidding me."

"Nope. Never seen anything like it. I set her up in the room with a stack of mugshot books. Usually, people take several hours to find the perp. She did it in fifteen minutes. She went speeding through the books like she knew who she was looking for. A kid named Carlos Vega. She signed the paperwork stating she was a hundred percent sure he was the guy who ran out of the store with the gun."

"Did you run him through the system?"

"Yup again. He has some low-end crimes, larceny, trespassing, breach of peace, and a couple of possession of narcotics charges. Never served any time. Was on probation for a year and completed it with no problems. There are no warrants out for his arrest. At his last arrest, he did have a tattoo of an eagle on his hand. It was his left hand."

"Do we have an address for him?"

"Sort of. When he was on probation, he lived with his mom. I called her. She said he moved out two years ago. Lives in an alley about half a mile down the street from the scene of the crime."

"Did you talk to his probation officer?"

"Yeah. He remembered him. Said he had a serious drug problem. Carlos made some improvement when he did a drug program for probation. Probation never took him as a violent offender; he never showed any signs of anger issues. It wouldn't be a surprise if he still had a serious drug problem. You want me to have the boys go get him?"

"Not yet... Let me talk to the state's attorney first. Let's see if we can get an arrest warrant."

"Think you got enough evidence for that?"

"Probably. Did Miggs get back from canvassing the area?"

"He did about an hour ago. I'll page him to your office."

Bynes got another Pepsi from the soda machine and met Miggs at his office. "Any luck?"

"Just about everyone heard the gunshots. Some looked out the window. Many just ignored it because they hear gunshots all the time. Just about everyone knew the victim and was shocked that he was dead. Nobody knew of anyone who would want to kill him."

"Anything unusual reported?"

"Two people who live in an apartment across the street from the front of the bodega heard the shots and looked out the window. They didn't see anyone."

"You think they were telling the truth, or do you think they were scared?"

"Most people in the neighborhood are scared and don't want to get involved in this."

"Let me ask you this... when you got to the scene, was Krystal already there?"

"Yeah. She was outside in front of the bodega."

"In the rain?"

"Yeah. I asked why she didn't go inside. She said that she didn't want to mess up the crime scene."

"Anything else?"

"That's it. Just the community is shocked. Everybody loved Julito."

Bynes picked up the phone and called Anne Rosen of the State Attorney's Office. She was still in the office, and he reviewed the evidence with her. She advised him to type everything up in an arrest warrant application; she also advised him to remove Krystal's name from the affidavit and refer to her as a confidential informant. There was enough evidence to get the judge to sign an arrest warrant. She would meet him at her office at 8 a.m. so she could sign the document before the judge signed it.

Drafting an arrest warrant application would take at least three or four hours. Bynes got another Pepsi from the machine. It was going to be a long night.

After completing the paperwork, Bynes managed to squeeze in some sleep before meeting Anne at her office. Anne's office was downtown at the courthouse on Washington Avenue. The marshals let him into the courthouse before they let the public in.

Bynes saw Anne and extended his hand out and said, "Counselor, good to see you again."

Anne shook his hand and said, "Good to see you, detective. Let's see what you have." She examined the document that described the crime scene and included the statement of Krystal with a K, AKA Confidential Informant, placing Carlos Vega at the scene of the crime, running away with a gun. "I think it will work," Anne said. "How do you feel about it?"

"I think it meets the standard, and the judge will probably sign it. Something about this case just doesn't seem right."

"You mean because Krystal with a K is your sole witness, and she has no credibility because of her substance abuse issues and her career choices, which have led her into several criminal convictions?"

"Yeah. That's part of it."

"Well...my advice is to have the judge sign it. You can bring this guy in and see what he says. If he's guilty, he'll probably plead. Krystal's name will be kept confidential for a while, but eventually the judge will force me to release it. At that point, we may want more investigation to see if we can get someone to support Krystal's statement. If not, I can probably convince a jury that Krystal is telling the truth."

Bynes left Anne's office and walked to the judge's office. He didn't like doing this, but he knew that this was the only way to bring Carlos in to talk. Also, if he got new evidence, he could ask Anne to withdraw the charges.

The judge signed the arrest warrant without question.

CHAPTER 11

"Wake up, sweetheart." There was no response.

"Let's go! Rise and shine!" Again, no response.

"GET UP, MOTHERFUCKER!!" Carlos opened his eyes slowly to see that he was staring down the barrel of a shotgun inches from his face. Hartford police had sent out their S.W.A.T. unit along with a few patrolmen and Detective Bynes to arrest Carlos in his alley. Once the warrant was signed, the team assembled and searched the alleys down the road from the bodega. Carlos was under arrest within an hour of the warrant being signed.

It seemed like just a few minutes ago when Carlos stood over the dead body of Julito. He was battling a ton of emotions and emotional pain. Carlos was withdrawing and in physical pain. His best friend was dead. Carlos began to review the incident over and over in his head. He panicked and left the store. Carlos recalled running into a woman and just kept on running. No way in hell she saw him, just as he did not see her. He just kept running.

Carlos had run out of the bodega and ran for about two miles until he arrived at Frannie's apartment. He knocked on her door. A tired college student woke up to see who was knocking on her door. She recognized Carlos and let him in. "It's not even 6:30 in the morning, Carlos," she scolded.

Carlos was crying and held on to Frannie tightly. He cried and cried, and she attempted to soothe him.

A college student who studied business and economics, Frannie had decided to sell drugs only to people that she knew in order to support herself. She had known Carlos for a few years, and he was a regular client of hers. Carlos was also a friend, but she had never seen him like this before.

"What's wrong?" she asked.

"Julito's dead."

"When? How?"

"Somebody shot him. Just a few minutes ago. I saw his body in the store, and I ran. I went to get some money from him because I was hurting and I needed a boost. He was just lying there. Someone shot him in the head. I ran. I didn't know where to go, so I just came here."

She held him close, and they sat on the floor until he calmed down and was breathing normally.

"I know I owe you money, but I'm hurting. Can you sport me an eight ball or two? I'm desperate. I just want to take something and knock out. I just want to get the image of Julito out of my mind. Please. I'm begging you."

Frannie was a businesswoman, but Carlos was a good friend. *That's the problem when your clients are friends,* she said to herself. *You extend them credit when you probably shouldn't.* Frannie opened her desk drawer and gave him the drugs.

He hugged Frannie again and thanked her for being a friend. Carlos walked back to his alley and got high. He wanted to feel nothing again. For what seemed like a brief moment, he was free of the pain, free of Julito, and free of his sadness. Carlos slept for almost twenty-four hours, only to wake up and find himself under arrest.

Getting a suspect to confess was like a game show among the detectives. Bynes currently held the record because he once got a murder suspect to give a written confession by promising to buy him

Chinese food. Detective Cross was a close second when he tricked a suspect into writing an apology letter to the victim's family for shooting their son, in hopes that the family would drop the charges.

Bynes walked down the hall to the interrogation room with a smile on his face. *Welcome to another round of Make the Drug Addict Confess,* he thought to himself. *Tonight's contestant is a drug addict who lives in an alley next to the Italian restaurant. Come on down.* He opened the door and was face-to-face with Carlos Vega. Bynes hoped Carlos was still intoxicated and would be more likely to talk. Bynes went into his best friend and ally mode, hoping to gain Carlos' trust.

"Hi Mr. Vega. May I call you Carlos?"

"Lawyer."

"Do you smoke? I can get you a couple of cigarettes if you want."

"Lawyer."

"Need to use the restroom?"

"Lawyer."

"Look, Carlos, before I talk to you, I need to go over your rights."

"Lawyer."

"What I would like you to do is review this document that lists all your rights and explains them to you. Will you review that?"

"Lawyer."

"Will you review the document for me, so that we can continue our conversation?"

"Lawyer."

"Mr. Vega, will you talk to me?"

"Lawyer."

"Are you requesting a lawyer?"

"Lawyer."

"If you get a lawyer, it's only going to make things worse."

"Lawyer."

"Look at me. Carlos, if you talk to me, I can help you out."

"Lawyer."

"Carlos, you're in deep shit right now. You need my help."

"Lawyer."

"If you don't talk to me then I can't help you."

"Lawyer."

"Carlos… I want to help you, but you need to talk to me."

"Lawyer."

"You really want a lawyer?"

"Lawyer."

"Are you saying you don't trust me?" Bynes said angrily.

"Lawyer."

"Fine!" Bynes yelled as he stormed out.

Bynes walked back to his office. *What do we have for the losers, Johnny?* Bynes mocked himself. *Well… Detective Bynes has won a day of testifying at trial in a murder case. But that's not all; he also gets to do further investigation to find another witness who will give more credibility than the unbelievable crackhead prostitute.* That's what he deserved when he played the game of charging someone with a crime when he was not certain they did it.

Thanks for playing, and remember, every contestant is a winner.

CHAPTER 12

Carlos sat in his cell reading *Tom Sawyer.* He checked the book out from the jail library because the selection was small, and the Stephen King novels were already taken. Only the classics were left. Carlos checked out the book a week ago and hadn't made much progress since his arrest and arraignment a month ago.

He shared a cell with Hooch, a "jailhouse lawyer" with a history of mental illness. Hooch killed two drug dealers because he believed they were demons sent by the devil to possess his soul. He told the police that he saved himself and humanity from these demons. A psychiatric evaluation showed that he was legally insane and could not be prosecuted. The prosecutor came up to Hooch and made him an offer: Hooch could either serve the rest of his life in a mental institution, with no chance of getting out, or he could serve two life sentences in prison. He was very familiar with mental institutions from his time spent in one as a child, and they scared him; prison was the obvious answer. Hooch spent the next thirty years reading law books and compiling a library of legal forms and articles. Inmates throughout the prison came to him for legal advice, and if they did not want it, Hooch would insist on providing it.

"When's your court date?" Hooch asked.

"Next week."

Hooch pulled out a stack of documents and handed them to Carlos. "Here. You have to make sure that your lawyer files these motions. It's very important to your case. Without these, you'll be screwed. Who's representing you?"

"I don't know. Some public defender."

"You got a public pretender? You'd better take over your case. Have you considered trying this yourself? I've represented myself several times."

"Really? Did you win?"

"Uh... no, but they knew I was good."

"Vega!" a voice from outside the cell yelled.

"Right here," Carlos replied.

"Legal visit. Let's go," the voice said.

Hooch grabbed the motions and placed them in Carlos's hand. "Have him file these for you."

The prison guard opened the cell door and walked Carlos through a maze of corridors and locked doors to the other side of the prison. The guard then opened a door to the visiting room and told him that his lawyer was in room four. Carlos opened the door to the legal visiting room. The room was small, with only three plastic chairs and a wooden table. Across the table was a short and skinny man in his late forties. The man held his hand out and said, "Hi. I'm James Jaynowski. People call me Jimmy J. I'm your lawyer."

Carlos shook his hand. "Hi. I'm supposed to give these to you." Carlos handed the documents to Jimmy J.

Jimmy reviewed the documents and said," I see you met Anthony Michael Beasley the fifth."

"No. I got them from Hooch."

"Right. That's Hooch's real name. He was nicknamed Hooch after a character on TV who was crazy. Anyhow… I filed several of these motions already."

"What's going on with my case, Jimmy?"

"I received all the information on your case from the state's attorney. I have brought all the police reports and statements. I have the coroner's report and information from the forensic labs."

"Well, here's what happened..." Carlos started.

"Stop. I don't need to know your story right now."

"What?"

"I know it sounds weird but let me explain. If this were a car accident, I would want to know all the information you could give me. Hell, we would probably even drive to the scene of the accident. The same would be true for any kind of case except a criminal case. I am bound by certain rules of ethics. If you tell me your story now, and then you decide to change your story later, I cannot ethically have you testify. Under the rules of ethics, if I believe you will lie under oath, I cannot ask you questions on the stand. It puts me in a legal bind and can do serious damage to you at trial. So, here's what we do. I will show you all the evidence in the case. Once you look over the evidence and know how this evidence can be used at trial, then you can tell me your story. The idea is that once you tell me your version of the facts, we are locked into that version of the facts throughout the case. Do you understand?"

"Yeah. I didn't know that, but it makes sense. So, what does the evidence say?"

"So far, the evidence tells me that the state does not have a strong case. I say 'so far' because evidence continues to come in, even during a trial. I've seen last-minute witnesses show up during trial who completely change the case. The state claims you walked into the bodega and pulled a gun on the victim. You had him open the safe, and then you put him on his knees and shot him once in the back and once in the back of the head. You took a few thousand dollars out of the safe and ran out the front door. On your way out, you ran into the state's only identification witness. After the murder, you celebrated by buying some eight balls and got high in an alley."

Jimmy J. continued. "The strength of the state's case is that a witness identified you and pointed you out from hundreds of pages of mugshot books. The witness also identified you with a tattoo of an eagle on your hand. This witness said she heard shots being fired and saw you running out of the store with a gun in your hand. If the witness is believed on the stand, she can convict you. Furthermore, you have a history of substance abuse. The state is going to try to argue that you are a junkie who committed this crime in order to get high. It gives you a motive to murder the victim."

"Don't they need more than that to convict me?"

"No. That *can be* enough to get a conviction, but it's pretty flimsy. There are problems with the state's case. They never found the murder weapon, nor did they find the money. Police searched your alley and the streets around it and the bodega, but they never found the weapon or the money. No fingerprints or any kind of physical evidence of yours were at the crime scene. Therefore, the case boils down to this confidential informant and what they will say on the stand. My next move is to have the judge order the state to tell me the identity of the confidential informant so that we can get more information about them."

"What do you need me to do?"

"Don't discuss your case with anyone. I can't stress that enough. If you talk to a cellmate or a friend about your case, they can end up testifying against you in court. Prison is filled with people who want to get out of prison. One way to reduce your jail sentence is to testify against your cellmate and tell the jury that you admitted to murdering the victim."

"Anything else?"

"Yeah. A woman keeps calling me; she said she's your mom. I can't discuss your case with her unless I have written permission from you. Do you want me to talk to her, or do you want to handle it? I don't like discussing my clients' cases with their parents. I feel that that is more of your responsibility than mine. What do you want me to do?"

"Tell her that I didn't give you permission to talk to her. If she wants to know about the case, she can come see me."

Carlos and Jimmy J. said goodbye and parted ways. Carlos walked back to his cell, where Hooch bombarded him with questions about his legal visit. He told Hooch that he was too tired to talk and went to bed.

Carlos spent the rest of the night staring at the ceiling. He replayed the incident of running into the confidential informant over and over in his head. Who was she? How did she recognize him in the fraction of a second when they ran into each other? Why was she lying? What happened to the money in the safe? When he left Julito, the money was still there.

CHAPTER 13

It was standing room only in the judge's chambers. Judge Hahn discusses every case on the docket in his chambers. Only after he speaks with all the attorneys on every case will he go on the bench and open court. These meetings in chambers are called 'pre-trying the matter' with the judge. There would be several of these meetings before the state or the judge would make an offer to the defendant.

Jimmy J. walked into Judge Hahn's chambers and stood against the wall, waiting for his case to be discussed. This was usually the most uncomfortable part of practicing law for Jimmy J. Judge Hahn, and most judges appointed to criminal courts are former prosecutors; they have no idea what it is like to defend a criminal defendant. Therefore, pre-trials often seem one-sided. First, the prosecutor reads the alleged facts of the case to the judge. The prosecutor usually throws in a couple of derogatory comments about the defendant. This usually gets a couple of chuckles from the court. The judge then looks at the defense attorney and asks about the defendant's story. Once the defense is explained, the prosecutor typically explains why they do not believe this story and that it is unlikely or far-fetched. Eventually, the prosecutor makes a ridiculous offer with excessive jail time, knowing that the judge will make an offer with less jail time. The rub is that the offer the judge makes is the one the prosecutor actually wants to be offered. The defense attorney can take the initiative and make an offer of their own, but these offers tend to be laughed at and ignored. Even the prosecutor knows, and usually brags, about the fact that they are in control; they are the offense, and the accused is the defense. The prosecutors determine what charges will be filed, they have the first and the last say in every hearing or trial, they have a natural trust of the jurors because they represent the good guys, and they have a stronger influence over the judge because they both prosecuted criminals and have an arrogant attitude that all defendants are guilty liars who need to be prosecuted to the fullest extent of the law. It's hard to sell your client to the court or prosecutor as an actual human being, placed in an unusual circumstance where they ended up making a poor decision. The world to them is black and white, with no shades of gray.

To Jimmy J., pre-trials are designed to be fundamentally unfair; that is why he hates them. Judge Hahn called Carlos's case. "Who's got Carlos Vega?"

"I do, Your Honor," said Anne Rosen. "This is a murder case over on the south side of Hartford. The defendant is a crackhead who was looking for his next high. He went into a small convenience store and held the owner at gunpoint. He made him open the safe and then shot him in the back of the head. The defendant stole about $3,000 in cash. The defendant was found the next day, only a few blocks away, sleeping in an alley; he was high when he was arrested."

The judge thought for a minute and then said, "This is a common story. I can't tell you how many of these cases I prosecuted when I was a state's attorney, and I continue to see these cases as a judge. These guys get high, commit a horrible crime in order to continue to get high, and when they get caught, they cry and claim that they suffer from this *disease* of drug addiction."

"Yeah," Anne chuckled. "We had an outbreak of that *disease* when I was in college. I think a few girls in my sorority caught it. Luckily, they found a cure by the time they graduated." The judge and the prosecutors had a good laugh.

Judge Hahn looked at Jimmy J. and said, "What do you have to say, Jimmy?"

"Well, the only evidence in this case comes from a 'confidential informant.' The informant is the only person to place the defendant at the scene of the crime. Other than that, there is no murder weapon, and no money was found. I need to know who the confidential informant is in order to properly build a defense."

Anne argued. "The confidential informant is scared. This defendant committed a murder, and she is afraid he will kill her before trial. I would ask that the name only be provided once a firm trial date has been set. This will give the defense a few weeks to do their investigation of the informant, while still protecting her from this violent felon."

The judge turned to Jimmy. "How do you respond?".

"I say no. The defendant is homeless, and his bail is set at $1 million. There is no way he will make bond. The state has to provide me with the informant's name now so that I can do my investigation and then properly advise my client."

Judge Hahn thought for a moment and looked at Anne. "He's right, Anne. Either provide him with the name of your confidential informant, or you can't call her as a witness in the trial."

"If I can't call her as a witness, then I have no case."

"Exactly," the judge said. "Either release the informant's name now or withdraw the charges against the defendant. You have no other options."

"It's Krystal Wiznet," Anne said. A chorus of snickers arose from around the room.

Judge Hahn smiled. "Your only witness is Krystal with a K?"

"Yes, but her story is very believable. This is a solid murder case. The photos of the crime scene alone will greatly impact the jury, and Krystal saw the defendant leave the scene of the crime with a gun."

"Maybe now is the time to make Jimmy an offer," the judge suggested.

Anne bit down on her lower lip, a habit she developed when pressured to come up with an offer at the last minute. "What if we drop the murder charge and have the defendant plead to manslaughter and illegal possession of a firearm for a sentence of twenty-five years?"

Judge Hahn looked back at Jimmy J. "It's better than the sixty-five years you would get for murder and an illegal firearm. I don't think I could give you a better offer."

"I'll run it by my client and see what he wants to do. How about if we continue the matter for a month, and let him think about it?"

"You got it, Jimmy," the judge said.

Jimmy J. left the judge's chambers and took the elevator down to the lock-up. The lock-up is the jail facility at the courthouse. The defendants who can't make bail are transported to court on the day of their hearing, and then they are transported back to prison.

The guards escorted Jimmy into the jail area, as there was no place for him to talk to Carlos alone.

"Hi, Carlos. They made you an offer today. Manslaughter and possession of an illegal weapon for a sentence of twenty-five years; they will drop the murder charge. Before you say yes or no, I will come up and meet with you to review everything with you before you make a decision. You have a month to think about it."

"I don't want the deal."

"Let's go over everything. I can't do that here. Once you have all the information, then decide what you want to do."

"Okay."

Jimmy J. and Carlos said their goodbyes.

CHAPTER 14

"Have you thought about an insanity defense?" Hooch asked. "I can work with you on it. We can draft a motion to have you evaluated by the court psychiatrist for diminished capacity. Then I can show you how to convince a psychiatrist that you don't understand right from wrong. Of course, you would have to spend some time in the mental hospital, but it might be worth it. What do you say?"

"I don't know," said Carlos. "If I'm truly innocent, why shouldn't I try my case? A trial is about finding the truth. Isn't that how it works?"

"Yeah," Hooch said. "For rich people who can afford an army of lawyers to defend them, along with a ton of expert witnesses to testify on their behalf. For the rest of us, not so much. It's about winning more than it is about getting to the truth. That's why I think you should give insanity a shot."

Carlos looked at Hooch for a moment and then thought that Hooch didn't successfully pretend to be insane as much as the psychiatrist noticed the obvious. "I don't think I could pull it off," Carlos said.

"Yeah, probably not," Hooch said. "It was a lot of work on my part to really get into that character and play the role of crazy, but it paid off. Not everyone can do that. Don't worry, though… we'll find you a good defense. What about a duress defense? Did someone make you do it?"

"I didn't do it. So, no one could have made me do it if I didn't do it."

"Yeah, but maybe you could say you did it, and then say someone made you do it."

"No. I think it is simpler just to say I didn't do it."

"How about self-defense? Did the victim try to shoot you, and you killed him to defend yourself?"

"He was shot in the back of the head at close range. Wouldn't he have had to have been facing me if it were self-defense?"

"Good point," Hooch said. "Maybe that's not the way to go. What about third-party culpability?"

"What's that?"

"It's where you claim the crime was committed by another person."

"Maybe. I mean… I didn't kill him, so it had to be someone else. The question is who?"

"Vega," a voice shouted from outside the cell.

"Right here," Carlos replied.

"Front and center. You got a visitor," the guard shouted.

"That must be my legal visit. It's been a week since our last court date."

Hooch said, "At least he visits you in jail. That's more than my lawyer ever did. Make sure you discuss the third-party culpability defense. Maybe the victim had some enemies who were out to get him."

The cell door opened, and a guard guided Carlos again through the maze of corridors, cell doors, and locked doors to the visiting room. "Which room?" Carlos asked.

"No visiting room today. Your lawyer's not here. You have a regular visitor." The guard pointed to an elderly and frail Hispanic woman sitting at a table across the room. "Her," he said. Almost all the seats were taken, but somehow, she managed to get a table alone.

Carlos's heart sank as he realized that his mom had come to visit. He had not seen her in two years, since he left home to live in the alley. She probably knew nothing about his charges, so he would have to explain everything to her. Maybe she is here to tell me how disappointed she is in me and that this is what I deserve, he thought to himself. Maybe she wants me to find God. On the other hand, maybe she wants to reconcile. Either way, it's time to face the music.

Carlos arrived at the table, and his mother stood up and put her arms around him and held him tight. Carlos put his arms around her. He could feel her sobbing into his chest. He continued to hold her tight. Carlos wanted to cry, but he held it in. He couldn't do that in front of his fellow inmates. He had to be strong and not show weakness. If others thought he was weak, he would be seen as an easy target and attacked on a regular basis.

They sat down and held hands across the table.

"Carlos… what happened?"

"I'm charged with murder. I didn't do it."

"Yes. I heard that they think you shot Julito. I contacted your lawyer. All he would do is tell me that you were here. I came to see you and see how you are doing. I also came here to talk about us, to see if we can fix our relationship."

"Momma. There's nothing more that I want."

"What happened to you, Carlos?" She cried as she spoke in broken sentences. "You were a smart young man in high school. You were a talented football player with scouts looking to offer you a scholarship to a four-year university. The world was in the palm of your hand, but you threw it all away. What happened?"

Carlos fought back tears as he answered slowly. "The easy answer is I don't know. Yes, it was the drugs. My addiction is strong, and it feeds on everything I love and everything that is important in my life. Friends introduced me to drugs in high school, and it wasn't a big deal. I would smoke some weed at parties on the weekends. When I got into college, I felt a lot of pressure. Classes were tough, most of my friends in high school went to other colleges; I felt alone. In high school, I was the man. I was a football star and did well in school. In college, I never stood out."

"But Carlos. That's just life. Your whole life is about starting over again, and again, and again. College is starting over from high school. Having a career is starting over after college. Getting married and having a family is also a big life-changing event," his mom explained.

"I guess I just wanted things to be the way they were."

"Yes, it's tough. But you also have the ability to decide who you want to be, the kind of man you will become."

There were a few moments of silence. Perhaps he should have been stronger. Maybe if he had talked with his mother more, he would have made better decisions.

"Mom… I felt alone, but instead of reaching for you, I turned to drugs. A friend gave me opioids to try to make college bearable. And for a while, it worked. Drugs made me feel like I could do anything, and it was great… until it wasn't. Eventually, all I wanted to do was get high. I stopped going to school. I stopped working. I stopped playing football. When I got arrested, I did okay on probation, but I couldn't wait to get high. The day probation ended, I used."

"Carlos, you stole from me."

"I did. I'm not proud of it. I stole a lot. At first, it was money from your purse. Then it was objects around the house. Then it ended with your ring."

"I never saw you after that. What happened?"

"I lived in an alley. I ate out of the garbage can behind the Italian restaurant. I did odd jobs here and there to buy drugs. I got arrested a few more times. My goal was to be high as much as possible. I tried rehab a few times, but I could never stick with it."

"Are you still using?"

"I've been in jail for about a month and a half. This arrest has been very sobering—in more ways than one. After I heard the charges, I stopped using. I've been clean since then, which isn't easy because it's easier to get drugs in here than it is on the street."

They faced each other in silence, wondering how they were going to repair this situation without hurting each other's feelings. Carlos stared into his mother's eyes and said, "I love you, Mom. I missed you so much. I can't tell you how much it means to me that you came today."

Mom looked up at Carlos and began crying again. "I love you too, Carlos. I want you back. How do we do that?"

"Well... I'm gonna be here for a while. But I am making the best of my time. I have not relapsed. I'm taking a junior college class. I'm on the list for a substance abuse program, which I hope to take soon. Seeing you as much as possible would be great."

"When are you coming home?"

"I'm not sure. It's a murder charge. If I'm found guilty, I am facing sixty-five years."

Mom pulled out her rosary beads and began praying. She started to cry again.

"Mom... I'm innocent. I didn't do this. I have faith in my lawyer." Mom began to rock back and forth in her chair, holding her rosary beads in a tighter grip and saying the Our Father prayer over and over. This always put the fear of God in Carlos. "Mom, I can win this trial."

Mom stopped and looked up at him. "Didn't your friend Alejandro say he was going to win his murder trial?"

Carlos looked away from her. "That was different."

"What about Pedro, who you played football with? He was offered five years, but he wanted a trial, and he lost. How much time does he have to do?"

"Thirty years," Carlos said, still looking away.

There was more silence. Carlos looked back at his mother. They made an offer. Twenty-five years for manslaughter instead of murder. Are you saying I should take the offer?"

"That's your choice, Carlos. If you get convicted, you will end up dying in jail. I would like to think that you will get out at some point in your life and make something of yourself. I would like to be there when you are released and watch you turn your life around. If you do twenty-five years, I will be seventy when you get out. If you do sixty-five years, I will be dead before you get out—*if* you get out."

"Are you telling me to plead to something I didn't do, just to get less time?"

"No. I'm telling you that we are the victims of the choices we make. I hope you win your trial, but if you don't, you will regret turning down the offer of twenty-five years when you are serving sixty-five. And you will have to live with it for the rest of your life. Can you live with yourself if that happens?"

"I don't know."

"It's a high price to pay. Do you want to be right and hope you win at trial or do you want to take the shorter sentence and get home someday?"

"I don't know, Momma. It's a lot to think about."

"No matter what, I will always come to see you. I want you back in my life, even if it is only for an hour or two a week."

"Time's up everyone. Time to say goodbye," a guard's voice shouted across the room. Carlos and his mom stood up and embraced one more time.

Mom looked up at him and put her hand lovingly on his face. "Make good choices."

Carlos was walked back through the maze and to his cell. He entered his cell and went to bed. Hooch was already asleep, so he did not harass Carlos about his case. Carlos couldn't sleep. He stared at the ceiling, thinking about what to do with his offer. Only a few hours ago, the choice was obvious; try the case. Now he was having second thoughts.

CHAPTER 15

Hooch was lying in bed, talking to Carlos in the bunk bed above him. "It's a brilliant plan. You have to do it."

"I don't know. They are asking me to plead to a crime that I didn't commit. I don't know anything about this habeas thing you want me to do."

"It's simple. You plead 'nolo contendre', meaning you accept no responsibility for the manslaughter, but you agree that there is enough evidence that could convict you. It's treated like a guilty plea, but you never plead guilty. You get sentenced to twenty-five years or even less if your lawyer can get you an even better offer. The day after you are sentenced, you file a petition for a writ of habeas corpus."

"What does that do?"

"It's a lawsuit. You are suing the warden to be released from prison for wrongful incarceration. Your lawsuit basically says that your lawyer screwed up and failed to properly advise you or failed to investigate your case. Then you use the habeas to get out even earlier or undo your conviction entirely. That way, you still have the benefit of the low offer."

"But my lawyer seems to be doing a good job."

"He'll understand when you raise this claim. It happens to all criminal defense attorneys. They get used to this. He'll get paid to testify on your behalf and talk about how he screwed up."

"He'll say that he screwed up?" Carlos said, not believing Hooch.

"Absolutely. Defense attorneys are trained in law school to 'fall on their sword' if it benefits their client. They will gladly agree with your petition that they made an error in order to get you out of jail. I know it sounds strange, but you're gonna have to trust my experience on this."

"I don't know, man. If it's so easy, how come I don't hear about people doing this all the time?"

"People do it all the time. They just don't do it right. They are not lucky enough to have Hooch, Legal Savant, as a cellmate to walk them through this."

"Vega! Legal visit," yelled the guard from outside his cell.

"Tell your lawyer that you want to cop out," Hooch said.

"We'll see," said Carlos.

The guard walked Carlos through the maze of corridors and closed doors. As the guard opened the door to the visiting room, he said, "Room number 3. Your lawyer is already there."

Carlos walked in and saw Jimmy J. standing up, waiting to greet him.

"Good to see you, Carlos." They shook hands and sat down.

"Okay, Carlos, let's go over the evidence."

"Before you start, I'm thinking of copping out to the manslaughter charge."

"Okay. Before you do that, let me tell you about all the evidence that they have so far. Then you can make an informed decision as to what you want to do."

"Alright. Whaddya got?"

"Well, the court ordered the state to release the name of the confidential informant. Her name is Krystal Wiznet. Do you know her?"

"No. I don't think I have ever met her." Carlos said disappointedly. He thought he had probably met her previously, which was why she was able to identify him from a split-second encounter.

"Krystal goes by the name 'Krystal with a K'."

"Ohhhhh. Krystal with a K. Of course I know her. She's a crackhead. I used to see her at some of the crack houses buying drugs and getting high. We got high together quite a few times. I haven't seen her for months. Now it all makes sense. She can place me at the scene because she knew that I lived in an alley a few blocks away. She knows what I look like, and she has seen my tattoo."

"Exactly," said Jimmy J. "She does not have a great track record. Krystal with a K has been an informant for the Hartford Police Department for years. On rare occasions, she has testified, but her credibility has been destroyed with her continuous drug use and spending her informant money on drugs, which provides a motive to lie."

"Jimmy, what do you think? Should I do the trial?"

Jimmy paused for a second and said, "Carlos, it's your decision. Here's what you're facing. If you try the case, they will have to call Krystal with a K to testify how she saw you run from the murder scene with a gun. I can discredit her testimony, to an extent. The question comes down to whether a jury will believe her testimony enough to convict you of murder. The offer of twenty-five years is a good offer, but you are the one who has to live with it."

"If I take the plea, can I file a habeas?"

"You can always file the habeas, but you will be in a position where you will have to prove that I made a mistake that was so bad that you should be allowed to withdraw your plea and try your case over again. That's a very high standard to meet, and most people can't meet it. I take it Hooch is giving you legal advice again?"

Carlos smiled and said, "Yeah."

"I highly recommend that you take legal advice from a licensed attorney." Jimmy J. then paused for a moment. "What are you thinking of doing, Carlos?"

"I think I wanna cop out. The twenty-five years sucks, but I don't want to do sixty-five years."

"That's the hook. The state does this to everyone. The state arrests them and throws every possible charge at them. Then they make an offer, which becomes tempting, because they are facing decades of jail time if they get convicted on the other charges. That's why they settle over ninety percent of their cases."

Carlos was silent for a moment. "I'll take the deal."

STEVE'S EDUCATION

CHAPTER 16

November came fast. Steve finally got the results of his bar exam at the beginning of November, and he passed. The swearing-in process was a formal admission before the members of the Connecticut Supreme Court, where the names of the new members of the bar were announced, and new members shook hands with all the members of the Supreme Court. Jenny attended Steve's admission ceremony, even though he said it was no big deal.

Steve, Jenny, and Buddy woke up early every Saturday morning and went hiking. Jenny took business advice from Steve and hired her first employee, a single mother whom she trained to do medical billing. This allowed Jenny to seek out more accounts and get more work done. Her business was beginning to boom.

Steve and Jenny's relationship continued to blossom. They had dinner together almost every night. Steve helped her business grow while Jenny showed Steve that there was more to life than working as hard as you can to achieve the goal of a coveted job, where you would continue to work even harder. Buddy was happy because he got to see mom and dad more often, and he got at least three days in the dog park, where he could run and play with other dogs.

Steve was starting to turn the office around. With help from Sam and the rest of the crew, Steve made a list of all the deadlines that were coming up on each case. This was the old-school method created for lawyers called a "tickler system." While most lawyers put these deadlines in a computerized day runner, Steve thought that this older system would work best for Sam and Steve, as Sam was not as computer oriented as Steve. The deadlines were posted in chronological order on a chalkboard for the whole office to see. Since Steve could not legally practice law until he was sworn in, he spent from August to November filing all the appropriate paperwork, motions, and briefs on each case as these deadlines arose. All deadlines were under control.

Steve's education was another story. Steve was great at paperwork but was unable to get the real-life experience of being a lawyer until he was sworn in as a full-fledged attorney. He did go across the street and watch Sam talk to some clients, but he didn't gain much from the experience. Steve was supposed to watch one of Sam's trials, but he ended up doing paperwork instead. While Steve knew the law, he had no experience talking to clients about their cases, nor did he have any experience in a real court before a real judge.

Instead, Steve took the business approach to his problem. Steve lacked experience talking to clients and trial experience. Therefore, he chose to give himself a rigorous trial schedule where he would prepare and try a case every week for the next several months. Placing himself in a situation where he would do nothing but trials and work directly with clients would give him a ton of experience in a short time.

CHAPTER 17

Bryce Jahari came to America from Haiti when he was ten years old. Although he spoke fluent English, it was difficult for others to understand what he was saying because of his thick accent. As a result, he was picked on by other children and was somewhat of an outcast. A local Waterbury gang, the Dakota Brothers, reached out to him because he was bigger than the other kids; he quickly added an element of fear to the gang, making them more than a group of young punks. Bryce was the "muscle," and all the children who made fun of him stopped. The Dakota Brothers gave Bryce respect.

As time went on, Bryce built a substantial criminal record. Since Bryce was still an adolescent, the court ordered him to attend Scared Straight, a program for juvenile delinquents. They would go to prison and hear lectures from the inmates about how scary jail can be. But the program didn't deter Bryce, and he continued to break the law. Each time he was arrested, he was sent to the Scared Straight Program. The first time, he actually was scared. The second and third times he attended, he was less so. After the fourth time, he was not scared at all. When he attended for the fifth time, he was friends with all of the inmates who were speaking.

By the time Bryce was twenty, the Dakota Brothers had a prospering drug business. The brothers had new recruits out on every street corner selling meth, crack, and heroin. Bryce handled turf disputes, which were common in Waterbury. Bryce's mere appearance would often be enough to the opposing gang to back down. But if it wasn't, Bryce was more than willing to take matters into his own hands. Eventually, he was charged with murder for shooting a rival gang member in a turf dispute. While Bryce claimed he was innocent, he was found guilty by a jury of his peers and sentenced to sixty-five years.

Steve sat in the prison's visitors' lobby along with parents, wives, and girlfriends of inmates, all waiting for their forty-five-minute visits. Steve watched the visitors interact. They all seemed to know each other, as if they had visited at this time on this day for years. They had formed a make-shift support group, and it no longer seemed weird for most of them.

But that wasn't the case for Steve. He still felt uncomfortable sitting and waiting for a meeting with a convicted murderer. There was always the element of the unknown. How would his client respond? Would he attack him? While this would be a remote possibility with most clients, this one had actually been convicted of murder.

"Jahari" yelled a voice across the lobby. Steve got up and walked across the room. He passed through the metal detector and went into the visiting room. "Room six, counselor," the guard said.

"Thank you," Steve said. Steve walked across the visiting room to the door with a big red six painted on the outside. Steve opened the door and saw a large man sitting in a plastic chair behind a round wooden table. As the man stood, Steve could see that he was about six foot, five inches tall and easily weighed 280 pounds. Steve extended his hand and said, "Mr. Jahari?"

"Yes," he said.

"I'm Steve Lansford. I'm your attorney."

"Is this about the guy I beat up in a bar?"

"No."

"You represent me in the rape case?"

"No."

"My violation of probation?"

"No."

"Is this about the time I was pimping my girlfriend out?"

"No."

"You're the appellate attorney for my drug possession conviction?"

"No."

"You represent me in my child support case?"

"No."

"You represent me in my DCF case?"

"No."

"Okay, then what are you here for?"

"I represent you on the case where you were convicted of shooting a guy in the face for selling drugs on your turf."

"Oh yeah. That one. So, what's going on?" They both sat down around the table.

"Well... I represent you in your habeas case. We have a trial coming up, and I wanted to talk to you about your case. While I have read all the transcripts and all the motions and briefs that were filed, I need to hear what you saw because you lived this, while I only read about it. Did anything strange happen in your case?"

Bryce took a minute to compose his thoughts and said, "Yeah. My lawyer fucked me. He didn't do anything for me. He did no investigation. He did nothing. He kept telling me to accept the plea, and I wouldn't because I didn't do it."

"Two people from your own gang testified that they saw you shoot this guy in the face. Do you have an alibi?"

"Hell yeah. That's what I've been saying. I was with my boy Crazy K. We were hanging out all day at his house in Hartford. The killing was in Waterbury, over thirty miles away. I wasn't even near there."

"Where can I find Crazy K? What's his real name? Is he a member of the gang?"

"His name is Kalvin Agholor. We grew up together in the neighborhood. When I was younger, other kids picked on me because I had an accent. He was the only one who didn't make fun of me and would listen. Kalvin never joined a gang because his dad would kick his ass. We were hanging out that day, washing his car and just talking. We ate dinner and watched football on TV all night. I told my lawyer about Kalvin, but he never talked to him."

"What about the two guys from your crew that testified for the state, placing you at the scene of the crime and killing the victim? We need to explain why their testimony is not accurate."

"They were working with the cops. They were both new recruits to the crew. They were arrested for selling to cops. In exchange for cooperating with the cops, their charges were dismissed. That's why they lied. My attorney never did any investigation into these witnesses to see if they had charges pending and what happened to those charges."

"Where can I find Kalvin?"

"He still lives in the projects in Waterbury."

"Okay. I'll check him out. I'll have him there for trial."

"See you then."

CHAPTER 18

Steve sat in his office preparing for Bryce's trial. There was a knock on the door jamb. "Say there, Mr. Steve, can I come in?"

"What's up, Leon?"

"Well, I completed the investigation in the Jahari case for you."

"Great. What did you find?"

"I found Kalvin. He was living in the neighborhood where Bryce used to live. I spoke with him, and he told me his story. He gave me the same story that Bryce told you. They were together that day, washing cars, at Kalvin's house. They spent the afternoon together, then they ordered a pizza and watched Monday night football. Bryce was with Kalvin from 11:30 in the morning until midnight. Bryce never left—he was with Kalvin for twelve and a half hours. The murder occurred between 7:30 and 8 at night; Bryce could not have committed the crime."

"Did you get a sworn statement from him?"

"Yup. He wrote the whole thing out and swore to it under oath."

"What about the two witnesses for the state?"

"They did have pending charges for possession of illegal narcotics with intent to sell. It was their first arrest. They pleaded and were allowed to go to a drug program instead of going to prison. They got a good deal, but it was their first arrest, and any lawyer could have gotten them the drug program. They didn't get any special favors."

"Did you talk to these witnesses?"

"I tried. They wouldn't talk to me."

"Anything else?"

"Kalvin doesn't come across as a great witness. He said everything that Bryce said he would, but it's his presentation. He had a hard time looking me in the eye. When he would tell his story, his eyes would look up and to the right. It seems like he is lying."

"Thanks, Leon. I appreciate your help."

Steve prepared his case.

CHAPTER 19

The time had finally come. Steve stood in the courtroom drinking water from a paper cup. He had poured it from the pitcher of water on the defendant's table, and it tasted stale. Nobody ever cleaned the pitchers.

In a few minutes, the judge would come out and start the trial. In Connecticut, all habeas trials are bench trials, meaning that there is no jury. Instead, the judge decides the case. Some lawyers believed that being a judge on the habeas court was a punishment or a job for the new judges. You spend your days listening to convicted felons whining about how they were mistreated. Obviously, it would get old after a while. Any judge with tenure never presided over a habeas court.

The state's attorney arrived. Jackie Garcon was six foot, two inches with a mop of dyed red hair.

"I'm Jackie Garcon," she said, reaching out her hand. "Nice to meet you."

"Nice to meet you," Steve replied.

"How long do you think we will be here today? I would like to get my dog from the vet before they close."

"Shouldn't be long. I only have two witnesses. How about you?"

"I have the original trial lawyer for Jahari subpoenaed in case I need him but no other witnesses."

Bryce was brought out and placed next to Steve. Judge Carver stepped out and took his seat on the bench. Steve was familiar with Judge Carver's decisions. Judge Carver retired several years ago but continued to hear cases as a retired judge. If he works 100 days a year, then he gets a full-time salary, just enough to milk the system. Judge Carver looked across the room and asked, "Counsel, are you ready to start?"

Both the petitioner and the state indicated they were ready. Carver looked at Steve. "Call your first witness."

"Petitioner calls Bryce Jahari to the stand." Bryce was brought to the stand and sworn in. He stated his name and address for the record.

"Good morning, Mr. Jahari."

"Good morning."

"Mr. Jahari, can you tell us why you are currently incarcerated?"

"I was convicted of murder."

"Do you remember the night of October 11?"

"Yes."

"What happened that night?"

"Well… that day I was hanging out with my friend, Kalvin…Kalvin Agholor."

"Okay. What did you do with Kalvin?"

"I went to Kalvin's house in Hartford. We spent the day together. We were just talking and washing cars at his house. We talked all day and played video games. As it got dark, we ordered a pizza and watched Monday night football until about midnight."

"What happened after that?"

"I went home. When I woke up, police officers were at my door, and they arrested me for a murder that happened the day before in Waterbury."

"Did you tell them that you were with Kalvin all day?"

"No. I kept my mouth shut and asked for a lawyer."

"Okay. And were you given a lawyer?"

"Yes. He showed up around a month later. After I was charged, he told me not to talk to anyone about the case."

"Did you ever tell him about being at Kalvin's house at the time of the murder and that you had an alibi witness?"

"Yes. I begged him to call Kalvin as a witness, but he never did."

"What happened next?"

"We went to trial. The state called their witnesses. We didn't call any witnesses, and I was convicted."

"Now the state had two witnesses testify who claimed they witnessed you murder the victim in this matter. Was their testimony true?"

"No. They lied. I was not at the scene of the crime that night."

"Why would they lie?"

"Lots of reasons. They were selling drugs for the gang. They picked up charges for possession of illegal narcotics with intent to sell. They had a reason to get me convicted because they didn't want to go to jail for the drug charges. Also, with me out of the way, they had the opportunity to move up in the gang and assume my position."

"What are you hoping that the court will do today?"

"I am hoping that this court would grant my habeas petition and open my original conviction, so that I could raise my alibi defense, which my lawyer did not raise in my last trial."

"No further questions, Your Honor."

Judge Carver looked over to the State's Attorney. "Attorney Garcon. Cross examination?"

Jackie looked at the court and said with a smile, "No, thank you, Your Honor."

Judge Carver looked over to Steve. "Next witness."

Steve stood silent for a moment. He knew he was walking into a trap, but he did not know exactly what it was. Why didn't she ask him any questions? She could have asked Bryce about the facts of the case that looked damaging to him. She could have asked him about his previous convictions. Instead, she chose to ask nothing. Why would she do that?

"Do you have another witness, counsel?" The judge asked.

"Yes, Your Honor. Petitioner calls Kalvin Agholor." Kalvin walked from the audience to the witness stand. He was sworn in and stated his name and address. "Good morning, Mr. Agholor," Steve asked.

"Good morning," Kalvin replied.

"Do you know the petitioner in this matter, Mr. Bryce Jahari?"

"Yes, we grew up together in Waterbury, Connecticut."

"You've been friends for a long time?"

"Absolutely. We graduated from high school together in Waterbury. I went to college in Hartford, so my mom moved to Hartford after I finished high school. I recently moved back to Waterbury."

"Do you recall the night of October 11?"

"Yes. I was hanging out with Kalvin that day. We were washing cars and talking all day. When it got dark, we ate dinner and watched Monday night football. The next day, I heard he got arrested for murder. I called the police to tell them that Kalvin was with me that day, but they wouldn't take my statement. Later on, I called Kalvin's lawyer and told him that he was with me all day and that I would testify to it; I was never called as a witness."

"I have no further questions, Your Honor."

Judge Carver looked over the top of the bench and said, "Cross-examination, Miss Garcon?"

Jackie Garcon stood up from her chair and approached the witness. "Yes, Your Honor," she responded. Steve watched and studied Attorney Garcon. Jackie stood before Kalvin and looked him in the eye. Kalvin could not hold her gaze; he kept looking over to his right to avoid eye contact. Jackie Garcon was an experienced trial lawyer and had seen hundreds of witnesses try to lie on the stand. She has made some liars cry on the stand and beg for forgiveness; the rest she just made look foolish. She started off with politeness. "Good morning, Mr. Agholor. How are you this morning?"

"Very good, ma'am. Thank you."

"My name is Jackie Garcon. I represent the state in this matter. I just have a couple of follow-up questions about your testimony."

"Um... Okay," Kalvin said.

"Now, Mr. Agholor, you testified that you were with Mr. Jahari all day on October 11. Correct?"

"Yes."

"Is it possible that you are confusing that day with another day?"

"No. I am certain it was that day."

"So, there is no possibility that you are confused about what date you spent the day with Mr. Jahari washing cars and watching football?"

"No. I am sure because it was the day before he got arrested for murder. I would never forget that day."

"Okay. And by any chance did Mr. Jahari leave you for a while then return later that day?"

"No. I would have remembered that."

"I see. Let me ask you this: have you ever been convicted of a felony?"

Kalvin paused for a moment and looked at Steve and Bryce. Steve knew there was nothing he could do. It was a fair question about Kalvin's credibility as a witness. Kalvin looked down and said, "Yes."

"What were you convicted of?"

"I was convicted of robbery in the second degree."

"Did you have to serve time for this conviction?"

"Yes."

"Do you recall when you served this time in prison?"

Kalvin was now looking away from Jackie. "I don't recall."

"If I showed you records from the Department of Corrections that show you were incarcerated from September of 2007 to January of 2008, would that refresh your memory?"

Kalvin understood that he was now facing a perjury charge. He looked directly at Jackie Garcon and said, "Now that you mention it, I believe that I am confusing the dates. I believe I was incarcerated during that time. I must have been thinking about a different day."

Attorney Garcon looked at Kalvin, knowing she had him where she wanted him: in fear of being charged of perjury. She asked him one last question to seal the deal. "So, is it fair to say that Mr. Jahari was not with you on October 11?"

"Yes. I was not with Mr. Jahari on October 11."

"Thank you, nothing further."

Judge Carver looked over at Steve. "Any more questions?"

"No, Your Honor."

"Anymore witnesses?"

Steve asked, "Your Honor, may I have a few minutes with my client?"

Judge Carver looked at the clock on the wall and said, "Let's take the morning break, and be back in ten minutes."

The marshal walked up to Bryce and had him stand up, so that he could be escorted into a prisoner holding area just outside the courtroom. "Do you need to talk to your client alone, counselor?"

"Yes," Steve said. The marshal took Bryce to the holding room while Steve went into the lawyer's entrance of the room. A metal screen separated them while they talked. Steve held his anger back in order to have a rational conversation with Bryce. He sat there, staring at Bryce for a moment.

Bryce looked back at Steve with a serious countenance, which slowly turned into a smile, and then turned into laughter. Bryce looked at him and said, "Hey man, are you pissed at me?"

Steve shook his head in disgust. "What's going on here, Bryce?"

Bryce smiled and said, "You know what they say. If you ain't cheating, you ain't trying. Look, I just want to get the fuck outta here."

"You put Kalvin up to this?"

"Look man, everyone in here knew I killed that kid. I told everyone in jail because it gave me a truckload of street cred, but I still wanted to get out of here. So, I asked Kalvin to lie for me. We got our stories straight, and then I filed the habeas. I never told you because I knew that you wouldn't be on board with it. Look... I know these things are hard to win; that's why I stacked the deck. I want to get out."

Steve stood up and said, "Well, I think we're done. Let's see if we can get out of here without me losing my license and without you picking up a new perjury or conspiracy charge.

Court reconvened. Judge Carver looked up from the newspaper in front of him and asked, "What are we doing, counsel?"

Steve stood up and said, "Your Honor, the petitioner rests at this point, and we waive closing arguments. We feel that the facts speak for themselves."

"Very well." Judge Carver looked at Jackie. "Any witnesses or closing arguments?"

"No, Your Honor."

Judge Carver studied his notes for a moment and then looked up. "After hearing the testimony, reviewing the briefs, and any and all evidence submitted, I find that the petitioner has failed to meet the burden outlined in U.S. versus Strickland. Therefore, I am denying the petition. Petitioner has a right to appeal this decision. Court is adjourned."

Steve and Bryce stood up. Bryce leaned over and spoke into Steve's ear. "Do you think I should appeal his decision?"

Steve looked at Bryce and said, "You have no chance of winning. The only thing that would do is make the state angry that they have to respond to your appeal, and they might decide to even the score by charging you and Kalvin with perjury and conspiracy to commit perjury. You have nothing to win, but you can file it if you want."

"I guess I'll pass, then." Bryce shook Steve's hand before the marshal took Bryce back to the holding cell.

Steve packed up all his papers back into Bryce's file box. As he turned to head out of court, Jackie approached him and said, "Is it your first time?"

Steve smiled and said, "First trial? Yes."

Jackie laughed and said, "No. What I meant was, is this the first time that your client lied to you and had someone lie on his behalf?" She paused and then said, "You don't have to answer that. It happens a lot. You're not the first victim, and you certainly won't be the last."

"Thanks. I needed to hear that. I appreciate your understanding."

Steve and Jackie walked to the parking lot together and then bid each other farewell.

CHAPTER 20

Steve arrived at the office, walked through the front door, and went upstairs. He took Bryce's file and placed it with all the completed files. He then erased Bryce's trial from the tickler list. Roxy walked into the file room and began rolling up the sleeve of her blouse. "Check this out," she said. "I have been doing an extra set of reps with the twenty-pound dumbbells for the past three months. Can you see the added definition in my triceps?"

"Looks great, Roxy. Can I get a few minutes alone? I had a rough day at court, and I need to think it through."

"Yeah, sure. I just wanted to share the good news with you."

"Your arms look awesome. Congratulations."

Roxy smiled and went back to her desk downstairs. Steve went to his desk and turned on his computer to check his e-mail.

Sam walked into Steve's office and said, "Hey, pal. As senior partner of this branch of Rockingham & Myers, I am instituting a new mandatory lunch meeting at Rico's every Friday. I like to call it 'fucked-up Fridays'. It's where we talk about our fucked-up week to each other, and then our mind is cleared so we can enjoy the weekend before we have to endure another fucked-up week. What do you say?"

"I say hell yes. I don't feel like working right now, and lunch at Rico's sounds good."

Steve and Sam walked next door to Rico's and grabbed a booth. Sam ordered a margarita to get his weekend started, while Steve ordered a Shirley Temple and then spent five minutes explaining that it takes a tough guy to order this drink.

"So, how was your trial?" Sam asked. Steve explained how his client had conspired to commit fraud and perjury in court. Sam had a chuckle. "It's a rite of passage. Clients will lie to you. Odds are that clients convicted of a felony are more likely to lie to you. Lastly, a client who has been convicted of a felony and wants to be released from prison is most likely to lie to you."

"Yeah… I get that. But I am just mad that it made me look like an idiot. Not only was my client trying to dupe the court into thinking he had an alibi defense, but he had convinced me as well."

"Here's the truth. Not all clients are going to see you as their lawyer; they just see you as part of the system. You are no different from the state's attorney."

"But I am their attorney.'

"Right, but if Bryce told you that he had lined up a friend to lie in order to get him a new trial, what would you have done?"

"I would have told him no."

"Exactly. You see, he doesn't want a criminal lawyer, he wants a *criminal* lawyer—a lawyer willing to bend the rules just like he has. He considers any lawyer who plays by the rules as part of the system." Steve sat quietly, thinking about what Sam said.

Sam continued, "You did the right thing. Your client put you in a bind. The fact that you escaped without you, the client, or the witness being charged with a crime is actually good lawyering. This happens to every habeas attorney."

Steve felt better. Sam said, "Next week, you have another trial. Your plan of gaining the maximum amount of trial and client experience in the shortest period of time is going to work out for you."

Steve and Sam finished lunch and went back to the office. Sam then left for the day. Steve closed out Bryce's file and then began reviewing the file box for next week.

CHAPTER 21

Elvin Gideon's substance abuse problem started when he was a child, showing off by stealing his stepdad's beers from the refrigerator and sharing them with his friends. They thought he was cool because he could get beer as a thirteen-year-old. Eventually, Elvin's stepfather caught on to what was happening and beat him with a belt. Elvin had to come up with another way of getting alcohol to impress his friends, so he got a job at the corner liquor store. He worked as a stock boy and figured that the owner wouldn't miss a few beers here and there.

Soon, he went from stealing a few beers to taking a bottle of vodka or tequila once a week. Elvin's problem snowballed. He went from drinking on Saturday nights to drinking several times a week. Elvin eventually got caught stealing a bottle of Johnnie Walker Blue. The owner fired him and called his stepfather, who laughed at the owner for hiring Elvin in the first place. His stepdad didn't care about Elvin's addiction as long as his beer was safe.

Marijuana, cocaine, and crystal meth quickly joined Elvin's roster. Elvin mugged people for money to get his next fix; he was in and out of jail as a teenager and into his mid-twenties. But then, his life turned around. He met Betsy, and she became the love of his life. They married and moved into a small apartment in New Britain. His daughter, Baby Betsy, was born on the day of their first wedding anniversary.

Elvin attended Narcotics Anonymous on a daily basis and got a job washing cars at the local car dealership. The owner of the dealership, Al Shazir, was aware of Elvin's past and was impressed with Elvin's commitment to a fresh start; he had Elvin do several jobs around the dealership, such as getting parts, delivering cars to other dealerships, and cleaning the waiting room. Mr. Shazir helped Elvin secure a large three-bedroom apartment at his mother's apartment building. Elvin would do some maintenance work around the building in exchange for getting a discount on his rent. From time to time, he would even get an advance on his paycheck.

One day, Elvin was delivering parts in the company truck and decided to run home and make a sandwich. Betsy was supposed to be at work, and Baby Betsy at school. But when Elvin walked through the door, he caught Betsy in bed with another man. Betsy tried to explain, but Elvin wouldn't listen. His rage built up to a level he had never experienced before, and he beat up both of them. Betsy moved to her mother's house in New York and took Baby Betsy with her. It didn't take long for Elvin to fall back on drugs and alcohol to kill the pain.

Still, he was careful not to be high or drunk while he was at work. He drank alone at night during the week and got high with his friend Peetey on the weekends. Gradually, the weekends moved from using once to a full bender from Friday night to Monday morning.

One Sunday morning, police came to Elvin's apartment. Elvin didn't answer the door because he and Peetey were too high to hear the doorbell. Police kicked in the door and arrested Elvin for murder.

Several days later, Elvin woke up in a jail cell, wondering why he was there. A lawyer came to visit Elvin and explained that he was charged with the murder of Al Shazir. The lawyer explained that Elvin had given a signed confession a few days ago, even though Elvin had still been under the influence of cocaine and heroin. He showed Elvin pictures of the crime scene. Mr. Shazir had been beaten to death in his office at the dealership on a Friday night with a hammer. Elvin's fingerprints were on the hammer, which was left at the crime scene. Elvin also had Mr. Shazir's blood on the clothes he was wearing when he was arrested, and Mr. Shazir's wallet was found in Elvin's pocket.

Elvin's head was spinning. He did not know what had happened over the weekend. All he knew was that he was getting high with Peetey on Friday and had no clue as to what happened until he woke up in a jail cell.

There was strong evidence implicating Elvin in the murder, including his own confession. The lawyer explained that he may be able to keep the confession out of evidence, but the other facts were tough to beat. Elvin considered trying the case anyway, until his daughter visited him and asked him to take the offer of manslaughter and serve thirty years so that she had a chance of seeing him outside of jail. Elvin could not resist the request of his daughter and took the deal.

Fifteen years passed. A jailhouse lawyer named Hooch advised him that he should file a habeas petition against his lawyer. Hooch explained that he should see if Peetey would be an alibi witness for him, explaining that Elvin was not the murderer because he was with Peetey all weekend. Elvin filed the petition.

Rockingham & Myers was appointed to represent Elvin. Steve Lansford sat in the lobby of the visiting room, waiting for his name to be called. This was his second case, and he was still nervous. Things could only get better from here, he thought.

"Gideon – Legal visit," yelled out the prison guard.

Steve stood up and said, "Here." The prison guard escorted Steve to the visiting room.

"Visiting Room Six," the guard stated as he pointed to the large red six painted on the door. Steve opened the door and saw a slender man sitting at the table. The file indicated that Mr. Gideon was a man of medium height with a strong build—strong enough to beat another man to death. Over the past fifteen years, Mr. Gideon had lost a lot of muscle.

"Who are you?" Elvin said with an attitude.

"I'm your lawyer. My name is Steve Lansford."

"What makes you qualified to represent me?"

"Well, the Connecticut Bar says I'm qualified."

"How many of these habeas cases have you won?"

"None. But then again, very few, if any, petitions are granted."

"I don't know if I want you as my lawyer."

"Okay. You can ask the court to appoint a new lawyer, but usually the court won't grant your request unless you have grounds. The court will give you the option of hiring your own attorney or representing yourself. Are you going to hire your own lawyer or represent yourself?"

Elvin thought for a moment. "I can't afford a lawyer, and I don't want to represent myself."

"Well… sounds like you're stuck with me. I have your complete file, which I have read. I am ready, willing, and able to try your case. Do you want me to try it?"

"I guess."

"Well, I need to hear what happened the night that Mr. Shazir was killed. What did you do that day?"

"I didn't kill him."

"I understand that. What I need to know is what you did that day. Let's start with the morning."

"I didn't kill him."

"Again. I understand that you didn't kill him. What I am trying to get at is, are there any witnesses we can question or things we can investigate to help prove that you didn't kill the victim?"

Elvin began yelling, "Look, I am not going to lie on the stand for you."

Steve kept calm and said, "I am not asking you to lie. I cannot ethically ask you to lie. I am asking you to tell me the names of any witnesses to bring to the trial to support your case."

"I didn't kill him," Elvin yelled.

"I agree, you didn't kill him. Aside from you testifying that you didn't kill him, who else can testify that you didn't kill him?"

"Peetey."

"Okay. I have Peetey's name and address in the file. I can send out an investigator to find him and bring him to court. What will Peetey say?"

"That we were getting high together all weekend. We hooked up with some prostitutes on Friday, but they left later that night."

"Do you know the names of these ladies?"

"No."

"Do you have any idea where I can find them?"

"No. Peetey does. They were friends of his."

"Let's retrace your steps. What did you do from Friday morning until you were arrested?"

"How many times do I have to say that I didn't kill him? Mr. Shazir was a friend of mine. I would never kill him. He helped me out. We were friends for over ten years. I went to his family's parties. I even went to Christmas dinner at his house. Why would I kill him?"

"I never said you killed him. The state says you killed him because you confessed to it, and when you were arrested, your clothes had his blood on them."

"Yeah, but I didn't kill him. I wasn't even there."

"I understand. Let's try this… When did you leave work that day?"

"I left around two in the afternoon. I picked up some booze from the liquor store on my way home. Peetey showed up at three."

"What happened next?"

"Sometime later on in the night, he called the girls over. They partied with us and then they left."

"What happened after that?"

"I just got high. Passed out. Woke up in a jail cell."

"Did you go out to eat?"

"Not that I remember."

"If you did, would you have paid cash or a credit card?"

Elvin looked up to the ceiling and thought for a moment. "I think I was light on cash after going to the liquor store, so I probably would have used my card. I am not sure. It's been fifteen years."

"Do you recall seeing anyone that night or going anywhere that night?"

"How many times do I have to tell you that I didn't kill him? I loved that man. He was my friend."

"I'm not asking you if you killed him, I'm asking you if there are any other potential witnesses to call other than Peetey and the two prostitutes."

"No. I don't remember going anywhere."

"Okay. What I am going to do is have the investigator find these people and see what they say. They may be able to have an explanation as to what happened that night. I hope to have some information soon, so I will be back in a few days to tell you what we found and to get you ready for trial."

"Great. That sounds good."

"Is there anything else I need to know?"

"Yeah… I didn't kill him."

"Yeah. I heard that somewhere."

Steve and Elvin parted ways, and Steve went back to the office.

CHAPTER 22

A week had passed since Steve's interview with Elvin. Steve put Leon and Roxy on the investigation. Leon would hunt down Peetey and the prostitutes and get their statements. Roxy would get Elvin's credit card information and see if he had any charges on the weekend of the murder. If he were at a restaurant or a store at the time of the murder, Steve would send Leon out to see if anyone recalled seeing Elvin.

But Steve was still stuck. How could he explain why Elvin had the victim's blood on his clothes and the victim's wallet in his pocket? The state contended that Elvin was looking to get high and tried to get an advance on his paycheck from Mr. Shazir. When Mr. Shazir refused, the state said that Elvin killed him in a drug-fueled rage. There was no evidence of Peetey in the victim's office.

Steve wondered: How can I explain Elvin's confession? Maybe he was high when he gave it, but the video of his confession shows him to be tearful and sad but coherent. This was going to be difficult, if not impossible, to win.

"What's up, Ace?"

Steve looked up from his computer and saw Roxy in the doorway, along with Leon. Steve smiled. "Okay. How did it go?"

Leon started. "I found Peetey."

"What did he have to say?"

"Nothing. He's dead. He's been dead for about three years. His body was found in an alley outside of a crack house. The coroner said he died of a drug overdose. Police think he died in the crack house, and nobody noticed until his body started to stink. Then the crack-heads probably dragged his body outside."

"Anything on the prostitutes?"

"Nope. No names. I asked a couple of the pimps I know in the area. They didn't recall Elvin or any girls who had him or Peetey as clients."

"What about you, Rox?"

"No credit card usage on that weekend. He had no money in the bank."

"So that would support the state's theory that he needed money and asked Al for an advance."

"I guess."

"Anything positive you have to tell me?"

Leon and Roxy looked at each other and shrugged. Roxy then spoke up. "I can now squat 280 pounds."

"Always glad to hear it, Roxy," Steve said.

CHAPTER 23

Steve made the trek across the street to visit Elvin. He waited in the lobby until they called his client's name. Steve was escorted back into visiting room six. Elvin sat in his chair and did not greet Steve.

"Good morning, Mr. Gideon. Good to see you."

"What do you have for me?" Elvin said.

"Well, I am sorry to have to tell you that Peetey is dead. He died three years ago of a drug overdose. My investigator talked with some people in the area, but they didn't know of any working girls who had you or Peetey as clients. We also checked your credit card; we didn't find any purchases over that weekend. Also, your bank account was empty, so you probably ate at home, or Peetey paid for food."

"Peetey never paid for anything. He was always broke. I always paid for him to get high. What do we do now?"

"Well, you can withdraw your petition and finish out your sentence."

"Not an option. I'm not giving up."

"Did you review the copy of the file that I gave you? Did you see anything that we should investigate?"

"I don't want to look at it."

"Well, then, we can go forward with what we have, which is your testimony. You can tell your story, and maybe the judge will believe you and reopen your case."

"Yeah. Let's do that."

"Alright. I thought we could work on your testimony today."

"I told you I am not going to lie for you on the stand."

"Yeah. I remember. But I'm not asking you to lie. When you take the stand, I'll ask you a series of questions about what you did that night and why you believe you did not kill Al Shazir."

"I didn't kill him."

"I understand. You have to be able to explain how you are innocent, even though you pleaded guilty to killing him."

"I said I didn't kill him."

"I never said you did. But when you pleaded guilty, you told the court that you killed him. I want to go over your testimony with you and prepare you for the state's cross-examination."

"I'm not going to lie on the stand for you. Do I need to get another lawyer?"

"I don't want you to lie on the stand. What I'm trying to tell you is that testifying in court is difficult and requires a lot of preparation. I would like to do a run-through of your testimony and practice some cross-examination questions that the state will probably ask you."

"Well, I'm not gonna lie for you, so I don't know what to tell you."

"Let me be clear. I am not asking you to lie. I want you to tell the truth."

"Good. 'Cause I'm not going to lie."

"Nobody wants you to lie. You can just tell your story about what happened that night and why you pleaded guilty when you were innocent."

"Yeah. I want to tell my story because I didn't kill him. He was my best friend."

"Okay. Shall we go over your testimony?"

"No. I don't want to."

Steve sighed. “Okay. Just remember to listen to the questions completely. Then answer the question.”

“I’m not an idiot.”

“I’ll see you at trial.”

CHAPTER 24

Steve sat down on the small metal stool in the prisoner holding room just outside the courtroom. He looked at Elvin Gideon through the million pinholes drilled in a thin sheet of metal that separated Steve from his client. "Mr. Gideon, are you ready to testify today?"

"Like I said man… I ain't gonna lie. I didn't kill Al. I loved him. I would never kill him."

"Okay. I'm not asking you to lie, I'm just gonna ask you a series of questions about what you did that night and why you know that you did not kill Mr. Shazir."

"Damn straight. I'm gonna tell that judge what it is."

"Okay. I will see you out there."

"I ain't gonna lie man. I didn't kill that guy."

Steve left the holding room and stepped into the courtroom. He shook hands with State's Attorney Garcon from last week's trial. Elvin was brought into the courtroom and sat next to Steve. A knock was heard, and the marshal stated, "All rise. Court is now in session. Honorable Judge Cohen is now presiding over all matters before this court today."

Judge Cohen was a young judge in her mid-thirties, Steve guessed. Steve had read several of her decisions and some of the transcripts from the trials that she presided over. She was a smart cookie and did not take any nonsense. It was going to be tough to convince her that his client was innocent.

Judge Cohen looked at both parties and said, “Are there any preliminary matters that we need to discuss this morning?”

“Nothing from me,” said the state.

“Ditto,” Steve said.

Judge Cohen looked over at Steve and said, “Okay then. Counsel, call your first witness.”

Steve stood up and said, “Petitioner calls Elvin Gideon to the stand.” Elvin walked up to the witness stand and was sworn in.

“Good morning, Mr. Gideon.”

“Good morning.”

“Did you know Al Shazir?”

“Yes.”

“How did you know him?”

“He was my boss. He was great to me. He knew that I was a recovering drug addict, and he gave me an opportunity to improve my life. He gave me a job, and eventually we became close friends. I did extra work around the dealership for a few extra bucks. Eventually, he got me an apartment at his mom’s apartment complex, where I would do some maintenance work around the building in exchange for paying less rent. We were close friends. He even invited me to some of his family functions, including his Christmas party.”

“Do you remember the day that Mr. Shazir died?”

“Yes, I do. I was working that day. I got off work around two and picked up some booze at the package store. I met up with my friend Peetey, and we partied that night. Peetey invited over some girls that he knew. We partied with them and had a good time until they left. We did some drugs and drank. Next thing I knew, I woke up in a jail cell charged with murder.”

“Do you remember who you were accused of murdering?”

“Al Shazir.”

“Did you plead guilty to this crime?”

"Yes."

"Why?"

"Because I had a conversation with my daughter and I told her of the plea offer that was made. She told me that she thought I should take the deal. I felt terrible having lost touch with her. I wanted to re-establish our relationship. She said that my attorney told her that I was going to lose the trial and that I should take the offer. She said she would visit me, and we could pick up our relationship where we left off. So, I took the deal."

"Do you regret this?

"Yes."

"Why?"

"Because I was over fifty years old when I pleaded to a thirty-year sentence. I will never have the opportunity to get out of prison." A tear started to roll down Elvin's cheek.

"Mr. Gideon, did you murder Al Shazir?"

Elvin sat quietly and stared at Steve. Then Elvin struck a pensive look on his face and began to stare at the ceiling, as if he were contemplating whether he killed Al Shazir. He sat and thought about the question. Steve, the state's attorney, and the judge all watched and waited for an answer. While Elvin's pause to consider the question was no more than thirty seconds, it seemed like an eternity. Elvin then looked back at Steve and said, "No, I did not."

"No further questions."

Judge Cohen turned to Attorney Jackie Garcon. "Any cross-examination?"

"Yes, Your Honor." Jackie Garcon smelled blood in the water. She knew that Elvin's pause was guilt. The tear on his cheek confirmed this. He was having doubts about going forward, and she knew it. It's time to step on his neck, but let's ease down the road, she thought to herself. "Mr. Gideon, I have just a few questions that I hope you can clarify for me."

"Okay."

"You were friends with Mr. Shazir, right?"

"Yes, that's what I said."

"He was a good man, wasn't he?"

Elvin paused to hold back some tears. "Yes," he said.

"And he helped you a lot, didn't he?"

"Yes." Tears began to roll down his cheek.

"He gave you a job when nobody else would, didn't he?"

"Yes."

"And he gave you and your family a place to live, right?"

"Yes," Elvin said, trying to keep it down to a small cry and not full-blown bawling.

"And from time to time he would lend you money or give you an advance on your paycheck if you were in a bind?"

"Yes. He was a good man."

"And you were suffering from a drug problem at that point in your life, isn't that true?"

"Yes," Elvin said. His crying was becoming louder and more obvious.

"You went to him that night to borrow money for drugs, didn't you?"

Elvin broke out into hysterical bawling. Jackie brought him a box of tissues. Elvin wiped his tears and began to compose himself. "I didn't mean to kill him. I was high on drugs. I couldn't even look at the evidence in this case because it was giving me nightmares." Elvin began to cry again. "I just don't want to die in here. I want to be on the outside before I die."

The courtroom was silent as Elvin tried to gain his composure.

Steve said, "Your Honor, at this point I move to withdraw our petition."

Judge Cohen did not wait for the state's response. "Granted. Court is adjourned." Judge Cohen got up and walked back to her chambers. Elvin stood up, and the marshals began to escort him back to the holding pen downstairs. Elvin turned around, while still crying, and said, "Thank you, state's attorney. Have a good day. Thank you so much."

Steve looked at Jackie and said," I guess you have a new pen pal."

Jackie chuckled. "It's been a while since I made a grown man cry."

Steve packed his file box and went back to the office.

CHAPTER 25

Steve sat at his desk and took stock of what had happened in court that morning with Elvin. It was bewildering to say the least. Then he heard a knock on his door. Sam stood in the doorway.

"Let's go, pal. It's fucked-up Friday. We gotta go to the bar slash restaurant and complain about the week."

Steve sighed. "I'm kinda tired."

"That's a direct order from your senior partner. It's not subject to negotiation."

"Fine. But you're gonna hear me complain a lot about this case I just finished."

"I wouldn't have it any other way. That's what fucked-up Fridays are all about. We purge all our anger and sadness so we can go into the weekend feeling happy and good about ourselves. Depression is only a Monday through Friday morning thing."

They walked next door to Rico's and ordered the all-you-can-eat enchilada and taco combo meal. Sam ordered a few margaritas for his lunch, while Steve stuck to Pepsi and Mountain Dew.

Sam started his second margarita and looked Steve in the eye. "So, tell me about your catastrophe today. What happened?"

"My buddy Elvin spent the week telling me that he didn't murder his boss, who befriended him and helped him out in a big way. I tried to have him review the evidence file in his case, but he wouldn't do it."

"Uh-oh," said Sam. "If they're afraid to look at the evidence, sometimes it's because they're feeling so much guilt about the crime that they can't look at it."

"Yeah. That thought ran through my mind, but he kept saying that he was innocent and wanted to continue with the trial, even when we had no witnesses to support his story."

"So, what happened?"

"We met a few times, and all he would say was that he didn't kill the victim. He takes the stand today and tells his story. I close with, Did you kill Mr. Shazir? He stares at the ceiling for what seems like an eternity, and he thinks about whether he really killed the victim. Even though he told me no, under the state's cross, he ends up confessing that he did kill him while he was on drugs."

"Wow. What a train wreck."

"Yeah but get this. At the end, he thanked the state's attorney for getting him to confess. He didn't say a word to me. Got any words of wisdom about that?"

"You have to build a rapport with your client. Sometimes the client doesn't want to build a relationship with you. You can try as hard as you want, but they still don't trust you. Sounds like you and Elvin never really connected. He probably doesn't trust lawyers to begin with, and he didn't trust you to tell you that he really did kill the victim."

"He didn't even want to go over the testimony with me. He thought he could do it cold."

"Remember… you are an outsider to their world. You can't relate to his drug addiction, his mental illness, or his murder. You can try to be understanding and have a relationship with your clients, but you have never lived that life. You'll always be an outsider to them. You can only help people who want your help. Sounds like Elvin really didn't want your help as much as he wanted to unload the burden of telling the world that he murdered his friend for no good reason."

Steve and Sam sat there in silence, thinking about the conversation. Sam finished his second margarita and said, "It's Friday. Time to start the weekend. What are you gonna do?"

"I'm going back to the office and review the case for next week. How about you?"

"Well, I spent the morning prepping my case for next week, so I thought I would get drunk over lunch and take a cab home."

"Sounds good for you. Tell you what. I'll keep you company through another two margaritas while I sip my Pepsi, and then I'll head back to the office."

Sam raised his glass. "To the clients. Let's focus on building more rapport."

Steve raised his glass of Pepsi. "I'll drink to that."

CHAPTER 26

Danny Mosier led a double life. When he was in high school, he got good grades and was on his way to junior college in hopes of moving to a four-year college. Danny's best friend was Tyrese. Tyrese was involved with a local gang that was selling drugs on the streets in Waterbury. While Danny was not in the gang, he was friends with everyone in the gang and would hang out with them. His parents knew Tyrese and thought he was a fine young man; they had no idea that Tyrese was in a gang and selling drugs.

While Danny was in junior college, he was struggling to work thirty hours a week at a grocery store and go to school full-time. He also had a girlfriend named Kristi. Danny wanted to work less but make more money so he could spend more time with Kristi and take her out more often. He also wanted to spend more time on his studies and maintain a high grade point average.

The answer to his problems was right in front of him. Tyrese sold drugs, so he made his own schedule and worked when he wanted to work. Tyrese did not attend junior college, but he lived the hustler life with his friends in the gang. Tyrese and the gang made a deal with Danny: they would front Danny some drugs to sell to his friends, and Danny would give the gang fifty percent of what he sold. So that his family still thought he was making money at the grocery store, he continued to work there part-time, but only about ten hours. And he still studied hard, keeping his grades up.

For a few months, the plan worked well. Danny had time to study, and he had money to take Kristi out to nice restaurants and some great concerts. But eventually, one of Danny's regular customers got arrested for possession of narcotics. The customer's lawyer got the state to agree not to press charges if the customer recorded a drug transaction between himself and Danny. Danny ended up being charged with the sale of narcotics.

Danny spent all his savings on a lawyer that the local drug dealers used: Ronnie Silver. Ronnie knew the drill. Danny was not going to snitch on his gang relationship in order to get a lighter sentence because Danny knew the code of the street: "Snitches get stitches." If Danny turned in the gang, his life was in danger. Ronnie Silver saw this all the time. Ronnie sold the state on the fact that Danny was in college and had a job, and he had a more promising future than the average drug dealer. Ronnie worked out an agreement with the state where Danny would plead guilty to drug sales in exchange for four years of probation and no jail time.

Danny's double life started to become a single life. He lost his job at the grocery store when his boss heard of his conviction. Danny gave up on school because he felt that he would never get a legitimate job with a felony conviction. Still, Kristi never gave up on him. She loved Danny and hoped he would find a good job doing construction with some of his friends.

Danny turned to Tyrese and the gang for more work selling drugs. Danny continued to make good money, but he told Kristi that it came from working construction.

Early on Saturday morning, police knocked on the door of Danny's home. When Danny's mom opened the door, police officers presented her with an arrest warrant for Danny. He was charged with selling drugs and home invasion. His parents could not afford to bail Danny out, so he had to wait in jail until his case was resolved.

Bridgette Lawson was the public defender appointed to represent Danny. She explained that, in addition to the drug sales and the home invasion, Danny would be charged with a violation of his probation from his previous drug charges. She showed Danny police reports and witness statements. Danny explained that while he was selling drugs again, which violated his probation, he knew nothing about the home invasion. Bridgette explained that Tyrese told police that Danny did the home invasion with him and the gang.

The state offered Danny fifteen years in jail for all his charges; if he went to court and was convicted, he could easily face fifty years. His lawyer advised him to take the state's offer. Even though Danny explained that he was with Kristi on the night of the home invasion, his lawyer said the alibi wouldn't hold up. Danny refused to take the plea offer, but his lawyer eventually wore him down, and Danny took the offer out of anger and frustration.

CHAPTER 27

Steve sat in the legal visiting room at the jail waiting to interview Danny Mosier. Steve liked to watch the inmates walk down the hallway and guess if the file matched the person. It was a game he played. Danny's file led him to envision two different people. One version was a smart college student who maintained a job at a grocery store while still being on the honor roll at school. This version of Danny, he thought, was probably a skinny kid who looked like a nerd and would be out of place in a prison environment. The other version was a young man who broke into a family's home with fellow gang members and tortured the family as they robbed them. They murdered the family dog in front of them to coerce them into telling where the valuables were kept. One of the gang members even defecated on the family dinner table. This version of Danny, Steve thought, would have a more muscular build with a dead-eyed stare. This version would be a more difficult person to deal with: his sociopathic nature may come out in his testimony.

A six-foot-tall man in his mid-twenties entered the room. He had a medium build, as if he had been skinny but had built some muscle while incarcerated. No dead-eyed stare. The nerd image seemed to be the winner. Steve stood up and said, "My name is Steve, and I was assigned to be your attorney in your habeas case."

"Danny Mosier. Nice to meet you. How do you want to start this?"

"Well, I've read the transcripts and read your file. I'm familiar with the case, but I didn't live the case. You lived this. You know more about this than I ever will. So, I would like to hear your story about what happened."

Danny spent the next forty-five minutes explaining his friendship with Tyrese and how he created two different lives in order to fool his parents into thinking he was working at a grocery store and going to school full-time. Danny went into detail about his relationship with the gang and his drug actions, as well as his first arrest.

Steve thought for a moment about Danny's story and then said, "How did you get charged with the home invasion? I understand the violation of probation and the second drug sales charge, but the home invasion just seems out of the blue."

"Selling drugs was only part of the gang's business. With the cell phone, they no longer had to hang out on the street corner, waiting for people to drive by and ask to buy drugs. Instead, clients just call and arrange a time and a place to meet to do the transaction. You can make a lot of money only working a few hours a day, so Tyrese and his gang started robbing houses to fill the rest of their days. But that's where I drew the line. I never took part in that."

"So how did the cops point the finger at you?"

"Cops keep track of the different gangs, but they have difficulty distinguishing who is a member of the gang and who is associated with a gang. I am not a member of Tyrese's gang. I don't have a tattoo of the gang symbol on my arm like all the others. I was never initiated like the others. I am a friend of the gang, and I do business with them. When the cops realized that Tyrese and the gang did the home invasion, they included me because they thought I was a member."

"Then why did Tyrese give a sworn statement that you were involved in the home invasion?"

"Tyrese told his mother, who told my mother, that the police kept him handcuffed to a chair for sixteen hours until he signed a confession that included me. Apparently, their goal was to take out the whole gang in this crime. Looks like it worked."

"Did your lawyer ever investigate your alibi?"

"No. I told her I was with my girlfriend that night. We were on the other side of town having dinner. We went back to her place just before the time of the home invasion. I was there until after midnight."

"Alright. So, it sounds like we need to interview Kristi and Tyrese and see what they will say at trial."

"How does my case look?"

"When I was in law school, I worked in a law firm over the summer. I had to work on a case that we all knew we were going to lose. The facts weren't in our favor. They filed a motion that I was having a hard time writing a response to because there was almost no law supporting our position. I explained the situation to my boss. He said, "Give the judge something to hang his hat on." What he meant was to build some kind of an argument that makes it possible for the judge to decide in our favor. With habeas cases, the state wins if the judge has something to hang his hat on. As a defendant, your case has to be one hundred percent solid. If it's only ninety-nine point nine, then the judge will rely on that point one percent to deny your claim. You have to build a case that is so solid that the court has no other alternative but to grant your habeas petition. Right now, your case is not one hundred percent solid. We need to do some investigation to see where we stand."

CHAPTER 28

It was time for what Steve called the weekly meeting of the brain trust. Steve, Roxy, and Leon would meet to discuss the investigation on this week's upcoming case. Leon sat in the conference room with his feet resting on the table. Roxy was admiring the definition she added to the inside of her biceps over the past several months. Steve walked in with his pad of paper in his hand and a pen tucked behind his ear. "Okay. How is our alibi defense coming along?"

"Not bad," Leon said. "I found Kristi. She's married now and has a two-year-old son. She remembers that day with Danny. He picked her up around five in the afternoon at her house. Her family was home. He came to the door, and they all saw him. They went a few towns over to an Italian restaurant, where they had dinner. At about 7:45 that night, they stopped at the gas station in Brookfield, next to the restaurant. They drove back to Danbury, where Kristi lived. On the way to her house, they got pulled over by a cop. He didn't issue a ticket but warned them that they had a taillight out. They go back to her house around 8:20, and they spend the next hour talking with her family. Danny and Kristi then go into her room and watch a movie until early the next morning. The home invasion started at 7:30 p.m. and ended around 8:00 in Waterbury. Kristi said that she and Danny were at the convenience store at that time. She's sure that they had video cameras. She said she told Danny's lawyer about the tape, but his lawyer ignored her."

"By any chance, do you have any physical evidence that supports her story?"

Roxy cleared her throat. "I checked with the gas station. They had video cameras at the time, and they worked, but the tape only lasted a couple of days before it recorded over itself. Any footage is gone by now. I checked on the police stop. No record of it. If they were given a ticket or ran the license, there would definitely be a record of it. Sounds like the cop didn't run anything, just warned them about the taillight."

"What else do we have?" Steve asked.

Leon continued, "I spoke with Kristi's family. They support her story. They remember Danny, and they remember him coming over that night. "

"Did you run a background check on Kristi and her entire family?"

"Yup. They are all clean. No criminal background. They are all employed, and they are very active in their church," Roxy explained.

"What about the Tyrese angle? Is he willing to say that Danny had nothing to do with the home invasion? "

"Yes and no," Leon said. "I spoke with him, and he told the whole story of how he and his friends did this home invasion. He explained how they picked this particular home, how they tied them up and intimidated them, and how they robbed them. Tyrese went into detail on how the cops interrogated him and roughed him up into saying that Danny was involved."

"Sounds great."

"Yeah… but when I asked him to write it up in a signed statement, he wouldn't do it."

"Why not?"

"Said he just couldn't do it, but he would testify at trial."

"That's gonna be risky. If I have a written statement, I can use it to correct his testimony if he starts to change his story. Without that, then if he lies and says that Danny was there, Danny will lose his trial. Having him testify is a gamble. Did you get a hold of the victims and see if they would say Danny wasn't there?"

"I called them and knocked on their door. They weren't interested in talking to me."

"Anything else?"

Both Roxy and Leon shook their heads no.

"Okay. Let's get subpoenas out to Kristi, her family, and Danny's former lawyer."

"What about Tyrese?" Roxy asked.

"Let's hold off. I have to think about that." Steve went back to his office and prepared for Danny's trial.

CHAPTER 29

Sam's door was open. Steve stood in the doorway as he watched Sam typing away on his computer. "What are you working on?" Steve inquired.

Sam looked up at Steve. "Just preparing a brief for trial. I am trying to keep up with the pace you're setting of one trial a week. Did you have a question?"

"Yeah, I just wanted to pick your brain for a minute."

"Well, I don't have much, but you can pick what little brain I have left."

Steve spent the next twenty minutes explaining his dilemma with deciding whether to call Tyrese at trial. Of course, Steve's twenty-minute explanation ended with "What would you do?"

Steve didn't even need to think about the answer. "Call him to the stand. You have nothing to lose."

"Nothing to lose? I'll lose the trial."

"Let's say that Tyrese does testify and says everything you want him to say. Do you think you will win?"

"Hell, yeah!"

"You think you have a winner?"

"Absolutely."

"Why do you think that?"

"Because all the witnesses will testify that Danny was on the other side of town with his girlfriend and her family. "

"And you think that's going to save the day?"

"Yeah. I mean, they are all clean. His girlfriend is married to someone else. Her family has no reason to lie. If Tyrese says that Danny didn't do the home invasion, then we are home free."

"Do you have any physical evidence? Anything other than what somebody *says*?"

"No. We checked. Nothing exists that we know of. I don't think we need it, but it would be nice to have."

"Kid, it's not nice to have. It's required to have. If you want to overturn the conviction, you will need physical evidence. Something tangible that the court can hold in its hands and say this shows me he is innocent."

"Where in the law does it say this?"

Sam chuckles. "It doesn't. If you look at the few cases where a conviction is overturned, the majority of them have some sort of physical piece of evidence that the court relies on to overturn the conviction. Testimony is nice to have, but habeas places an incredibly high burden of proof on the defendant to show that his lawyer made an error that ruined his trial. The only slam dunk that exists in the habeas world is when you have DNA evidence that shows your client could not have committed the crime. To make matters worse, your guy took a plea and never tried his case."

"I disagree. I think the judge is gonna hear this testimony and overturn the conviction."

"Okay but remember this. About five years ago, I represented a kid who was convicted of raping his cousin at a family gathering on Easter Sunday in Connecticut. He had at least ten alibi witnesses: friends, family, and the local pastor, who could have been called as witnesses but were never asked to testify. They all would have said that the defendant was in North Carolina on that Easter Sunday. I brought every one of those witnesses up to Connecticut to testify.

Every one of them said the same thing: the defendant was with them that day in North Carolina. He stayed overnight and left the next morning. Therefore, it was impossible for him to have raped the victim at 9 p.m. on Easter Sunday. The court listened to all of these witnesses and still determined that there was insufficient evidence to prove the alibi. The judge didn't even bother to write a decision; he just heard that case and then told me that we lost. Still think that you have a winner?"

"Yeah," Steve said, but now with less confidence.

"Okay then, but when you get the decision, instead of going to Ricos and getting all-you-can-eat tacos for f'd up Friday, we go to the fancy steakhouse in downtown Hartford. Loser buys steaks and drinks."

"You're on."

CHAPTER 30

Danny's trial was going well. Kristi and her family testified as expected. Kristi explained that she had done all she could to help Danny. She tried to get the video from the gas station, but they would not do it without a subpoena. Kristi talked to Danny's attorney, but she dismissed Kristi and what she thought was important for Danny's case.

The state had very little cross-examination of these witnesses. Testimony was going well for Danny. The next witness was Bridgette Lawson, Danny's former lawyer. "Good morning, Attorney Lawson."

"Good morning," Bridgette said to Steve.

"Do you remember representing Mr. Mosier?"

"Yes."

"What do you remember about his case?"

"I remember that he had drug charges and a home invasion."

"Did he also have a violation of probation charge?"

"I think so, yes."

"What investigation did you do in this case?"

"I read the police reports, and I talked to Mr. Mosier."

"Did Mr. Mosier ever tell you that he had an alibi for where he was on the night of the home invasion?"

"He did. He said something like he was with a girlfriend."

"Did you talk to the girlfriend?"

"Yes."

"In fact, she came to you; you didn't seek her out?"

"I'm not sure. I know that I talked to her."

"Did you talk to her family and see if they corroborated Danny's alibi?"

"No, but we were not going to trial at that time. I had time to do the investigation."

"So, when he eventually pled to these charges, you had not investigated his alibi defense to see if it had merit?"

"No, but like I said, I had time to do it before the trial."

"Would you agree that he did not have that knowledge when he pled?"

"Well, he knew what he was doing."

"What does that mean?"

"He knew where he was that night. He knew if his alibi existed or not. He didn't need me to verify it."

"So, it's fair to say that you never gave him your opinion on whether he had a valid alibi defense?"

"I said he already knew. He didn't need me to tell him."

"So that's a no?

"It's not a no as much as it was something that didn't need to be done."

"So, you would agree that it wasn't done?

"Sure."

"Okay. Let's talk about the plea. Did Danny tell you that he was guilty of selling drugs?"

"Yes."

"But he also told you that he did not commit the home invasion?

"Yes."

"So why did you advise him to plead to all the charges?"

"Because that was the offer."

"Okay, let's unpack that. Did you tell the court or the state that Danny would plead to the violation of probation and the drug sales but wanted to take the home invasion to trial?"

"You can't do that."

"Why not?"

"Because that's not how it's done."

"Says who?"

"It just is."

"So, you are saying that it would be impossible to resolve all the cases except one?"

"Yes. You resolve all the cases. Not just some of them."

"Why?"

"You just do. The state won't give you an offer for some of the charges. You try them all or none of them. There's no splitting them up."

"Did you ask?"

"No."

"Could you have asked?"

"No. They don't do that."

"Why was it impossible to ask?"

"It just is."

"Could you have had him plead guilty to the violation of probation and the drug charge without a deal in place?"

"No."

"Why not?"

"You just can't."

"Why?"

"You just can't."

"So, you didn't try?"

"No, because you cannot split up cases."

"Okay... if I showed you actual case law where cases were split, with some charges settled with a plea and the remaining charges resolved with a trial, would that change your mind?"

"No. You can't split up the charges."

"No further questions, Your Honor."

Judge Minko looked over to the state and asked, "Any cross?"

The state's attorney stood and said, "Thank you, Your Honor. Attorney Lawson, why did you advise Mr. Mosier to plead to all the charges for a sentence of fifteen years?"

"Because it was a good offer. If he had tried all the charges and lost, he could have gotten fifty years."

"Nothing further, Your Honor."

The judge asked Steve, "Any redirect counsel?"

"Sure. Just one more question, Attorney Lawson. What would the offer have been had he just pled to the drug charge and the violation of probation?"

"I don't know."

"Is that because you never asked?"

"Yes."

"Nothing further."

The judge looked at Steve. "Any other witnesses?"

"Yes. Petitioner calls Tyrese Jones." Tyrese was brought from jail and escorted to the witness stand, where he was sworn in to tell the truth. Steve saw Tyrese for the first time. Tyrese was the same age as Danny, but he appeared to have aged pretty badly. Tyrese had some scars on his face, and his hair was graying while he was in his late twenties. It appeared that he had been beaten in jail and was under a lot of stress. "Good morning, Mr. Jones," Steve said.

"Good morning."

"Are you currently incarcerated?"

"Yes."

"What are you incarcerated for?"

"Drug sales and a home invasion."

"What sentence did you receive for these charges?"

"Fifteen years."

"Did Danny Mosier take part in the home invasion with you?"

"No."

"Did you tell the police that he was involved in this home invasion?"

"Not at first. I was arrested for drug sales and for the home invasion. Cops kept me in the interrogation room for hours. I told them everything I knew. I implicated everyone who was involved in the drug sales and the home invasion. But that wasn't good enough. I didn't have any more information to give them, but they wanted more. They handcuffed me to the table and told me to give them more information. I was there for hours. They started to beat me until I told them what they wanted to hear. I told them Danny did the home invasion with me."

"Why did they want you to implicate Danny?"

"They wanted me to implicate the entire gang in the drugs and the home invasion. They thought Danny was a member, so they wouldn't let me leave until I implicated everyone, including Danny."

"Did Danny sell drugs with you and the gang?"

"Yes. I fronted him the drugs, and he sold them. We split the profits. He was never a member of the gang, but we worked together when it came to selling drugs."

"Did he take part in the home invasion?"

"No. That is something that me and the gang did. He wasn't part of it. Danny never worked nights."

"Was your interview with the police videotaped?"

"I saw all the evidence in my case, and a video of my confession was not part of it. They only had my written confession as evidence."

"No further questions."

The judge looked at the state's attorney. "Cross-examination?"

"Yes, Your Honor. Mr. Jones. You are a convicted felon, aren't you?"

"Yes."

"You're lying right now, aren't you?"

"No."

"You're friends with Mr. Mosier?"

"I don't know. We were before I implicated him in the home invasion. I think he might be pissed at me that I implicated him, but I only did it under duress."

"So, you're trying to regain his friendship by saying that the police made you implicate him in the home invasion?"

"No. I'm just trying to set the record straight."

"You're still lying, aren't you?'

"No."

"Nothing further."

Steve and the state's attorney had brief closing arguments. Judge Minko stated that he would write a written opinion shortly and send it to the office.

"How long will that take?" Danny asked Steve.

"He has 120 days to decide, so anytime between now and four months from now. When I get a decision, I will come see you and we will discuss what our next step will be."

"Well, how do you think we did?"

"I feel that it went well, but I don't want to get your hopes up. My suggestion is to keep your mind on other things. You'll end up driving yourself crazy trying to relive the trial and imagining what the judge is thinking. We'll get an answer soon and then decide our next steps. Until then, there's nothing we can do.

Danny and Steve said their goodbyes. Steve packed his file box and briefcase and went back to the office.

CHAPTER 31

Steve sat in his office, going through his post-trial ritual. He replayed the trial in his head and tried to guess how the judge would decide. Essentially, everything that he would tell his client not to do. How can I lose this trial, he thought to himself. In order to lose, the judge would have to give no credit to all the alibi witnesses who testified on Danny's behalf. The trial attorney presented like an idiot, essentially saying that she did nothing to investigate his case and nothing to separate the drug charges from the home invasion. It's clear that the only thing his initial trial lawyer did was pressure Danny into taking a deal. Tyrese also came through. He sounded very credible.

Sam walked into his office. "Playing your usual post-trial game, second-guess the judge?"

"Yeah."

"How did the trial go?"

"It went great. Everyone testified like I thought they would."

"Good luck."

Steve and Sam began to discuss the remaining scheduled cases for the month and the progress they were making to get caught up. Roxy walked into the office. "Steve, this was just faxed to you. It's from the court." She handed the document to Steve. Steve read the three-page decision of the day's trial. He lost.

"Is it a decision?" Sam asked.

'Yeah. I lost. The court gave no credibility to any of the witnesses and said that I did not present enough evidence to show that the attorney erred by not investigating the alibi defense or that she did not properly represent him during the plea bargain."

"I'm sorry."

"How did I lose?"

"Very few habeas cases ever win. There is a reason for that. It's because the standard of law for a habeas is so high that it's not impossible to win, it's just next-to-impossible. The case you put on would have won at the original trial, if there had been one. The problem is that the habeas court wants more evidence than that. Showing that the attorney made an error is challenging, but demonstrating that the error cost the defendant the trial or compromised the plea bargain is a high standard. No judge wants to overturn someone's conviction and say that the justice system has failed someone so badly that they need to have a new trial. They will only do it if the lawyer's representation was so terrible that they have no alternative but to give the defendant a new trial. Are you starting to see what it takes to win one of these?"

"I am now."

"Focus on giving your client the best trial you can. After that, it's in the court's hands, and there's nothing you can do. You can rest assured knowing that you did the best you could."

"Yeah… but it sucks."

"Why, because you owe me a steak?"

Steve chuckled a little. "It just seems unfair. This guy should never have been charged with the home invasion, but his conviction will stick, and there's nothing I can do about it."

"You're right. But, you did all that you could do."

"I gotta go across the street and tell Danny we lost."

"He'll wait until the morning. You got the wind knocked out of you. Go home to your girlfriend and your dog, who are waiting to see you. Spend the evening with the people you love. Get your spirit back. Go see Danny in the morning and discuss his options. Then you can buy me that steak."

CARLOS'S EDUCATION

CHAPTER 32

It was recreation time at the prison, and Carlos was spending his two hours of recreation talking to Hooch about his case. Carlos was sentenced a week ago and was thinking about his next move. "So how does this habeas thing work?" Carlos asked.

"It's easy. You file a form with the habeas court saying that your lawyer fucked you. I have the form in my file box under my bunk, if you need one."

"What should I say in the form?"

"Well, I thought we would talk to my associates and discuss this."

"Who are your associates?"

"Right this way." Hooch led Carlos across the yard to three middle-aged men sitting in a circle. "These are my associates. This is Ice, Crazy-K, and the Blade."

The Blade, who had a long scar on the side of his face from being cut with a knife, stood up and faced Carlos. "Hey, boy. You know why they call me 'the Blade'?"

"Because of your illustrious figure skating career?"

Everyone stood in silence as Carlos and the Blade stared at each other. After a moment, Blade began to laugh. Everyone else realized it was okay to laugh. "I like the new guy. He's funny."

Carlos sat down with the crew and began to discuss his legal dilemma. He explained what happened and how he pleaded to twenty-five years for manslaughter. The gang sat quietly and thought about Carlos's options.

"You can ask for a sentence modification," Ice said.

"What's that?"

"It's a form you fill out. It asks the state's attorney and the judge to lower the amount of time that you were sentenced to," explained Crazy K.

"Yeah," said Hooch. "The motion to modify is usually denied because everyone asks for one. There are usually two ways to have your motion approved: One, you inform them about a crime that you have specific information on, usually a murder. Or two, you file the motion halfway through your sentence and explain that you are, in fact, guilty of your crime and that you learned the error of your ways."

"I don't have any information on any murders."

Blade said, "Well, you can try to build a relationship with some of the inmates who are going to trial and get them to confess. Then you can snitch on them in exchange for some time off. But if you do that, you risk getting murdered yourself."

"That's probably not a good idea for me if I have to spend twenty-five years here."

"You can file for a pardon from the governor," said Blade.

"How does that work?"

"It's a form you fill out that asks about why you should receive a pardon. If the pardon is granted, then your crime is erased, and you can walk out a free man."

"What do you have to write to get it granted?"

Ice, Crazy K, Blade, and Hooch looked at each other. "Nobody knows," said Crazy K. "I've never heard of anyone getting one while in prison. Most of the time, the people who get a pardon have already completed their jail sentence and are trying to get a job."

"I thought you had to have a political connection or contribute a bunch of money to a campaign in order to get a pardon," Carlos said.

Blade explained. "That only works when the president is about to leave office. It may still work that way for people who have a lot of money, but now a board of state employees decides who gets a pardon and who is denied."

Carlos sat and thought for a moment. "What do you guys think I should do?"

Hooch and his associates huddled together for a few moments and discussed the situation. Hooch then cleared his throat and made his presentation. "We believe that you should file a habeas petition. I have a form that you can use. We can fill it out tonight."

Ice said, "The grounds for the petition are that your lawyer failed to properly investigate your case. You allege that he did not gather enough information on Krystal. If you had known how weak a witness she was, you would not have taken the plea."

"Yeah, but he did tell me that she was a weak witness. I just didn't want to lose the deal and risk more jail time."

Blade said, "You can also claim that he failed to investigate the crime. It's possible that Krystal was the killer or maybe even someone else."

"That sounds good. Let's go with that."

Crazy K said, "That may be your best bet. Let's get your petition filed."

CHAPTER 33

Carlos lay in his bunk reading a book entitled *How to Represent Yourself in Court.* It was one of the books that circulated inside the prison among inmates. Hooch found it in the prison law library and checked it out, but he never returned it. Instead, the book joined Hooch's personal law library. This book was the beginning of the jailhouse legal education. It served to teach inmates the basics of what they should know about the legal system. Eventually, Hooch's students moved on to some books on criminal law.

Carlos had filed his habeas petition several months ago and was waiting to hear from an attorney. He ended up claiming in his petition that his attorney should have done a better investigation into his criminal case.

"Vega," shouted a voice from outside the cell. "Legal visit." Carlos hopped down from his top bunk and walked with the corrections officer through the maze of corridors and locked doors to legal visiting room number six. When he opened the visiting room door, he saw a heavy-set man in his late fifties standing up to greet him.

"Hi. I'm Robert Maghee. Please call me Bob." Bob Maghee had been a criminal lawyer for more than thirty years. His first job out of law school was as a prosecuting attorney in downtown Boston. He kept that job for ten years, which was just long enough for him to develop and maintain a heavy Boston accent that made it difficult for those in Connecticut to understand him. Bob began practicing in a small firm. After five years, he started his own firm and began focusing solely on criminal defense, which included a habeas contract with the public defender's office.

Bob and Carlos shook hands and sat down. Carlos told his story from how he got into drug use to how he and Hooch filed.

"That's an amazing story. What do you know about this Krystal with a K?"

"I knew her from crack houses. We would get high together sometimes. She probably saw my tattoo before."

"I think that the first thing we should do is get an investigator to question Krystal and see if we can shake her story. Maybe we can find a way to get a forensic accountant to see if she received a lot of money around the time of the murder. If she suddenly had money and happened to put it in a bank, she would have a lot to answer for."

"You don't think she killed Julito, do you? Krystal with a K is a lot of things, but I can't imagine her killing Julito. Then again, I can't imagine anyone doing it."

"Well, we have no idea who killed Julito, but if you want to win your case, it's helpful to be able to point a finger at someone else who could be the killer."

"That's a good point."

"Regardless of whether Krystal killed Julito, we need to investigate Krystal and figure out why she lied. We need to find out if she had a motive to tell the police that she saw you run out of the bodega with a gun. On top of that, we need to do another canvas of the neighborhood to see if we can turn up any witnesses that the police may have missed during their investigation."

Carlos looked at Bob and felt at ease. For the first time, he felt that there was hope of getting out of jail sooner rather than later. Bob asked, "Are you aware of how a habeas case works?"

"Yeah. Hooch gave me the lowdown on all that."

"Yes, I know that Mr. Hooch is a good attorney, at least in here, but let me just review a few things with you. Have you ever heard of the New Age Rapist?"

"Not really."

"Back in the eighties, the New Age Rapist committed a bunch of sex assaults in New Haven over two years. Eventually, he was caught by police and pleaded guilty to eight sexual assaults in New Haven. After he served about ten years of jail time, he decided to file a habeas case. He got a good lawyer, and his lawyer found that the court failed to ask him certain questions when he pleaded guilty. Since these questions weren't asked by the judge, all the New Age Rapist's cases were reopened. Instead of giving him another plea offer, the state decided to try all eight of his cases in a jury trial. It turned out that the New Age Rapist lost all eight cases. This time, the court sentenced him to twenty years for each case. That meant he was sentenced to serve 160 years. He turned his original sentence of twenty years into a 160-year sentence."

Carlos was shocked. While Hooch had told him that this was possible, Carlos had never heard of this actually happening. "If I win my habeas case, doesn't the state have to make another offer on my case?"

"No. If you are able to win your case, you can be recharged with your original charges. The state may make you an offer, and it may be a better offer than you had before, but they do not have to make you an offer other than a plea to the maximum sentence. They can force you to participate in a trial that you may not want to do. The point I am making is that if you are able to overturn your conviction, you may end up doing more time than you are doing now. In Massachusetts, we'd call that a *wicked pissar.*"

"Are you saying I shouldn't do this?"

"No. What I'm saying is let's get an investigation started and see what we can find out. You may have a lot of good information that was never uncovered by your previous attorney. We may come up with nothing. Either way, you don't need to make a decision about whether to move forward with your case until much later. I say let us do some research and investigation and see what we can find out, so that when we make the decision, you'll have a better idea of what kind of case we can put together."

"Sounds great. What can I do?"

"Well, you can start by writing your story down on paper. Sometimes writing it down helps you remember things. Write down everything you can recall about Krystal with a K. These things may be helpful in trying to find her. If you can remember where she said she lived or what town she was from or what street she lived on, write it down. Things like where she was born or where her family lives may seem useless now, but they could end up being a lead that the investigator could use to find her, especially if she suddenly leaves town."

"I can do that. But what do I write?"

"Anything and everything you know about Krystal, Julito, and what happened the day Julito died."

"Okay. I'll start on that when I get back to the cell."

"Good. Also, for a habeas, we have to file a brief. If you write down your story, I can use it to write the fact section. The bottom line is this: you lived this case. I only know your case from talking to you and reading police reports. You have the most insight on this case of anyone. So, the more you write down, the better I can prepare your case."

"Got it."

"In the meantime, I will get a private investigator to start getting information on Krystal with a K. I'll visit you in two or three weeks to discuss where we are with the case.

Carlos and Bob stood up. Carlos shook Bob's hand. "Thank you, Bob. I am really excited about this case. I will write down my story." Carlos and Bob said their goodbyes, and Carlos navigated his way through the maze of corridors and locked doors back to his cell. It was late, but instead of going to sleep, Carlos went to his desk and began to write down his thoughts.

CHAPTER 34

Mark Hutch was slowly building his private investigation practice. Mark had been a cop for twenty-five years. When he celebrated his twenty-fifth anniversary of being on the job, his life was at a crossroads. Mark was in the middle of a divorce. He had two grown children who had both been out of the house for a couple of years. Anna, his wife, left him for another man. They were selling the house and splitting the proceeds. Mark thought that this would be a good time to collect his retirement and open a private investigation firm.

Mark had several friends who were former police officers who became private investigators. All of them got their start by writing a letter and mailing it to the licensed attorneys in the state, offering their services. Eventually, they all built up a clientele and had steady work. Mark did the same and soon began steadily working on habeas cases for Bob Maghee.

Krystal with a K was no stranger to Hartford police officers. Mark had known Krystal with a K for most of his police career. Mark had questioned her dozens of times and could successfully get her to talk every time. It could be that Krystal talked because he possessed excellent witness interrogation skills. Or maybe it was because Mark had been a defensive tackle on his college football team and was still physically intimidating. Most likely, though, Krystal spilled her guts to

Mark because she had practically made a career out of being a professional witness in criminal cases.

Mark drove to Krystal's apartment in Hartford. He had questioned her there several times. Mark had spoken to Krystal over the phone, and she agreed to talk to him about Julito's murder case. Mark knocked on her door, and Krystal answered.

"Mark. How are you? It's been so long." She quickly wrapped her arms around Mark and held on tight. Mark was caught off guard. He went through the motion of hugging her back and then patted her on the back, signaling her to let go.

"Krystal… thanks for doing this."

"Sure. No problem. Always glad to help you out." Krystal led him to a chair so he could face her while she sat on the couch. Krystal made small talk, asking Mark about his new business and retirement from the police force. Eventually, Mark brought the conversation back to the purpose of his visit.

"So, Krystal, I am working for a lawyer who represents Carlos Vega. Do you remember Carlos?"

"Yeah. I met Carlos at a crack house. We would get high together from time to time."

"What do you remember about the day that Julito died?"

"Same as I told the police on that day."

"Okay… and what was that?"

"I was walking down the street around six in the morning. I was looking to get a cup of coffee and a doughnut. I heard gunshots that sounded like they came from the bodega. As I was about to go into the store, a man ran out of the door and knocked me down. I saw that it was Carlos Vega. He was carrying a gun. I walked into the store to check on Julito. I did not see him in the store, so I walked toward the back of the store and saw his body on the floor. I ran out and called the police."

Mark looked at Krystal. He said nothing. Nothing is sometimes the best tool to get people to talk. When someone lies to a police officer, they feel uncomfortable. Mark learned that if he stared at someone and stayed quiet after they lied to him, it would create an uncomfortable silence. In order to break the uncomfortable silence, the liar would begin to talk and eventually lead the liar to come clean.

Krystal felt the uncomfortable silence. At first, she smiled and looked Mark in the eye and remained quiet. Then she said, "I know it was Carlos. I saw the tattoo on his hand."

Still dead silence from Mark. "I know I didn't get a good look at him because he knocked me down, but I could tell it was him. I remember the tattoo on his hand. He was carrying a bag of money, and he had a gun."

Mark upped his game. He responded by looking at her with one eyebrow raised, as if to say, "Oh really?"

Krystal's hands started to shake. She looked at Mark and said, "Honestly, I saw Carlos leave the bodega carrying a gun and a bag of money."

Mark knew that using words like seriously or honestly was a dead giveaway that you were lying. Liars use them to convince someone of a lie because they are worried that you're not believing them. Mark knew this from personal experience, having tried it on his mom when he was a teenager. "Honestly, Mom, I didn't have girls in the house while you were gone. Seriously… I didn't." It never worked. Mark continued to stare.

Krystal's eyes started to get watery, and then she started to cry. "I saw Carlos leave the bodega. He ran out the door and ran into me. He kept on running, and he never looked back. I didn't see a gun. I didn't see him carrying money. He was just running away. I told the police that he had a gun and the money."

Mark broke his silence. "Why did you say this to the police?"

Krystal looked in his eyes and began to bawl. Mark did not do a touchy-feely type of interrogation. He did not hold her until she gained her composure. He knew that now was the time to get the answers.

Krystal took a deep breath and said, "Because I took the money. I went to the back of the store and saw that the safe was open. There was a lot of money in it. I took the money out of the safe and wrapped it in my coat. I carried it under my arm and walked down the street a few blocks away. I shoved it under a dumpster in an alley. Then I went and called the police. I went back to the bodega and met the police there. I told them that I saw Carlos leave with a gun and the money because I didn't want to be a suspect. If they knew that I took the money, they would think that I killed Julito first and then took the money. When I left the bodega, I was supposed to go to the police station and look through the mug shots. I asked if I could go to my apartment first. On the way to the apartment, I went back to the alley and got the money and took it home. Then I went to the police station and looked for Carlos in the mugshot books."

Mark remained quiet, but he shifted his countenance to a look of feeling sorry for Krystal.

Krystal got a hold of herself and got her crying under control. "I felt terrible for what happened to Carlos. I was going to change my story, but then he pled guilty to the crime. Then I thought maybe he did it. I still feel bad for lying. I should never have put Carlos in that position. If you see Carlos, please tell him that I'm sorry. I'll testify on behalf of Carlos and try to fix what I did. I can't live with myself for doing this."

"Would you be willing to help Carlos by signing a statement as to what you just told me?"

"Oh absolutely. I wanna help him."

"Great. I will write down what you just told me. I would like you to review it. If what I wrote is the truth, then go ahead and sign it."

"Okay."

Mark spent the next thirty minutes writing Krystal's new version of facts on paper. Krystal reviewed the statement and said, "This is what happened. I'll sign it."

Krystal walked Mark to the door.

"Thanks Krystal," Mark said. "You're doing the right thing by helping out Carlos. Thank you for meeting with me." They said their goodbyes. Mark drove back to his office and emailed Krystal's statement to Bob Maghee.

CHAPTER 35

Carlos was in his cell, discussing case law with Hooch. They were debating how a change in the statute for strangulation would be interpreted by the Supreme Court. Carlos had come a long way in his legal knowledge and was starting to give adequate legal advice to other inmates. It made Hooch proud that his prodigy was now becoming a fellow jailhouse lawyer.

"Vega," yelled a voice from outside the cell. "Legal visit."

Carlos grabbed his notes and a book on criminal law and then followed the corrections officer through the corridors until they reached legal visiting room six. Carlos opened the door and saw Bob Maghee sitting at the table. Bob got up and shook Carlos's hand. "Good to see you, Carlos."

They both sat down. Bob slid a copy of Krystal's statement to Carlos. "I think we have a new development in your case. Read this statement from Krystal."

Carlos took the statement and read it. Then he read it again and again. He couldn't believe what he was reading. He looked up to a smiling Bob Maghee. "Krystal stole the money?"

Bob chuckled. "I guess so. I had my investigator go out and talk to her. He's a former cop and had questioned her several times in the past, so he knew how to handle her. At first, she repeated the story she told to police, but she eventually broke down from all the guilt of framing you and told the truth. Then she put it in writing. What do ya think?"

"I'm happy, and I'm angry. I'm glad she is going to help us out. I'm pissed off that she lied to the police and implicated me as the killer. I mean, how could she do this to me? We were friends. I would never do something like that to anyone. How can she live with herself?"

"Well, it looks like she is trying to make amends."

"So, how does this affect our case?"

"It shows that the only person who linked you to the murder lied to cover up her own crime. She is more likely to be the killer. If she only stole the money, then what was your motive to kill Julito and leave the money? The state's case is that you were a drug addict desperate to get his next fix. The state's case is destroyed with Krystal's statement because you had no reason to kill Julito and *leave* the money."

"But I went in the building first and saw that Julito is dead, so it couldn't have been Krystal who killed Julito."

"That's true, but you never gave a statement. You were smart and lawyered up. As a result, we go back to the only eyewitness who places you at the scene of the crime, and that's Krystal. This statement destroys all of Krystal's credibility. Therefore, there is no *credible* evidence placing you at the scene of the crime."

"So, what will this trial look like?"

"I think it's going to be simple. First, we call Krystal and have her testify to her new version of the facts. If she changes her story again, we call my investigator, and he will testify as to what she told him. At the end, we call your attorney, and he can state that he did not have this information; if he knew that Krystal lied, he would have advised you to try the case. I think we have a shot at this."

"Am I going to testify?"

"Not in this case. With most habeas cases, you would need to testify, but in this case, no. If you testify and indicate that Julito was already dead when you got there, then it's less likely that Krystal is a possible suspect to be the killer. Your testimony would start to give credibility back to Krystal's statement. So, in your case, it's better to let Krystal do the talking and admit she stole the money."

"Are we gonna win?"

"I can never guarantee something like that. All I can tell you is that you have a good case to argue. You have the only witness who places you at the scene of the crime, admitting to lying and confessing to a felony."

"So..." Carlos asked coyly.

Bob smiled. "I'm not saying you got a winner. I'm only saying you have a chance, which is more than what most habeas cases have."

Bob continued to talk about trial strategy and the evidence he would present at trial. Carlos looked him in the eye and nodded along but did not really pay attention. He was taking a trip to fantasy land, where Carlos imagined himself a free man. He envisioned himself walking out the prison doors. Then he thought about what he would do first. What would he do with his life, now that he had several years of sobriety? Maybe he'd go back to school, he thought. He could get a degree and start his own business. He had a good background in law, thanks to Hooch; maybe he could become a lawyer. The world was an open door; all he had to do was walk through it.

Bob suddenly stood up and held out his hand. Carlos quickly came back to reality. Carlos shook his hand and said, "Thanks for everything, Bob. I really do appreciate it." They said their goodbyes, and Carlos made his way back to his cell. Hooch was already in bed. Carlos climbed to his bunk and thought about what life may soon be like.

CHAPTER 36

Carlos woke with a smile on his face. It was a good day to be alive. For the first time in a long while, Carlos had a reason to believe that his future was bright and promising. Each day was only going to get better and better.

It was recreation time at the prison, and this is when Carlos would join the gathering of jailhouse lawyers in the prison yard. Hooch and Ice were in a serious debate over whether they could sue the state for the prison not giving them a kosher meal when they requested one, even though they were not Jewish. Ice believed that you had to show that you were a practicing Jew in order to have the prison provide kosher meals. Hooch argued that it was a right for all prisoners, not just Jewish prisoners.

Carlos walked up to the group and could not stop smiling. "What's wrong with you?" Blade asked. "Why do you have that stupid grin on your face? Did your Playboy magazine arrive early this month?"

"No. I got good news from my lawyer last night."

"So, give us the message. What did he say that's got you grinning like a madman?"

Carlos explained the new evidence in his case.

"Looks like you've taken a trip to LaLa Land," Ice said, laughing.

Hooch laughed too. "I bet the minute he told you that, all you were doing was picturing yourself on the beach, strutting around with a bunch of beautiful ladies wearing bikinis. Am I right?"

The group stared at Carlos. Carlos began to grin again, and everyone laughed. "How did you know?" Carlos asked.

"We've all been through that," Hooch explained. "You finally get some good news after years of getting nothing but bad news, and you feel like your whole life is going to change. Unfortunately, for most people, that's not true."

Blade said, "Every year, thousands of inmates file a habeas petition. You have to remember that habeas petitions are rarely granted. The odds of you winning this case are one in several thousand. You have to ask yourself, is your case *that* good?"

"Yeah, man," Ice said. "I thought my case was that good."

"So did I," Hooch agreed.

The air went out of Carlos's sails. He began to question whether his case was truly *that* good.

"Look," Blade explained. "You have good evidence on your side, but you have no idea how the state is going to defend this. Your case isn't over yet. You need to focus, come back down to planet earth, and get your game face on."

"Hey man, let me ask you this," said Hooch. "Is your evidence so great that it will make the judge forget that you pled guilty to manslaughter?"

What Carlos thought would be a celebration ended up being a sobering intervention. His trial was starting soon, and he needed to be ready.

CHAPTER 37

"Get up, ya sack of shit," yelled the corrections officer. It was three in the morning. "Get ready for a wonderful day of court." Carlos slid out of bed and got dressed for court.

Today was his trial, and possibly the day his life would change. He gathered his legal documents and his criminal law textbooks and placed them in a garbage bag. The Department of Corrections would not give the inmates a briefcase or a backpack. Instead, the jailhouse lawyers had to use clear garbage bags so that the prison guards and marshals could see if the inmate was carrying something illegal.

Carlos was tired. He hadn't been getting much sleep because he was so nervous. Like other inmates taken to court, he had one hand cuffed to a rail in the van so he couldn't fight another prisoner or attack the guards. Then, he was taken to another prison and placed in a holding pen. After a while, he was routed to a different van to head to his court. The whole process is laborious, enough to wear down some prisoners who will plead to a crime just so they can finally get some sleep.

Carlos arrived at court at nine thirty and was taken to the courtroom a half hour later. He was escorted into the courtroom by two marshals and seated next to Bob.

"How ya holding up?" Bob asked.

"Tired, nervous, excited."

"You don't have to testify, which should be a load off your mind."

"Yeah, but I'm still nervous."

Attorney Jackie Garcon walked into the courtroom, carrying a box of documents. "Good morning, Bob. I got your list of witnesses. Are you really going to call Krystal with a K?"

"Of course," Bob said.

"I'm just used to trying to give her credibility. I've never had the pleasure of tearing her credibility apart."

"Well, it sounds like you're in for a special day."

"All rise," shouted the marshal. Judge Larkin came into the courtroom, walked up to the bench, and sat down.

"Good morning, counsel. What are we doing today?" He asked.

Jackie and Bob stood up. "Good morning, Your Honor, we are here for Vega versus the Warden," Jackie said.

Judge Larkin looked at Bob. "Are you ready to go forward?"

"Yes, Your Honor," Bob said. "I have all my witnesses here outside the courtroom."

"Great. Any exhibits going into evidence?"

"I have a statement made by Krystal Wiznet that is Petitioner's Exhibit One."

Judge Larkin looked at Jessica. "Any objection?"

"No, Your Honor," she said.

"Admitted as full. Call your first witness, Attorney Maghee."

Bob stood up and said, "Petitioner calls Krystal Wiznet."

The marshal went outside the courtroom and called for Krystal. Carlos looked at the entry doors to the courtroom. Krystal with a K walked into the courtroom and took the stand. Carlos had not seen her for at least three years. Although it had only been three years, she looked as if she had aged ten. Drugs had taken their toll on her. She wore heavy makeup to try to turn back the clock, but it didn't help much. Krystal took the stand, raised her right hand, and swore that her testimony would be truthful.

"Good morning, Ms. Wiznet," Bob started.

"Good morning."

"Do you know my client, Carlos Vega?"

"Yes."

"How do you know him?"

"We used to get high together."

"When was that?"

"About three years ago."

"Did you know someone by the name of Julito Hernaiz?"

"Yes."

"How did you know him?"

"He ran the local bodega. I would see him almost every day. I would go to his store and buy a cup of coffee and a bagel in the morning. Sometimes, he would loan me money if I was short. He was a nice man."

"Do you remember the day Julito died?"

"Yes."

"What happened that day?"

"It was early in the morning. I was walking down the street to the bodega to get coffee and a donut. I heard a couple of shots fired. As I approached the store, Carlos ran out of the store and knocked me down. He was carrying a gun in his right hand and a bag underneath his arm. He kept on running. I went into the store and found Julito dead on the floor. The safe was open, and all the money was gone. I ran down the street to a pay phone and called the police."

Carlos was startled. This was exactly what she told the police.

Bob took Krystal's statement to Bob Hutch, exhibit one, and walked towards the witness stand. "Your Honor, may I approach the witness?"

"Sure," said Judge Larkin.

Bob handed Krystal the statement that she had made for Mark Hutch. "Ms. Wiznet, is this your signature on this statement?"

"Yes, it is."

"Do you remember signing this statement for my investigator?"

"Yes, I do."

"Would you agree that this statement is different from your testimony today?"

"Yes."

"Which statement is the truth? The testimony you gave today or the statement you made to my investigator?"

"The testimony that I gave today."

"Then why did you sign this statement that you now say is inaccurate?"

"Mark Hutch came to my home and we talked. I mentioned that I had been struggling with my bills lately, and he told me that he would pay me $1,000 if I signed this statement. I was desperate, and I agreed to sign the statement, even though it was a lie."

"So, you're saying that my investigator, Mark Hutch, a former police officer, came up to you out of the blue and offered you a thousand dollars in cash in exchange for signing this statement. Is that what you're saying today?"

"Well, I wouldn't say it's out of the blue. I've known Mark for years, and he has helped me out from time to time over the years."

"In this statement, you admit that you stole the money from the safe."

"That's what the statement says, but it's not true. I signed it because I needed to pay my rent, or I was going to get evicted. I was desperate for money, and Mark offered me this opportunity."

Bob asked, "May I have a moment, Your Honor?"

"Absolutely," the judge said.

Bob leaned over to Carlos. "What the hell is going on?" Carlos whispered.

"She flipped back. The only way we can un-flip it is to have Mark Hutch testify. He's a cop, so he may have the credibility to fix this for us."

"This totally fucks my case," whispered Carlos angrily.

"Maybe not."

Bob stood up and said, "No further questions, Your Honor."

"Any cross-examination, Ms. Garcon?"

Jackie stood up and smiled. "Just a couple of questions, Your Honor." Jackie walked over to the podium in front of the witness stand. "Ms. Wiznet, you testified that you have known Officer Hutch for years."

"That's true," Krystal said.

"How did you know him?"

"He once arrested me for prostitution. We became friends. He would come by the apartment from time to time over the years and have sex with me in exchange for money. He's a sweet guy."

"So exactly how did this deal go down when he wanted you to sign this statement?"

"He came over to my apartment, and I thought he was looking for some company. We were chatting, and I was explaining how the landlord was going to start the eviction process against me and that I was scared. He offered to give me $500 if I would sign a statement saying I stole some money. I said no. He then offered me $800. I didn't want to go to jail for signing a statement saying I committed a crime. He said that it couldn't be used against me because it was not a statement I made under oath. I still didn't want to do it, but I needed the money, so I agreed to do it for $1,300. Mark said he would only pay $1,000, and I had to have sex with him to seal the deal."

Jackie explained, "No further questions, Your Honor, but I would like to point out that while this document is signed by the witness, it was not signed under oath. This document supports her version of the facts."

Bob stood up. "Your Honor, given the circumstances, may I have fifteen minutes to talk to my witnesses and the client?"

Judge Larkin looked at the clock. "Okay, but only fifteen minutes."

Bob stormed out of the courtroom and walked up to Mark Hutch, who was sitting on a bench outside the courtroom. "Mark, let's talk."

The court had several small rooms so attorneys could speak confidentially with their clients. Mark and Bob walked into a small room. "Did you know Krystal was going to lie?" Bob asked.

"No. I thought she would testify to the story she gave in the statement. What did she say?"

"Well, she said that you paid her $1,000 to sign a statement that you drafted, which was a lie."

"That's not true. She told me the story of how she stole the money and lied about Carlos."

"She also said that you and she have had a sexual relationship for years in exchange for money."

Mark looked away from Bob and sat quietly.

"Are you kidding me?" Bob asked.

"Look. Krystal and I have been friends for years. I was in a bad marriage, and I would go see her from time to time. I paid for her services. But everything in my investigation is true. She told me that story on her own. I never paid her for it. I didn't have sex with her that night. She voluntarily signed that statement because she wanted to do the right thing. I don't know why she lied."

Bob's face fell into his hand. "We're screwed."

"I can testify and straighten this out. I used to be a cop. The court will believe me."

"If you testify that you paid her for sex, you will be confessing to a crime. Your testimony will give her story credibility, and you could go to jail. I can't call you as a witness. You need to leave the courthouse in case the state tries to call you as a witness and have you incriminate yourself."

"I'm sorry, Bob. I should have told you that I had a relationship with Krystal."

Mark walked out of the courthouse. Bob asked the marshal if he could speak with his client and was led to a room where he could speak with Carlos through a screen on the wall.

"What's happening to my case?" Carlos asked angrily.

"We're screwed," Bob responded. "Krystal is lying about being paid money to sign the statement."

"Okay, so Matt will testify to this. He used to be a cop, so the court is going to believe him. We should be okay, right?"

"No. Unfortunately, Krystal was telling the truth when she said that she used to have sex with Matt."

"Are you kidding me?"

"I was shocked, too. I can't call him to the stand because he is only going to give some truth to Krystal's new version of facts. I know that Jackie will ask him if he had sex with Krystal for money. He will have to tell the truth, which is that he did. I told him to leave. We can't call him as a witness."

"So, what can we do now?"

"Not much. We can call your trial attorney, Jimmy J., and see if this statement would help his case." Bob was trying to be cheerful.

"So, we're screwed?"

"Yeah. I'm sorry. This is not how I wanted it to go. If Mark had told me that he had a relationship with Krystal, I would have used a different investigator."

Carlos hung his head low. Hooch, Ice, and Blade were right. He had gotten his hopes high, and now he sank to the depths of reality. It hurt. It's easier to deal with a loss when you're expecting it.

Bob and Carlos called their last witness, Jimmy J. Jimmy agreed that if he had known that Krystal had stolen the money from the safe, the information would have helped his defense of Carlos's case. On cross-examination, Jimmy said that he never spoke with Krystal because Carlos wanted to take the deal.

Judge Larkin decided Carlos's case from the bench, meaning he didn't write the decision; he just verbally gave his decision to deny the petition and explained that it was denied because Krystal's new statement was not believable. The transcript of his verbal decision would be used as his written decision.

Carlos and Bob talked again in the holding room outside of the courtroom.

"I'm sorry the case didn't go your way."

Carlos sighed. "I know you did what you could. I appreciate everything that you did for me, Bob."

"You're welcome, Carlos. My advice to you is to file another habeas petition against me. I'll testify that Mark hid the fact that he had a relationship with Krystal, and that I was unable to put him on the stand since he told me that he paid her for sex."

"We'll see. Maybe I should just give up and focus on making the most of my time."

They said their goodbyes. Carlos got in his van and took the five-hour trip back to his cell.

CHAPTER 38

Hooch, Ice, and Blade were on the ground of the prison yard, laughing.

"Awwwww. Carlos got his cherry popped," Ice said.

Laughter started again. Carlos was a good sport and did not get angry at his friends after he told them what had happened at his habeas trial.

Blade said, "Maybe we can take up a collection and get another $1,000 to see if Krystal will change her story back."

Laughter continued. Hooch had tears rolling down his cheeks. He kept laughing and then said, "Hey man, these are tears of sadness. I really do feel bad for you, man. Really." He then burst into laughter again, causing Ice and Blade to laugh again.

Carlos kept quiet until the laughter stopped. Once he had everyone's attention, he asked, "What should I do now? Should I file another habeas petition, or should I just focus on serving the rest of my time?"

"How dare you?" an insulted Hooch stated sternly. "I took you under my wing and taught you how to be a top-notch jailhouse lawyer. Now, you're thinking of throwing all that away and knuckling under to our oppressors? How dare you."

"Yeah, man. That kinda burns. You're doing Hooch wrong. Me and Blade, too," said Ice.

"Uh, sorry, guys. I didn't mean to hurt your feelings. I'm just depressed that Krystal with a K screwed me again."

Blade patted him on the back, "At least she didn't charge you."

The laughter started again.

"Seriously, guys, what should I do next? I was thinking of filing again, claiming that my habeas lawyer was ineffective for failing to conduct a proper investigation."

Once again, the brain trust stopped laughing and thought about what he was saying. Hooch said, "You definitely need to file again. The court is starting to dismiss these cases, and the court itself may try to dismiss your case or not appoint you a lawyer."

"So, what would I have to do?"

"Before they can dismiss your case, they usually bring you up to court and give you a chance to argue your position and tell them why your case should not be dismissed," Hooch explained.

Carlos thought about it while the brain trust discussed other matters. When he went back to his cell, he drafted another habeas petition.

CHAPTER 39

Carlos had filed his second habeas petition a few months ago and was waiting for a response. Every day, around one in the afternoon, he would be on edge, waiting for the mail and a response from the court.

Counselor Mendoza walked by his cell. "Hooch, you got mail."

"Anything for me, Ms. Mendoza?" Carlos asked.

"Yup. Here you go." She passed a letter through the bars of the cell door.

It was a letter from the Rockville habeas court, the only habeas court in the state of Connecticut. Carlos opened it up and read it. He would have to go before the court to make the case about why he should be allowed to pursue a second habeas petition.

Carlos sat down in the one chair in his cell.

"What's wrong?" Hooch asked.

"I got the notice from the court. They want me to explain why my new habeas should not be dismissed."

"Fun. Let's get prepared."

"I don't think so."

"What? You're not going to prepare."

"I think I'm ready. I'm gonna go in there and tell them what happened and why I deserve a second chance. Nobody knows my case like I do. I don't think there's any case law that will help me."

"Okay. Just one thing. Be aware that the court will dismiss your claim if it is not different from your previous claim. They won't let you try the same case twice; they say it's a waste of their time.'"

"So, I need to explain that this case is not the same case I tried last time?" Carlos asked.

"Well, look how the student has become the teacher. That's exactly what I meant. The court will try to get you to say that this case will be the same issue as your previous habeas case. It's a trap that the court uses to trick a lot of these guys into saying it will be the same case. The court then dismisses the petition."

"That's kinda sneaky, isn't it?"

"Yup. Watch out for it. The court will apply pressure on you to get you to say it's the same case. A lot of people go along with what the court says because they are afraid to challenge the court's authority."

"I think I can handle it," Carlos said confidently.

CHAPTER 40

It was 2:45 a.m. Carlos sat in his chair waiting for the prison guard to escort him to the van, so he could argue his case at court. He played out the oral argument over and over in his mind. He needed to be respectful, but at the same time, he needed to get his point across that this was going to be a different case. On the ride there, he continued to tweak his argument. He focused on possible questions he might be asked and how he should answer them.

At the Rockville Court inmate holding center, he watched as inmate after inmate was brought before the court and then put back in the cell. Each one complained that they were treated unfairly by the court, and their cases were dismissed.

"Vega," a prison guard shouted.

"Over here," Carlos responded.

"It's show time. Let's get you up there."

Carlos was shackled and brought upstairs to the judge. He was escorted into the courtroom. As he entered the courtroom, he noticed Jackie Garcon standing at the state attorney's desk. Carlos could feel his hands shaking. He started to get nervous, but when he stood at the defense table, he felt a wave of calmness come over him. He knew that he was innocent, and he was not afraid to explain how his last trial went wrong and was deserving of another. He was calm. He got out his pen and paper and was ready to take notes.

"Good morning, Mr. Vega. I am Judge Sullivan. I brought you here today because you have filed another habeas petition. There are currently over 2,500 habeas petitions on our docket, which means that it takes about four years for a person to get a trial after filing a habeas petition. My job is to reduce the docket so that everyone who deserves a trial can get one as soon as possible. One of the ways we reduce the docket is by dismissing cases that ask us to retry the same case we already heard. That's why you're here. I want to hear why your case is different. First, I will hear from the state."

"Good morning, Your Honor. Jackie Garcon representing the state. I tried Mr. Vega's case just a few months ago, and he is already asking for a new trial on the same matter. This case should be dismissed."

"Okay. Mister Vega, how do you respond?"

"Good morning, Your Honor. I am Carlos Vega. First, the state is correct in that I filed another habeas immediately after my first habeas trial. This case, however, will be different because a serious error was made in my case that could not be corrected during the trial. As I'm sure Attorney Garcon will recall, the only witness who could place me at the scene of the crime later gave a statement where she confessed to stealing the money from the safe at the scene and falsely accusing me of leaving the scene of the crime with a gun. At trial, this key witness changed her story, claiming that she was paid money by my attorney's investigator in order to give a false statement. My attorney never brought this investigator to the stand to question him about bribing the witness. If the court had heard this testimony, it would have given less credibility to the witness's testimony and more truth to her statement."

"Attorney Garcon?"

"Well. My interpretation of the facts is that this is the same issue. The issue is the credibility of the witness. The Petitioner is correct in that the witness gave two different versions of the facts, but she explained that she was given money to recant her original statement. The Petitioner had his investigator on the witness list, and I saw the witness waiting outside the courtroom. The Petitioner had an opportunity to call this witness and did not do it. He shouldn't get another chance."

"If I can respond to that, Your Honor?" Carlos asked.

"Go ahead."

"Well, the issue switches from ineffective assistance of trial counsel in my first case to ineffective assistance of habeas counsel. These are two different issues. If the state is correct that the witness was outside in the hall, then why didn't my habeas attorney call him to clarify whether the witness told the truth? Instead, he dismissed the witness, resulting in me losing the trial. It's a different trial at this point, Your Honor. I ask that you not dismiss my case and appoint me an attorney."

"Attorney Garcon?"

"Your Honor, it's the same case. The Petitioner called the eyewitness as their witness. They had the opportunity to discredit their own witness and chose not to do it. He is not deserving of another trial."

"If I may respond, Your Honor?"

"Go ahead."

"Thank you. Counsel is correct that this was our own witness, and my attorney did not discredit our own witness. This strengthens my argument that this witness lied on the stand, and my lawyer should have called the investigator to testify against her. Also, the investigation in my case turned up evidence that the eyewitness stole the money from the safe, which was alleged to be the reason the victim was murdered. If the witness stole the money, then money could not be the motive for me to murder the victim; it had to be another reason. That is why I ask for another chance, because this investigation was never completed."

"Any response from the state?"

Jackie Garcon replied, "I stand by my position, Your Honor."

Judge Sullivan looked at both sides and said, "I am not going to dismiss the petition at this point. I will appoint an attorney for you, Mr. Vega. Good luck."

Jackie Garcon was miffed. She had never lost an oral argument to anyone who was not a lawyer, much less a jailhouse lawyer.

Carlos thanked the court and walked back to the holding cell. He fell asleep feeling proud of himself for having stood up to the court and the state's attorney.

A DAY WITH DR. BOB

CHAPTER 41

April in Connecticut is usually when the weather warms up to the 50s, and everyone believes that the snow is finally gone. Sometimes, they are right, but on a few occasions, Mother Nature shows everyone who's boss with one more snowstorm.

Steve had found his stride at the office. He was eight months into his contract and was picking up steam toward the finish line, having completed more than fifty trials. The firm was in good shape. All the habeas cases were up to date; all the paperwork was filed, clients were happy, and Rockingham & Myers was on top of their habeas contract. The crisis that Steve was asked to fix had been fixed. Steve was the missing ingredient that got the *other office* of Rockingham & Myers humming again. His energy got Sam to focus more on his work and increase his productivity. Now Steve's focus was to complete as many cases as possible before his contract was over.

It was Saturday. Jenny, Steve, and Buddy grabbed their gear to hike the Sleeping Giant trail in Hamden. They left at five a.m. so that they could have coffee and breakfast on top of the Sleeping Giant Mountain at sunrise. Jenny planned to take some pictures while Steve held Buddy and took in the beauty of the sunrise coming across the land from far away. The glory of the red and purple colors in the distance, illuminated by the sunlight, made Steve respect the fact that his life was part of a larger world and that the problems and pressures he faced in his life were truly no different than anyone else's. The sunrise made his pressure and problems seem small and insignificant.

Jenny, Steve, and Buddy finished their hike and spent the afternoon in Jenny's apartment, conducting their typical Saturday afternoon business meeting, which was usually a nice lunch that they prepared together, followed by trading back massages. Jenny's medical billing business had expanded to five full-time employees. With Steve's help, Jenny was mastering her skills of bringing in more work for the firm and keeping clients happy. Jenny now spent her week meeting with clients and supervising her employees, who took care of the medical billing. They had come to the conclusion that it was time to have one of the employees do the supervision and management, while Jenny devoted her time to bringing in new clients.

Steve was rubbing Jenny's back at the close of the business meeting. "What are you going to do when the contract ends?" Jenny asked.

"Well, I'm waiting to see what options are put in front of me. The habeas contract is in good shape. It's likely that Big Frank is going to offer me a job with the firm. In the alternative, he will make the million-dollar phone call."

"Is that what you want?"

"In June, that is exactly what I wanted. Now, I don't know."

"So, what do you want?"

"In terms of a career, I don't know anymore. My office is in the DMZ and across the street from the jail. My paralegal is a self-absorbed nut. My investigator is a former drug addict and has ties to almost every drug dealer in the city of Hartford. My immediate boss is an alcoholic. In spite of all that, I actually like the people I work with. They're great. We work well as a team. They all work hard for very little pay. And Sam has gotten his alcoholism under control, and he really is a valuable mentor. Plus, he stresses the importance of maintaining a personal life. I know that if I were working in the *other* Rockingham & Myers office, I wouldn't have a boss like that."

"So, that's important to you?" Jenny asked coyly.

"Before I met you... no. It wasn't. My life was about law and business. But now things have changed. You know that I love you, and I enjoy our relationship. I wouldn't give up my time with you for the world."

Jenny smiled. "It makes me happy to hear you say that."

"The problem is that more than likely, I will be handed everything I have ever wanted, and now, I may not want it anymore."

"Just remember, Big Frank doesn't have all the answers. You still have other options other than what Big Frank offers," Jenny said. "You have a ton of trial experience. You could work for a different firm. You could start your own firm. You could even work with me in our business and take it public."

"I mean, I know what I want in my personal life," said Steve. "The question is what kind of work life do I want? Will that work life be compatible with my personal life?"

"You'll figure it out."

Buddy lay on Jenny's back, breaking up the conversation and focusing their attention where it belonged—on him.

CHAPTER 42

Steve received an email to meet Big Frank at the main office for lunch at noon. Luckily, Steve had an office day and could fit Big Frank's request into his schedule.

Steve spent the morning preparing cases, but the meeting kept nagging him. In the back of his mind, he kept wondering what the meeting could be about. Did I screw up? Is Big Frank going to fire me now that the habeas problem has been resolved? Maybe he just wants to chat. Steve tried to focus on the things that he could control: preparing cases for trial. When 11:30 arrived, he grabbed his suit jacket and started to leave.

"Going to lunch without me?" Sam asked from across the hall.

Steve poked his head into Sam's office and said, "The powers that be summoned me."

"Big Frank?" Sam asked.

"Yeah. Do you know why?"

Sam shook his head back and forth, "No. I've been giving you nothing but green lights in my discussions with him. He shouldn't have any complaints."

Steve shrugged his shoulders and said, "I guess I'll find out."

Steve made the short drive across town and made it to the waiting room of the other Rockingham & Myers office with a few minutes to spare.

Magda told him that Big Frank would be out momentarily.

A few moments later, Big Frank opened the frosted glass door and walked into the lobby. "There he is. The man of the hour. Follow me. We're gonna go to lunch."

Steve followed Frank to the elevator and then down to the lobby to Marty's restaurant. Marty's is the firm's "go-to restaurant." Marty's was the place to bring clients and potential employees for a power lunch. Marty's also catered the firm's annual Christmas party and special events.

Steve and Frank walked through the entrance of Marty's where the maître d' immediately escorted Steve and Frank to a booth by the fireplace. The waiters saw Big Frank and quickly brought him menus, water, and silverware, and then took his drink order.

"I'll take two fingers of bourbon. What do you want, kid?" Frank asked.

Steve refused to order alcohol while he was working. "I'd like ice water please."

"You can order a beer. It's okay on a business lunch with me."

"I'm good."

"Suit yourself," Big Frank shrugged. "So, how are you and Sam making out over there?"

"Nothing different than the weekly reports I've been sending you. We have the case load under control. The public defender seems to be happy, and their office continues to send us new cases. Clients seem to be happy, despite the circumstances."

"What circumstances?" Frank asked.

"The fact that we have lost every single case, which is normal for the situation. They understand that but would be happier if their convictions were overturned."

Big Frank chuckled. "Yeah, that's not gonna happen anytime soon."

Steve nodded his head. "They know that. They seem to be happy with our work, just not the results."

Frank took a sip from his bourbon and said, "I gotta tell ya that I am really impressed with the impact you've had on the firm over there. It seems like Sam is a new man. Since you arrived, it's like the difference between night and day. Productivity is up and you are making a decent profit for the firm. I'm very impressed."

Steve smiled. "Thanks. I'm happy to hear that. We really have a good team over there."

Big Frank nodded and said, "I brought you here to thank you for what you've done for the firm. I also wanted you to know that there is an opening in mergers and acquisitions."

Steve was caught off guard. He thought for a moment and said, "What happened? Those people have been together for years. I'm surprised someone left."

Frank nodded, "We let David go last week."

Steve was shocked. "David, the first-year associate who was hired with me?"

Big Frank nodded his head. "Yup. He promised millions of dollars of work for the firm but produced nothing. Turned out his father's software company was using Carson and Palmer for their corporate takeovers instead of us. David had told us that we would get all this work, but we found out that his dad's company was taking over five other software companies and we didn't get any of the business. Not even a chance to show them what we can do. We asked David why his father didn't hire our firm, considering that his son worked here and promised us the work. David hemmed and hawed about it and then said that his father thought it was a conflict of interest to send work to his son's firm."

"What was he doing the whole time?"

"Not much. His billable hours were shit. He spent most of his time updating his Facebook profile."

Steve shook his head back and forth. "That's terrible."

"Yeah. We are reconsidering our hiring policies when it comes to hiring associates based on their ability to provide income to the firm, thanks to David."

"I'm sorry to hear that."

Big Frank was quiet for a moment and stared at his bourbon glass. Steve did not say a word and let Big Frank guide the conversation.

"You're not gonna ask me more about the opening in the mergers and acquisitions department?"

Steve took a sip of water and said, "I'm committed to the team across town. My plan is to finish the contract and see what happens after that."

Big Frank sipped his bourbon and sighed. "I wanted to talk to you, and tell you that we did you wrong. We all knew that you were the best candidate for David's position, but we were blinded by his false promises. I know we hurt you in the process. I'm sorry."

Steve smiled and said, "Don't be. I have a great team. I've grown as an attorney. I earned more trial experience in less than a year than most lawyers get in a lifetime. I've also grown as a person: I have never enjoyed life more than this year. I wouldn't change that for the world."

Their meals arrived. Frank talked about all the work happening in the mergers and acquisitions department. Steve listened intently.

The check arrived, and Big Frank left a sizeable tip and signed the bottom of bill as it will be added to the firm's tab with Marty's restaurant.

Big Frank and Steve stood up at the table as they prepared to leave. Frank cleared his throat and said, "So do you want the mergers and acquisitions position?"

Steve reached out and shook Big Frank's hand. "I have no job offers beyond the contract. I plan on finishing the contract. When the contract is up, I will consider all offers and options that are before me at that time. Regardless of what offers I have, I still expect you to keep you word and make that phone call if I need it."

Big Frank laughed his signature belly laugh and said, "Fuckin' kid still refuses to be humbled. You know I will keep my word."

Steve chuckled and said, "I got humbled last time."

CHAPTER 43

Steve walked across the street and sat in the lobby of the jail, waiting to be called into the legal visiting room. Steve reviewed Carlos's file and read the trial transcripts. He knew that this trial would be difficult for many reasons: It was Carlos's second habeas case, making the burden twice as high as the first habeas. Bob Maghee only had to show that Jimmy J had erred; Steve would have to prove the errors of both Bob and Jimmy. Second, he would have to get to the bottom of the Krystal with a K situation.

"Legal Visit for Vega," shouted one of the prison guards. Steve got up and walked through the metal detector. He was then escorted into visiting room number six. Steve walked in and laid down his file and transcripts. He waited patiently for his client, trying to imagine what his client looked like. Steve pictured Carlos as six feet tall with a strong build from his football days in high school and college. I bet he is still fast, Steve thought to himself.

A five–foot–six skinny Hispanic male entered the room. Steve stood up and shook his hand.

"My name is Steve, and I've been assigned to represent you on your second habeas case."

Carlos was very gracious and thanked Steve for taking the time to meet with him. "I reviewed your file and the transcripts from your habeas case. What I need to know is your story and what happened from before the crime until the present day."

Carlos looked at Steve and said, "Where exactly did you want me to begin?"

"Let's start from when you started using."

Carlos spent the next hour telling Steve his story, from how he became an addict, to how he found Julito dead in the bodega, to how he pleaded to killing Julito, and eventually to his habeas trial. Steve listened and took notes.

"So, what's the deal with Krystal with a K?" Steve asked.

"She gave a statement to the investigator saying that Julito was dead and she stole the money from the safe. At the habeas trial, she went back to the story that she told the cops and said the statement was a lie."

"That was a big deal in the habeas world," Steve explained.

"What do you mean?" Carlos asked.

"Since Krystal's testimony, Mark Hutch has been charged with bribing a witness. Any attorney who used Mark Hutch on a case has been told to have all their investigations redone."

"He got charged for what Krystal said?" Carlos asked.

"Yeah. The state took her testimony to be true and charged him with a crime. He may actually go to jail."

Carlos was stunned. "They believed Krystal?"

"I guess," Steve explained. "It could be a strategy to strengthen Krystal as a witness. They charge Mark Hutch to give her credibility. If he gets convicted, then she remains a credible witness in your case and in all the others in which she has given testimony. If they hadn't charged Hutch with a crime, then I could argue that even the state thought Krystal was a liar."

"You think it's a strategy to charge Hutch?"

"More like self-preservation. The state has invested heavily in Krystal as a witness over the years. Everyone knows that she is unreliable, but the state still uses her. If they don't charge Hutch with a crime, they are conceding that she is a liar."

"So, what can we do?"

"I think we need to find out why Krystal lied and what the truth is. I think we should avoid talking to her, at least at first. "

"What?"

"I think talking to her is a waste of time. She'll give us the run-around and eventually claim that *we* bribed her. It's a waste of our time and dangerous to us. We need to investigate her: look at her financial records, criminal history, and any other information we can get on her. Then we need to talk to everyone she knows to see what information she told them. Maybe she told someone else she stole the money from the safe."

"Is that it?" asked Carlos.

"No. Krystal is not enough. Even if she took the stand and said that she stole the money, that won't be enough. We need to find someone else who could have killed Julito."

"How can we do that?"

"I'm not sure yet. This is a crime with two witnesses: you and Krystal. Neither of you saw who shot Julito. We need to do a canvas of the area to see if anyone remembers seeing anything unusual that day. We need to investigate Julito and his family to see if anyone had the motive to kill him."

Carlos thought for a moment and then asked, "Why can't we just focus on Krystal and show that she lied? Since her testimony was not credible, the state then had no credible witness to put me at the scene of the crime."

"That was Bob Maghee's theory at your trial. It's not bad, but a court can listen to Krystal's version of the facts and believe parts of it. They can believe that she saw you leave with the gun and the money and that she stole the money from the safe. That still makes you the potential killer. I think it's a serious gap in your case where the court can still believe you are the killer. And remember... you did plead guilty to killing Julito."

"Yeah. That's a good point."

"I think we need to come up with a potential suspect. Someone who was more likely to kill Julito than you. Your case is going to involve a ton of investigation and research. I have a good crew, and we can start on this right away. What do you think?"

Carlos was stunned. None of his lawyers ever asked him about his opinion on what trial strategy should be used. "It makes sense. I think we should investigate as much as we can and see what we come up with."

"My thoughts exactly," Steve said.

They both stood up and shook hands and said their goodbyes. "Thanks for listening," Carlos said. "You're easy to talk to."

"Thank you, Carlos."

Steve left the jail and walked back across the street to his office. It was after five, and everyone was gone. He laid Carlos's file on his desk and wrote down more notes on his conversation.

Steve had heard the stories of more than fifty clients. Most of the stories were unbelievable. A habeas client tends to take all the facts of the case and create a story that explains all of the facts.

For example, Steve once represented a man who was convicted of meeting with several gang members who conspired to murder a rival gang member. The co-conspirators placed the client at the meeting and at the murder scene. The client's story explained that he went to the meeting but stepped out of the room and happened to miss all the discussions that involved planning the murder. When the client drove the co-conspirators to the murder, he said he didn't know they were going to commit a murder. The story sounded unbelievable. The only point of the meeting was to plan the murder. It seemed unlikely that the client attended the meeting but missed all the discussions on planning the murder.

Carlos is innocent, Steve said to himself. Carlos's story was believable. He didn't hide the fact that he had a serious drug problem and lived in an alley. He was going to Julito for money because he needed to get high, like the state said. Carlos didn't have a motive to kill Julito. Also, his story didn't have an answer to everything. The court would still be left with no motive for the murder of Julito.

Steve had come to realize the old adage that it was easier to represent a guilty person than an innocent person. Steve believed Carlos was telling the truth, but he also knew it would be very difficult to prove his innocence. He asked himself if he lost this case, would he be able to live with himself?

CHAPTER 44

"Get in here, son," Roxy said.

Steve poked his head in the conference room. "You talking to me?"

"Hell, yeah. Let's get our meeting on."

Leon walked into the conference room. "Is it time?"

"Yeah. It's brain trust time," Roxy said.

"Okay. Well, I'm glad that you are so motivated to get started. I read Mr. Vega's file, and I talked to him about what we need to do. There is a lot of investigation that needs to happen. Leon, have you read the file?"

"Yeah. I reviewed the police reports and the statements from the original attorney. I'm still making my way through the transcripts."

Steve said, "I think there are two areas we need to investigate. First, we need to investigate Krystal with a K. She placed Carlos at the scene and told the police that she saw him fleeing the scene of the crime while carrying a gun and a bag under his arm. Then, she changed her story and said that she stole the money and lied about seeing Carlos leave the crime scene with a gun. But at Carlos's habeas trial, she said that what she told the police was true. She claimed that she took money from Carlos's investigator in exchange for signing a false statement. She also claimed that the investigator paid her to have sex with him. I think it would be in our best interest to find out more information on Krystal with a K without talking to her; I don't want a repeat of false accusations. Maybe we can interview some of her friends and go through her financial information and criminal records."

"I'll scour the computer for her financial information and personal information," said Roxy.

Steve looked at Leon. "In your former life, did you know Krystal with a K?"

"Yeah. I was friends with her roommate, Crystal with a C."

"Seriously?" asked Roxy.

"Uh huh. That's how they got their nicknames, Krystal with a K and Crystal with a C, because people would always confuse their names."

"Any chance you could meet up with Crystal with a C and do some inquiry? Maybe see if there are other people you can talk to that would support this idea that she stole the money out of the safe?"

"Sure. I think she's still in Hartford. I can drop by and get caught up with her."

"We also need to investigate Julito, his wife, his family, his friends, and the people who worked for him. Somebody had to have a motive to kill him. We need to find anyone and everyone with a motive to kill him and see if they had the opportunity to do it."

"I knew Julito," Leon said. "I know a lot of people who knew him. I can ask around and see if they know of anyone who had an issue with him."

"I'll check his business records. See if he has any outstanding debt. He may have been in deep with a loan shark who ended up robbing him." Roxy said.

"Okay then. Let's get started," Steve said.

CHAPTER 45

Steve looked into Sam's office and saw that he was reviewing a file. He gently knocked on the door so as not to disturb him if he was deep in thought, but to let him know that he wanted a word with him if he had the time. This was an old habit from law school that he never quit. "Come on in."

Steve walked into Sam's office. "What's on your mind?" Sam asked.

"I wanted to pick your brain about the Vega case."

"All right. What's up?"

Steve proceeded to tell Sam the facts of the case.

Sam thought for a moment and then said, "They never found the gun?"

"Nope."

"But they did find the bullet?"

"Yup."

"So, you are trying to show that the original trial attorney failed to do a proper investigation, because if he did, he would have either found the real killer or someone else who could just as easily have killed Julito?

"Essentially."

"How did you plan on proving this?" Sam asked.

"I thought I could compare ballistics from this bullet to the bullet in other cases to see if we could find a match. If we can find a matching bullet from a murder where they found the killer, then we could potentially find a third party who could be a suspect in Julito's death."

"How would you go about getting this information?"

"Well… I thought that we could subpoena the information from the forensic lab."

Sam thought about it for a moment and said, "Well, you can send the subpoena, but you'll end up arguing this in court."

"Why?"

"This is where you get to meet the city attorney."

"What does the city attorney have to do with this?"

"In our line of work, we come across the city attorney when you subpoena something that they don't want to produce."

"Meaning what?" Steve asked.

"Well, back in the day, I represented a guy who was convicted of walking up to a couple and robbing them at gunpoint. He told me that he was several miles away in downtown New Haven, walking the streets and shopping. I asked the New Haven Police Department to provide me with all the video footage from all cameras located at each streetlight for the time that the crime took place. This would prove his alibi."

"So, what happened?"

"I subpoenaed the information, and the next week I had to show up in court and argue why I was entitled to it. The city claimed that the subpoena was too broad and would take a great deal of time to gather all this evidence. The judge agreed with the city, saying it would place an undue burden on the already overworked police department. I was never given the footage and could never prove his alibi."

"Do you think I'll get the same result?" Steve asked.

"Yeah. You are going to ask the forensic lab to look through every murder case involving a gun and compare the ballistics tests for similarity. I can practically guarantee you that the request will be denied.

Your client, however, may be grateful that you tried and appreciate your effort, so it may be worth a try."

"What if I asked other law firms to send me information from their murder cases? There are only about thirty law firms in the state that do habeas work on a regular basis, and I have met most of these lawyers. They may agree to this."

Sam shook his head back and forth. "Think about what you're asking them to do. You're asking them to produce evidence that may prove one of their clients committed a murder."

"You're right. I was just thinking out loud."

Sam thought for a moment. "Did you look at the ballistics report?"

"Yeah. It doesn't say much. It was from a .38."

"It was done in the state forensics lab in Meriden?"

"Yeah. Isn't that the only forensic lab in Connecticut?"

"It is. I just wanted to be thorough. Sounds like you need a day with Dr. Bob."

"Who's Dr. Bob?"

"Dr. Bob is the firearms expert for the state of Connecticut. He is a doctor of mechanical engineering with an emphasis on the science of firearms. He worked for several years as an engineer and consultant for a firearms company in Connecticut. For the past thirty years, he has been the expert on firearms for the state forensic lab and has been in charge of the ballistics tests."

"He's a friend of yours?"

"Yeah. We belong to the same emotional support group. That's code for we used to meet at the Gas Chamber in downtown Hartford and get drunk together on Friday nights after my wife died. His wife passed away around the same time as mine, and we ended up commiserating together. We still get together about once a month."

"If the city attorney will deny the subpoena, what is Dr. Bob going to do for us?"

"He owes me a few favors from over the years, and he's a close friend. If I ask him what we can do, he may be able to come up with a solution. Let me give him a call."

Steve sat in a chair listening as Sam explained the situation to Dr. Bob. In that moment, it occurred to Steve how important relationships were in law. An investigation of this nature would never happen because the state would not pay the money to produce information that could prove a man innocent, yet it pays tens of thousands of dollars every year to keep the same man in jail. Only because Sam happened to be a drinking buddy with an expert from the forensic lab is there a chance that an investigation will take place.

Sam hung up the phone and looked at Steve. "I think we have a solution. Dr. Bob said that the lab is closed on the weekends. We can come up next Saturday and go through the files. He will tell us what to look for and will watch as we go through the relevant files. If we find any potential matches, he'll get the original bullets and compare them and let us know if they are from the same gun. Maybe we can bribe Roxy and Leon to join us and make this thing go quicker?"

"This is great. Thank you," said Steve.

"Friends in low places," Sam said. "Whatever you do, don't tell anyone about this. Dr. Bob is not supposed to allow civilians in the lab, especially on weekends. We don't want to get him in trouble."

"Not a problem."

CHAPTER 46

Steve brought bagels and doughnuts from the local bakery, along with coffee. It was a small token of appreciation for everyone spending their Saturday in the lab. Steve, Sam, Roxy, and Leon got into Sam's car and made the fifteen-minute drive from Hartford to the lab in Meriden. A short bald man wearing a lab coat and a bowtie stepped out of the car parked next to them. He walked up to Steve and said, "Pleased to meet ya. I'm Dr. Bob."

"Nice to meet you, Dr. Bob. What's your last name?"

Dr. Bob chuckled. "It's Bob."

"Oh, I'm sorry. What's your first name?"

"Joe."

"Dr. Joe Bob?"

"At your service."

Sam approached Dr. Bob and shook his hand. "Thanks again, Joe, for doing this."

"My pleasure, Sam. Glad I can help."

Dr. Bob opened the front door and invited everyone into the lab. The building was dark inside, and Dr. Bob led them down the long, dark corridor to the file room. The file room was large and seemed almost endless. "This is the master file room. We keep the original copies of all our lab reports in this room. We have files going all the way back to the first report we ever made."

Dr. Bob explained how the lab processes a bullet. "First, we receive a bullet and place it in an evidence bag. We take the bullet and look to see what kind of gun it came from. This is called rifling. Every barrel of every gun has a series of grooves and ridges that cause the bullet to start to spin inside the barrel. When the bullet leaves the barrel, it's spinning. This spin can be a tight spiral, which is used for accuracy, similar to a hunting rifle. The spin can also be loose to create what's called a wobble. This is a spin with a looser spiral, so that when the bullet enters the target, it turns in a larger circle inside the target; this causes the exit wound to be larger than the entry wound."

"Each manufacturer has a specific and unique pattern for rifling each of its weapons. So when we look at a bullet, we can see the pattern of rifling as it went through the barrel of the gun. We can then determine which manufacturer made that particular weapon."

"After that, we use what is called a comparison microscope to see if the bullet was fired from a particular suspect weapon. We compare the bullet, usually taken from the body, to a bullet we fire from the suspect gun and see if the bullets match."

"Now, the comparison microscope has a camera that can take a picture of the suspect bullet and the comparison bullet. I take a picture of every bullet that I test, then I keep the pictures in a file in case someone wants to do a reverse gun check, like in this case, where you have a bullet and you want to see if there were other bullets fired from the same gun."

There were several long tables in the master file room. Each table had a small, green banker's lamp in the center for extra light. Steve thought that the forensics lab could double as a law library.

Dr. Bob gathered everyone around a row of file cabinets. "I pulled Julito's file, and he was murdered with a .38 caliber pistol made by the Davidson Gun Corporation. This row of twelve file cabinets contains every ballistics report with a bullet fired from a .38 caliber pistol made by Davidson. I made copies of the comparison picture from the bullet taken out of Julito. Each of you has a copy. Each file in these twelve cabinets contains a ballistics test. When you open the file, the comparison picture will be attached to the left side. Compare that picture with the picture of Julito's bullet. If it's the same or similar, call me over, and I'll take a look and decide if it's similar enough to do a comparison analysis. Once you're done with the file, put it back in the exact place you found it. Any questions?"

Everyone looked at each other, but nobody had a question. Dr. Bob said, "Okay. If you need me, I will be on the far end of the room trying to meet women online. According to television, there are hot women in my neighborhood who are dying to meet me."

After four hours, there was a small stack of possible matches on the table. Dr. Bob picked up the files and walked to his lab.

Steve and the crew decided to take a lunch break. When they got back to the file room, Dr. Bob was still gone. They spent the next couple of hours going through the remaining file cabinets but didn't find any other matches. They waited quietly in the file room for Dr. Bob.

Finally, he entered the room with a stack of files. "Were there any other possible matches from the remaining file cabinets?"

"We nailed them all out. You have all possible matching files," said Roxy.

"Okay," said Dr. Bob. "You folks gave me sixteen possible matches. Of those matches, I went and got the actual bullets from those cases and compared them to the bullet that killed Julito. Of the sixteen potential matches, there were two matches that were fired from the same gun that killed Julito. One of the bullets was from a murder that happened a month before Julito was killed. The other bullet was from a homicide that occurred a few weeks after Julito was shot. I made copies of the file for each of these cases, because I knew you would want that. Anything else I can do ya for?"

Sam walked up and shook Dr. Bob's hand. "Thanks, pal. Let's go out tonight and get a steak. My treat."

"That sounds swell," said Dr. Bob. "Maybe we'll meet some ladies."

Sam drove the crew back to the office. He thanked everyone again for their help. Sam went off to meet Dr. Bob at the Dakota Steak House. Roxy and Leon went home. Before Steve headed to see Jenny and Buddy, he wanted to review the files.

The murder before Julito's death was only a couple of miles from the bodega. It was a gang shooting that resulted from a dispute over which gang would sell drugs on a street corner. The victim was from a small Hartford gang called the LaFayette Boys, named after the street they believed they controlled. The shooter was from a Latin gang called the Columbian Lords, a very large and well-organized crime family with chapters all over New England. The defendant was sentenced to sixty years for the murder. He is serving his time in a prison close to Rhode Island.

As Steve reviewed the second file, the murder after Julito's death, he was shocked to learn that he already knew this case. The defendant was Bryce Jahari, the first habeas case that he tried. The bullet that killed Julito was fired from the same gun that Jahari used in his turf dispute. Steve would have to pay Mr. Jahari a visit on Monday.

CHAPTER 47

Steve recruited Leon to go see the shooter of the murder before Julito was killed. Meanwhile, Steve walked across the street to meet with Bryce Jahari. He sat in the lobby with the other lawyers, all waiting for their turn to meet with their clients. Steve waited for about two hours until a room became available. He passed the time talking with other criminal lawyers. Many criminal lawyers are solo practitioners, and Steve enjoyed talking with them about how they developed their practice. He found that the other lawyers loved to talk about how they built their business and were proud of the hard work they had put in to build their own firm.

"Legal visit for Jahari," yelled the prison guard. Steve walked through the metal detector and was escorted to visiting room number six. Steve entered the room and made himself comfortable in one of the chairs and waited.

Bryce entered the room. "What's up, man? Why are you here?"

Steve got up and shook his hand. The prison guard left them alone. They both sat down.

"Bryce, I need your help on a case."

"What? How can I help?'

Steve gave Bryce the short version of Carlos's story and how he pled guilty to shooting Julito. Steve kept the names out of it in case Bryce knew someone involved in the case.

"What does this have to do with me?"

"The gun that was used to kill the victim in my client's case is the same gun that was used to kill the victim in your case."

Bryce stood up and began yelling. "I'm not going to confess to killing someone else. Do you think I'm an idiot? Even if I did do it, I wouldn't confess. I would make them prove it."

Steve stood up and put his hands on Bryce's shoulders, attempting to calm him down. "I'm not asking you to confess to anything."

Bryce pushed Steve back, "Get off me, man."

"Bryce, I am still your lawyer, and we have a confidential relationship. I can't tell anyone anything you tell me unless you ask me, too. I'm not asking you to confess to anything."

"Then what are we doing?"

"Like I said. I need your help."

"So, what do you want?"

"I want to know who you got the gun from."

"Why?"

"Well, I can't use it as evidence, but it can give me an idea of where to start looking. If I know who gave you the gun, then odds are that they are the killer in my case, or they know the killer in my case."

"Well, if I tell you, then I'm a snitch. You know what they say: snitches get stitches."

"If you give me the name, I can't repeat it to anyone outside of my office. I can't tell cops. I can't tell anyone. I can't even interview the person unless I have a more legitimate way of saying how I came up with them as a suspect."

"Then why should I tell you if you can't even use it?"

"Because I can use it. I can use it as a guide to find the potential suspect. Once I have an idea of who the killer is, I can try to find more information about them and see if I am able to tie them to the crime with other information and other evidence. Your name would never be mentioned."

"I don't know, man. I'm not a snitch."

"I'm asking you to help clear a guy who is truly innocent and should not be in jail."

"What's in it for me? I can help get some guy out of jail, but I can't help myself even get any time off from my sentence."

"If you help me, I can try—and I emphasize the word 'try'—to negotiate a sentence modification for you. While it is not overturning your conviction, we may be able to take some time off your sentence. If you help me out, I will try to get some time removed from your sentence."

"Okay. I believe you. If I tell you the information, you are not going to use it without my permission. And you don't have my permission at this point."

"Exactly."

"Alright." Bryce sat for a moment and collected his thoughts. "I know a guy who's in a different gang. He was a cellmate of mine when I was in the state juvenile facility. He's a member of the Columbian Lords. I saw him from time to time when I would go to Hartford. My crew is in Waterbury, so there were no conflicts between us. So, I'm at a party over on the West side of Hartford, and he shows up. We start talking, and he tells me that he has a gun he wants to get rid of. I know it's probably hot, but I needed a weapon for myself. He offers to give it to me for twenty bucks. I take it."

"When did this happen?"

"A few weeks before the murder in my case."

"This guy needs to get rid of the gun, and you bought it for only twenty bucks?"

"Yeah. I knew it was probably used in other crimes. But I couldn't get a clean gun because I was a convicted felon. I needed a gun to defend myself."

"I understand. Who *is* this person?"

"Mike Munoz. Word on the street is he's a high-ranking member of the Lords."

"He lives in Hartford?"

"Last I heard."

"Thanks for your help."

"Don't forget about me in here."

Steve smiled. "Nobody can forget about you, Bryce."

Bryce and Steve said their goodbyes. Steve walked across the street to his office, sat in his chair, and wrote down some notes on his conversation with Bryce.

Leon knocked on the door frame of Steve's office. Steve looked up and said, "How did you make out?"

"I'm not going to use the words he used, but he invited me to have a sexual relationship with my mother."

"Did you get anything from him?" Steve inquired.

"Nope."

"Thanks for the effort, Leon."

"How did you make out?" Leon asked.

"He said he got the gun from Mike Munoz."

"The dude from the Lords?"

"You know him?" Steve asked.

"Know of him. He's seriously connected."

"That's what I hear. We need to get more information on him. Sounds like the Lords may be involved in Julito's murder."

"Sounds like a Sam thing," Leon replied.

"How would Sam know?"

"I'm sure he knows a guy."

A DAY WITH THE F.B.I.

CHAPTER 48

Sam took Steve to Ernie's Taco Factory in West Hartford. It was time for Steve's review, and Sam thought he would make the occasion special by taking Steve to a restaurant that did not have a dollar menu. Sam and Steve were seated in a booth toward the back, where they could talk in private.

"Who died?" Steve asked. "Why are we driving twenty minutes away to eat at a fancy taco joint instead of going to Rico's next door? Am I getting fired?"

"No. This is your annual review."

"I thought I would get that with Big Frank in a few months."

"Oh, you will. This is your review from me. The firm wants me to give you a review as your boss. At the end of your contract year, Big Frank will give you your review and will discuss the next step."

"Next step?"

"Next step, meaning Big Frank will tell you if he is making you an offer after your contract expires. He might offer you that associate position with the firm; he could try to extend your current contract; he may not renew your contract or offer you a position. All that is up to Big Frank. I am here just to tell you how you are doing."

"Okay. How am I doing? Is my review written down on an actual piece of paper that I get to keep?"

"Dude. Do I look like a guy who gives written reviews?"

Steve thought about it for a moment and said, "I guess not. I thought maybe, since you stopped coming to work wearing sweatpants."

Sam and Steve laughed. They ate their lunches and ordered margaritas to celebrate.

"So, how am I doing?" Steve asked.

"You're doing great. You've done a fantastic job. The habeas department has been turned around. We're on top of our deadlines. We are currently on target to close 100 files this year. I don't think that has been done before by any firm. The office of the chief public defender loves us again. So, I wanted to take you here to say thank you. I even sprung for the $10 taco place."

"Thanks, Sam. That means a lot to me."

"Look. One of the reasons I brought you here is because I have a business proposition for you."

"I'm listening."

"What if you continued to work here with me in the habeas firm? I've been thinking of developing and expanding this branch of the firm. We can start to take direct criminal trials, criminal appeals, and expand our habeas work. I spoke with the chief public defender; she agreed to give us more court-appointed work. I can even broach the idea with Big Frank to get an advertising budget and some private cases. What do you think?"

"It's a lot to think about. In what capacity would I be doing this? Would I still be under a contract? Would I be a partner? Would I be an associate?"

"I'm not sure. It's something that I would have to talk to Big Frank about. I haven't pitched the idea to him yet. I wanted to talk to you first and see if this is something that you are interested in doing."

Steve sipped his margarita and thought for a while. "My dream has always been to do mergers and acquisitions. I've focused my life on that."

"But now your life has changed. You are getting a new perspective on life since you started your contract. You found a girl and fell in love. You've finally taken time for yourself and realized that there was more to life than work. You have a knack for doing criminal law, and you're good at it. I think that despite how you got screwed by the firm, you're actually happy with your life for the first time in years."

"That's true. But the question is… is the time I spent here a layover in the airport on my way to another destination, or have I found home?"

"That's your call. I don't want to pressure you into doing something that you don't want to do; I know all about that. I just want you to know that you have a home here with me. I think that we can do something great, but we build it on the concept that our families always come first; business is second. If we get overwhelmed, we hire additional help to keep our sanity."

Steve sat in silence and thought for a moment. It is one thing to work in a successful firm and do what you love. It's another thing to build the firm from the ground up. "I don't know, Sam. I need to think about it, and I want to know what Big Frank has to say."

"I respect that. You want to weigh all your options before you decide what you want to do. You might also want to confer with Jenny and Buddy."

Steve chuckled. "One thing I want to talk about is the Colombian Lords."

"What about them?"

"I think they were involved in the murder of Julito."

"So, what do you need?"

"I need to talk to a gang member who will tell me if someone from the gang murdered Julito, but I want to do it without raising any alarms."

"Sounds like you need a day with the FBI."

"The Feds?"

"Yeah. The Feds have managed to gain leverage over someone in every major crime organization in America. They trump-up federal charges on someone and convince them to become an informant in exchange for holding off prosecution; they also pay money or turn their head while the informant sells narcotics."

"Any chance I can talk to the informant for the Colombian Lords?"

"I'll call a friend of mine in the bureau. He should be able to hook you up. Understand something. None of this information you get is admissible in court. It's all hearsay. Even if this guy says that he killed Julito, he is under 'Queen for a day' status."

"Queen for a day?"

"That means that whatever crimes he may confess to you, he can't be prosecuted based on the statement he gave you during the interview. If you find a way to prosecute him without his own statement, then he can be prosecuted, but the statements he makes on that day cannot be used against him."

"Okay. Got it."

"Any information you get from this is only to help you look in a certain direction."

CHAPTER 49

Sam made arrangements for Steve to meet an FBI informant in the Colombian Lords, and a few days later, Steve drove to an address in the Spanish section of Hartford, near Trinity College. It was in the middle of the afternoon, and he was meeting the informant in an apartment in the projects. Although he was not wearing his suit, Steve still stuck out like a sore thumb.

Steve was trying to locate apartment 178. As he got closer, he realized that apartment 178 was the maintenance office that housed the cleaning equipment and grounds maintenance machines. He walked into the room, which was really just a small warehouse. In the very back was a small office. There were no windows, and it was out of sight from anyone looking in the apartment as they walked down the street. He knocked on the door. A black man dressed in khakis and a button-down shirt opened the door.

"Are you Steve?"

"You're Mr. Washington?"

"Hell yes." They shook hands, and Steve was invited into the small office, which contained a desk, a desk chair, a water cooler, and three wooden chairs arranged in a circle, like the last thing to happen in this office was a discussion among three people.

"Do you guys always have your meetings out here?"

"Sometimes. It's easier to meet in a common place in the community than in a police station or a Starbucks. If they are seen talking to someone who looks like a cop, they will be considered a snitch, even if they never snitched. This way, they are still in the community, and nobody will be the wiser."

"So, who are we waiting for?"

"His name is Hector, but he pronounces it without the 'H.' So he goes by 'Ector'. He is a member of the Lords, along with all of his brothers, cousins, and an uncle. He agreed to come over and talk to us. I didn't tell him what this was about. I'll let you do the talking. He should be here any minute."

They continued to make small talk for twenty minutes. Suddenly, there was a knock on the door. Before the agent could answer the door, a skinny Hispanic man entered the room and looked around.

"Hector, good to see you," said Agent Washington. "Have a seat and join us."

Hector looked outside to make sure nobody saw him enter the room. He sat down and continued to look around, acting jumpy like a mouse placed in a snake pit, knowing he was going to be eaten alive; he just didn't know when.

Agent Washington looked Hector in the eyes. "Hector, this is a friend of mine named Steve. He is doing an investigation into the murder of Julito Hernaiz. We want to know if you have any information on that."

Hector looked away. "I might have some information on that."

"Well, you know the deal," said Washington. "Queen for a day. We can't use this information against you or against anyone you implicate because it is hearsay. Please be honest with us, and we will continue our relationship with you. You can continue to sell drugs in the area where we allow you to sell."

Hector looked back at Steve and Washington. "Okay. What do you want to know?"

Hector looked as if he were withdrawing from drugs and needed his next high. Steve asked, "Did you know Julito?"

"Yeah. Everyone knew Julito. He knew I was a junkie and gave me a couple bucks when I was hurtin'."

"Did you work for him?"

"No. He hired guys to help him from time to time, but I never worked for him."

"What do you know about his death?"

"Mike killed him."

Steve's hands began to shake a little from the excitement. He could feel himself getting closer to freeing Carlos. "Who's Mike?"

"My cousin. Mike Munoz."

"Did Mike tell you this?"

"Yeah."

"Tell me about that."

"We were down in his basement watching football. I hadn't seen him in a while, so we got together. He was happy and was celebrating his engagement to his girlfriend. I didn't even know he was dating anyone, when all of a sudden, he was engaged and had a baby on the way."

"What does this have to do with anything?" Washington asked.

"I'll explain. Just sit tight," Hector said. Hector turned back to Steve. "So, we're chillin' on the couch, drinking beers, eating pizza, and watching the game. So, when he tells me he's engaged, I ask him all the usual questions. Who is she? Where did you meet her?"

"Go on," Steve said.

"He tells me that he's engaged to Carmen Hernaiz. Well, I asked him if that was Julito's widow. He says yeah. And I say, well, Julito died like a month ago, and you're already going to marry Julito's wife."

"And what did he say?" asked Washington, who was now giving Hector his undivided attention.

"He says that he had been having an affair with Carmen while she was married to Julito. She got pregnant and was scared.'

"Why was she scared?" Steve asked.

"Julito had a vasectomy years ago and couldn't get her pregnant. So, if he found out that she was pregnant, he would know that Carmen cheated on her."

"Yeah, but they could have gotten an abortion," Washington said.

"Mike and Carmen are both Catholic. They don't believe in abortion."

"That can't be a big deal to Mike. I know he's killed other people or had them killed," explained Washington.

"It's not like that. Killing a rival gang member or drug dealer happens all the time in this business. Killing an unborn child is not the same. That baby did nothing to deserve this. Abortion was not an option. Mike looked at it like he had to choose between killing his own child and killing Julito. And when you look at it like that, it was actually an easy decision. He wasn't going to kill a family member."

"But why kill Julito? What was the point? This kind of stuff happens all the time. There was no reason to kill Julito over this."

"No. Mike was scared of Julito. He would have to deal with him when he found out his wife was pregnant. Mike was afraid of what Julito could do. Julito may not kill Mike himself, but Julito had a lot of his crack-head friends who would do it for him."

Steve thought for a moment. "Did Mike tell you how he did it?"

"Yeah. When Carmen told him that she was pregnant, they came up with a plan."

"Wait. Carmen helped him kill Julito?"

"Hell yeah. She was just as scared of Julito and his crack-head friends, too."

"So, what was the plan?" Washington asked.

"Julito would get to the store early, usually 5:30 or a quarter of six. He would set up the register and then open the door. Carmen gave Mike the security code and the key to the back door of the bodega. Mike got there early and waited for Julito. He put a gun to Julito's head and said that it was a stick-up. He had Julito open the safe. He put Julito on his knees and shot him. Mike left the money in the safe and then opened the front door."

"Why would he do that?" Steve asked.

"Because Mike figured that a few crackheads would come to the store when it opened, looking for money from Julito. Mike thought that if one of these crackheads saw the money in the safe, they would take it. Then the crime scene would be fucked up and maybe make the crackhead appear to be the killer. And I guess that's exactly what happened. Some other guy got convicted."

"Did they get married?"

"Yeah. I went to the wedding. They're still married. She had a baby girl named Anna. They bought a house with the insurance money."

"Come again?" Washington asked.

"Julito had taken out a life insurance policy. He did it years before he was killed. The insurance company paid out on the policy. Carmen sold the house that she had with Julito and used the insurance money to buy a big home in West Hartford."

"What did Mike do with the murder weapon?"

"Whenever there's a killing, the Lords have a rule that we get rid of the murder weapon immediately. You can do that by burying it or throwing it in a river. Some guys sell it. I don't know what Mike did with the gun."

"Any other questions for Hector?" Washington asked Steve.

"Yeah." Steve turned back to Hector. "Do you know Krystal with a K?"

"Yeah. Everyone knows Krystal with a K. We got together once or twice."

"Did she have anything to do with Julito's murder?"

"Not that I know about."

"Do you know if anyone helped Mike kill Julito?"

"Only Carmen. She helped plan it and gave Mike the code to the security system."

Steve, Hector, and Washington stood up. Steve thanked Hector for his help. Hector opened the door and cautiously looked outside. When the coast was clear, he left the building.

"This is an FBI safe house. Only one person leaves at a time. We wait for fifteen minutes after each person leaves. I'll lock up and leave fifteen minutes after you," Washington instructed.

Steve and Washington continued to chat until the fifteen minutes were up. Then Steve thanked Agent Washington and left the safe house.

CHAPTER 50

Steve sat in the legal visiting room waiting for Carlos. As he waited for Carlos, he replayed Hector's interview in his head over and over again. This was the first case where he knew that his client was actually innocent. At first, he was overjoyed to represent a man he knew was innocent. Then the burden set in. What if he couldn't get Carlos a new trial? How could he live with himself if he couldn't help an innocent man?

Carlos opened the door and walked in. Steve stood up, and they shook hands. "Good to see you. I was just thinking about the case. Any progress on the investigation?" Carlos asked.

"I have good news and bad news," Steve said.

"Okay. What do ya got?"

"I know who killed Julito."

Carlos gasped in disbelief. He was not prepared to hear this news and was taken aback. Carlos paused for a moment and then said, "What do you mean?"

"First, understand that whatever I tell you, you cannot repeat. Not even to your fellow jailhouse lawyers. People have risked their lives to get this information, and me telling you is putting their lives in your hands. If word gets out that you know this information and leaked it, these people could lose their jobs—or be killed. Do you understand that?"

"Yeah. I won't tell anyone."

"This is a leap of faith that I'm making."

"I get it. What happened?"

"With the help of some friends, we were able to compare the ballistics results from every murder weapon in every murder and assault in Connecticut for five years before and five years after Julito's death. We found two other cases where the same gun was used that killed Julito. One of the assailants said he got the weapon from a member of the Colombian Lords. I then spoke with an informant in the Lords who knows who killed Julito. He told me that Julito's wife and this gang member were having an affair. She became pregnant with this guy's child and was scared about how Julito would react if he found out, so she and the gang member killed Julito."

"Are you sure he wasn't making this up?"

"That's what I thought. So, I had him describe the killing, and he did. His wife gave the killer the security code to turn off the security system and a key to the building. The killer got there before Julito arrived. He pretended it was a robbery. He had Julito open the safe, and then he murdered him. The killer intentionally opened the front door and left the safe open so that someone would come in and take the money, in order to infect the crime scene and cause the thief to appear to be the killer."

"Who is the killer?"

"Mike Munoz of the Colombian Lords."

"The Mike Munoz?"

"Yeah. Apparently, he was having an affair with Carmen Hernaiz, and she got pregnant. Julito had a vasectomy so he would know that he wasn't the father. Apparently, Carmen and Mike got married shortly after the murder."

Carlos's head was spinning. The story started to make sense. Now he knew why the killer had left the money in the safe and unlocked the front door. He was silent for several moments, and Steve knew to keep quiet while Carlos soaked it all in. After a few minutes, Carlos said, "Sounds like we have a strong case."

"That's the bad news. Everything that the informant said is hearsay and inadmissible in court. As for the guy with the gun, he was a client of mine and would only cooperate if I promised to help him with another criminal matter. None of this can be used in court."

"We know what happened, but we can't prove it?"

"At this point, we can't. But now we know the truth. So, we can focus on proving this story. We can focus our investigation on Mike Munoz, Carmen Hernaiz, Krystal with a K, and Julito. We need to get as much information as possible on these people and see what it tells us. We're still far away from being ready for trial, but this is a vital first step."

Steve and Carlos stood up. "I want you to know that I really appreciate all that you have done. If nothing else comes from this, at least I know what really happened. Thank you," Carlos said.

"Carlos, it is my pleasure. Remember, you can't speak about this to anyone."

Carlos and Steve said their goodbyes. Steve walked across the street to his office. It was after six in the evening, and everyone in the office had already left for the day. He sat in the chair in his office and reviewed the events of the day, from the interview with Hector to his discussion with Carlos.

CHAPTER 51

"What's wrong?" asked Jenny. "You're awfully quiet."

It was Saturday, and Jenny and Steve were having their weekly business meeting to discuss the progress of Jenny's medical billing company. Of course, the meeting took place over mutual massages and a bottle of wine.

While Jenny was getting her massage from Steve, she talked about the events of the week and the steps she was taking toward her company's goals. Steve normally loved to discuss the numbers and her company's progress but today was different. He was unusually quiet.

"I'm sorry. I just keep going back to a case that I've been working on. It's all I've had on my mind for the past couple of days."

"That's odd. Once you got settled at the firm, you stopped taking your work home with you. Now you have a case that you can't stop thinking about. What's up with that?'

Steve explained, "Well, I have a case where I found out that my client is actually innocent. That's not usually the situation. Usually, I don't know for sure if they are guilty and just lying to me or if they are innocent. In this case, I truly believe he is innocent."

"Isn't it good that you know the truth?"

"The problem is that I'm not sure if I can convince a judge to overturn his conviction. I don't know if I can actually *prove* his case."

"But you haven't tried his case yet?"

"Right. But it's the fact that I now know he is innocent. It's bad enough getting a beating in court when you know your client is guilty. It's worse when you lose a case where your client tells you they are innocent, but you don't really know for sure. But if I fail in this case, I feel that I will have denied him justice that he should have under the law."

"Look at it this way… in all your other cases, was there anything more that you could have done that you didn't do?"

"No. I gave them the best trial that I could put together."

"Are you going to give this client the best trial you can produce?"

"Of course."

"So how is this different than any other case that you have done or that you will do?"

"It's not different. It's just that the stakes are higher."

"How are they higher? Aren't they the same as in every case that you have done before?"

Steve thought about it for a while. "I don't know. It just seems different. The fear of losing is starting to consume me. It's the only thing I've thought about for the past few days."

Jenny and Steve were quiet for a moment. They switched positions, and Jenny began to massage Steve's back. She could feel the tension in his muscles. "You know, now that I am in the field getting more clients, I talk to a lot of doctors on a daily basis. They have people's lives in their hands every day."

"Yup. I understand that."

"They do this by learning to separate themselves personally from the problem. They look at the human body as a problem that they're trying to fix. They don't focus on the human being, just the problem. If you were a doctor and really got to know your patients, you'd have a hard time cutting them open and performing surgery. That's why many doctors don't want to know their patients too well because, when emotions start to become involved, it affects their judgment. Surgery becomes harder to do when you're performing it on a friend."

"And the point you're making is…?" Steve asked.

"Maybe you're getting too personally involved in this case. Maybe you're risking letting your emotions affect what you are going to do."

"So, what should I do?"

"Don't focus on the fact that you know he's innocent. Focus on giving him the best trial you can, like you always do. As long as you try your hardest, you have nothing to lose. Build the best case you can and then kick some ass."

Steve was quiet and let the words of Jenny's wisdom roll through his mind. He knew she was right; he just needed to hear it from someone else. A calmness came over him, and he began to feel at peace. For the first time in a few days, he smiled.

"You know something? You always manage to keep me grounded. I love you for that. You put my mind at ease. Please tell me again about your week at work. I promise that you now have my undivided attention."

Buddy woke up from his nap on the floor and stretched out. He walked over to Steve and Jenny and lay down next to Steve, indicating that he wanted his back massage, too.

CRYSTAL WITH A "C"

CHAPTER 52

Steve put his hand in the air and began to turn it in a circle, like he was holding a lasso over his head with an invisible rope. "Rally! Everyone… Rally!" He began to clap his hands loudly. "Come on. Let's go. It's Monday morning. It's time for the Brain Busters to have a meeting."

Leon slowly walked into the conference room and took a seat. Roxy entered walking even more slowly. Roxy had dark sunglasses over her eyes, her hair was in pigtails, and she was sporting a sleeveless blouse so she could show off her new tattoo. Roxy sat down and looked up at Steve. "You are way too chipper for 8:15 on a Monday morning."

"We've got a lot to do today. We need to get going," replied Steve.

"Okay," said Roxy. "I am a little hungover from yesterday, but I'll make it. I had to drink last night to kill the pain from my new tattoo." Roxy's tattoo was a picture of handcuffs underneath the words, "Society made me do it."

"It's very nice."

"Thanks," said Roxy. "I was thinking of my ex over the weekend and decided to commemorate our relationship with this tattoo. The artist put it on my bicep so when I flex, I can make the handcuffs dance."

"Okay," Steve started, trying to get the image out of his mind. "Let's talk about Carlos Vega. We know that Mike Munoz is the killer. We also know that Carmen Hernaiz, Julito's wife, helped plan the murder."

"What was the motive?" Leon asked.

"Carmen was having an affair with Mike. Carmen became pregnant with Mike's baby. Julito had a vasectomy, so he would have immediately known she was having an affair. Mike murdered Julito to prevent retaliation."

"So, how do we prove it?" Roxy asked.

"Well, that's the question we have to answer. I think we start by getting all the information we can about Julito, Carmen, Mike, and Krystal with a K. Let's get criminal records, medical records, financial records, newspaper clippings. Let's talk to neighbors, let's talk to family, friends, enemies—basically everyone who knows anything about them. But I can't stress this enough. We have to keep it quiet. We don't have to announce who our witnesses are until two weeks before the trial. Let's not give anyone a heads-up that they are a witness until they receive a subpoena. We know that the Lords are involved in this matter, and we may get some splash back. That's why we need to make sure that we don't tip anyone off that we're looking to point the finger at Mike Munoz and Carmen Hernaiz."

Roxy said, "I'll get a copy of the files from everyone's criminal charges through the Freedom of Information Act. That should give us a list of co-defendants who may have some dirt on these people—if they have criminal records. I can get a copy of the birth certificate for Carmen's baby from Vital Statistics. Let's see if she named Julito or Mike as the father."

Leon said, "I have been in contact with Crystal with C. We're friends on Facebook and have been chatting it up over the past couple of weeks. We're going out for drinks tonight. Maybe she can give me some dirt on Krystal with a K. Anything else I can do at this time?"

"Yeah. Roxy, can you see if Detective Bynes will speak to me about Julito's murder? See if Leon and I can meet with him about the investigation. Maybe he was uncertain that Carlos was the killer."

Leon spoke up. "Cops usually don't want to be questioned about their detective work. They think you're going to use it against them in a habeas case."

Steve asked, "How do you suggest we approach him?"

"What if we get Roxy to use her 'lady jazz' to get him to talk to us?"

"What the hell are you talking about?" asked Roxy.

Leon explained, "What I mean is, cops are not going to talk to me and Steve if we approach them straight up and say, 'Tell us about the investigation.' But if you and I approach him and you flirt a little, he may be a little more receptive. If Steve approaches him and starts getting all lawyer on his ass, then he'll shut down and give us nothing."

Steve looked at Roxy. "Are you willing to go with Leon and see what you can do?"

"Yeah. Why not? I got mad skills when it comes to lady jazz."

"This I gotta see," said Leon.

"It's true. It's easy for me to pick up a guy. The difficult part is staying with him."

"Okay," said Steve. "While you do that, I am going to scour the autopsy report and medical records for Julito to verify that he did have a vasectomy and when. Maybe we can subpoena the doctor to testify to this."

"Sounds good," said Leon.

"What time is your date with Crystal with a C?"

"Drinks at 7 at some restaurant in East Hartford. We'll see."

CHAPTER 53

Roxy and Leon walked down the road from the office and into the Hartford Police Station. This was not Roxy's first trip to the police station, but the circumstances were different this time. When they entered the building, nobody was sitting at the front desk. After a few minutes, an officer approached the front desk and asked them if they needed assistance.

"We have an appointment with Detective Bynes," Leon explained.

"And you are?"

"Leon and Roxy. We called earlier today."

The officer walked away and then walked back to the front desk. "You can go back and see him. He is in the third office on the right."

Roxy and Leon walked past the front desk. Roxy cleared her throat as she approached Bynes's office. The door was open, and a blonde-haired man sat at the desk, typing on a computer. "Detective Bynes?" Roxy asked in a lower-than-normal voice.

"Yes. Are you Roxy?"

"I am."

"I like the sound of that name," Bynes said, flirting back.

"If you like that, you oughta hear my phone number."

Bynes and Roxy giggled like a couple of school kids. "What brings you here? Something about the Hernaiz murder?" Bynes asked.

"Yeah. This is my partner, Leon. We're doing some research on the Julito Hernaiz murder, and you were the lead detective on that case. Can you tell us about the investigation?" Roxy wanted to keep the questions simple and calm. She didn't want to upset Bynes.

"Not much to tell. Mr. Hernaiz was robbed by a junkie named Carlos, who was looking to get his next fix. Carlos murdered Mr. Hernaiz for the money in the safe. A witness saw Carlos leaving the place with a bag of money. We got a warrant and found him sleeping in an alley. He pled guilty. Really nothing more than that."

"How did he say that he committed the crime?"

"He didn't. He never confessed. He pled guilty, but he never told us how he did it."

"Do you think he acted alone?"

"Yes. A witness saw him leave alone."

"Do you know how he managed to get in the building?"

"Not for sure. He would never talk to the police."

"How did you feel about the case when it was over?" Roxy said with a subtle smile on her face.

Bynes looked at Roxy's smile. He couldn't help but smile back. "I felt like the case had a lot of unanswered questions. We had enough to get an arrest warrant. I wanted to talk to him and hear his side of the story, but he lawyered up. And then he pled. Nobody ever got the story from him… unless you've talked to him."

"He said he's innocent."

"He's full of crap. I had an eyewitness who saw him leave the building."

"Yeah, but wasn't the only witness Krystal with a K?"

"True. But why did he plead?"

"I don't know. He doesn't say."

There was a pause as Roxy was caught taking a not-so-subtle look at Bynes's biceps through his tight-fitting button-up shirt. Roxy took the file folder she was holding and used it as a fan while giving Bynes a subtle smile. Bynes gave a little chuckle and smiled back.

"Let me ask you this," Roxy continued. "If Vega hadn't pled, who would you have investigated?"

"You're asking me to guess what I *would* have done? Well, since we had an arrest warrant for Vega, I would have continued to investigate the case and search for more evidence—which is what I did. My investigation stopped quickly when he pleaded guilty to the crime. But if I *had* continued the investigation, I would want to know how he got into the building. Did he just walk through the front door with a gun, leave the door open while he killed Julito, and then run out the front door? It didn't make sense to me, but on the other hand, you don't go to jail because you're brilliant. I've seen people commit dumb crimes. They even have TV shows dedicated to stupid criminals. Who's to say this isn't one of them?"

"How did you feel about the widow? Did you talk to her?"

"I interviewed the widow. I was the one who had to break the news to her."

"What did you think of her?"

"I'm not gonna answer that. That's not important."

Roxy was wearing her button-up sleeveless blouse. The blouse was her go-to weapon. She had recovered the money she spent on the blouse ten times over in free drinks at the bar. She wore the blouse with the top two buttons unbuttoned. As she talked, she held onto the third button of her blouse. This never failed to bring a man to his knees.

"Detective… I want you to know that I value your opinion. I know you've questioned hundreds, if not thousands, of people. I know that your experience in questioning people and your gut instinct make you a good judge of people. It would really mean a lot to me if you could tell me about your meeting with Carmen Hernaiz, and what you thought about her statement." Roxy held onto her button and gave a subtle pouting look.

Bynes held eye contact with Roxy. He knew he was being played, but he also figured there was no harm in giving his opinion. The case was closed, and Vega had already lost his habeas trial. Bynes smiled and said, "Fine. After I examined the crime scene, I went over to the Hernaiz house. I told her what happened, and she burst into tears and got very upset and cried for a while. When she composed herself, there were no tears. Her makeup was perfect. Not a sign of a smudge."

"What if she had on waterproof makeup?"

"I've told dozens of women that their husband or child is dead. The best makeup in the world can't survive the tears and eye rubbing that come with this news. I could be wrong, but I've seen fake crying before, and it looked like fake crying."

"Why do you think she faked it?"

"I don't know. I never investigated further."

"Was there any sign of gang involvement?"

Bynes thought for a moment. "No. Not really. The only thing that sticks out is the fact that the victim was put on his knees and shot in the back of the head. That suggests that the killer was deliberate in his actions, like maybe he had killed before."

Roxy paused and then asked, "Like maybe a guy who was desperate for his next fix wouldn't have acted in such a deliberate fashion. That someone who was desperate would not have thought out and executed such a plan?"

"Exactly. It could have been a gang killing, but not necessarily. The act looks more planned and perfected by someone who had done this before, not necessarily a gang member."

"And not necessarily Vega?"

"Except for the fact that he pleaded to it."

"Touché"

"Anything further?" Bynes asked.

"Krystal with a K. Did you do any further investigation on her?"

"There was no need. She's an open book—literally. The department's file on Krystal is probably a foot thick. I'd be shocked if she had any part in killing Julito. She's a career low-end criminal and drug addict. Krystal is now in her late 40s and still using meth and racking up prostitution charges because she turns tricks to pay for her habit. Murder is not part of her act."

Roxy looked at Leon. "Do you have any questions, Leon?"

Leon looked at Roxy. "No. I'm just the chauffeur driving Ms. Daisy."

Roxy stood up, and Bynes followed her lead. Roxy held out her hand and shook his. Bynes was impressed by her strong grip. Roxy gave Bynes the full smile and said goodbye. Roxy turned around and said, "Let's go, Leon," as she walked out of the room.

"Yes, Ms. Daisy," Leon replied.

After they left the police station, Leon said, "Nice move with the third button."

"Oh, you caught that?"

"Yeah, you have serious lady jazz skills."

"Told ya so."

CHAPTER 54

Leon sipped his beer and looked again at the clock on the wall. He was at a popular East Hartford sports bar called the Husky House. Connecticut hadn't had any major league sports teams since the Hartford Whalers left the state in 1997 to become the Carolina Hurricanes. As for college sports, there were two major colleges with NCAA teams: Yale and the University of Connecticut, with Quinnipiac University trying to catch up. UCONN has consistently had championship women's basketball teams. While the men's team has had a few titles of its own, the UCONN Women's Basketball team has been the pride of Connecticut for the better part of the last twenty years. Husky House was one of many sports bars to dedicate their business to Husky fans.

It was 7:15, and Leon was wondering if he was going to be stood up. He continued to sit while he went over his game plan. They would reminisce about the past and talk about the old days. He would eventually lead the conversation to Krystal with a K and then go where the road took him.

A petite woman wearing a beret and a vest walked into the bar. Leon walked up to her. "Crystal with a C, you look great."

"Leon, how've you been?"

"Good. Even better now that you're here."

Leon and Crystal sat at a table and talked about the good old days and what they were doing now. Crystal had been going to school off and on when Leon last saw her. She told him how she eventually finished nursing school and worked her way up through different nursing jobs. She started as a nurse's assistant in several retirement homes and eventually became a visiting nurse. She shared some scary stories about being alone with different patients who attempted to attack her. Finally, she snagged a job at Hartford City Hospital; it was a great job with great benefits. Now she was studying to become a physician's assistant. Leon was proud of her.

Crystal was happy to learn that Leon had turned his life around, too. He was off drugs and had a full-time job working as a private investigator.

"Do you ever see Krystal with a K anymore?"

"No. I haven't seen her in years."

"You guys used to be close. What happened?"

"She got to be too much to deal with."

"How so?"

"Well, we all knew that she had a drug problem. I tried to get her into treatment, and sometimes she would go, but she would always fall off the wagon."

"Yeah. We all saw that it was heading in that direction."

"Well, she continued to borrow money from me and not pay me back. Eventually, she started to take my stuff or steal money from my purse. I was sympathetic and continued trying to get her into treatment. She still wouldn't go."

"Why not?"

"Her addiction was strong. She was having sex for money in order to pay for her addiction. I know she got caught several times stealing stuff from department stores."

"How did you know that?"

"I bailed her out a bunch of times. I kept trying to help her, but she wouldn't get the help she really needed. As things got worse, my jewelry went missing, and my money kept disappearing. I was getting furious, but I tried to be understanding."

"And then what happened?"

"I was struggling to pay the rent one month. I was afraid we were going to be evicted, so I thought I would go through her purse to see if she had any money to pay the rent. When I opened her purse, I found almost $2,000 in cash. I didn't take it, but that was the last straw. We were gonna have it out, right then and there. I walked into her room. She was passed out on her bed. I went into the kitchen and got a pitcher of ice-cold water and poured it all over her."

Leon started laughing, which caused Crystal to laugh.

Crystal continued, "She woke up and started yelling at me. I told her that I had spent tens of thousands of dollars on her. Bailing her out of jail, covering her rent for the better part of a year, paying some of her bills, not to mention all the belongings she had stolen and sold for drugs. I couldn't stand it anymore. I told her that I found a ton of money in her purse."

"Let me guess," said Leon. "She got pissed at you because you went through her purse and made you out to be a criminal."

"Exactly. She tried to turn the tables on me, but I wouldn't let it happen. I unloaded and vented about all the bad things that she had done to me. She stood there and began to cry, and then she got mad again. She grabbed her purse and said, "If you want my money, then here it is," and she reached into her purse and took out the roll of money, and she threw it at me. She then stormed into her room and came out with a box. I asked what she was doing and she said, 'I'm paying you back for all the terrible things I did to you.' And she began throwing rolled coins at me."

"Really?" Leon asked.

"I'm not kidding. She had boxes of rolled coins and was throwing them at me. And I mean hundreds of dollars' worth of coins."

"What did you do?"

"Well, she was throwing rolls of coins at me, and it hurt. So I just bull rushed her and pinned her against the wall."

"Little tiny you bull rushed her?" Leon started to chuckle again.

"I have wiry strength for a tiny gal. I have to defend myself against patients sometimes, so I did the same to her. I pinned her against the wall. Then I grabbed her by the hair and dragged her to the front door and pushed her outside. I told her to come back in an hour."

"Why? What did you do in an hour?" Leon asked.

"I grabbed all the garbage bags in the kitchen and packed up all her stuff in the bags and threw them on the front porch. When she came back, I told her to take her stuff now and never come back."

"What did she do?"

"She was calm and said that she would go into rehab. I said that's great, but it's too little too late. She had to take her stuff and leave. She said she couldn't do it in one day. I said get it done because anything left on the porch tomorrow morning was going in the trash."

"So, what happened?"

"She got mad. But she took her stuff and left. When I went to work the next morning, everything was gone. I don't know where she went, but I never saw her again. The lease was up in about a month. I used the money she threw at me to pay off the remaining rent and put down a deposit on an apartment over here in East Hartford. It was closer to work, and I didn't want any problems with Krystal. I didn't know if she would do something when she got high, so I thought it was a good idea to sever all ties with her and move over here."

"Were you afraid of her?"

"No, I just didn't want to deal with her. I kept feeling sorry for her, and she used that to her advantage. I never took her as a violent person, but I just didn't want to have her come around and beg me for money anymore."

"When did this happen?"

"I don't remember the date."

"Was it around the time that Julito died?"

Crystal sipped her beer and thought for a moment. "Yeah. It was because I remember the day he died. The bodega was around the corner from the apartment. I went by the bodega to get a cup of coffee and grab some milk on my way home. I got off work around one in the afternoon and saw the police all around the store. Someone told me that Julito was dead. I was upset and walked home. When I got there, I walked in, and Krystal told me that she had to go down to the police department because she may have seen the killer. We were both sad that Julito was dead because he was a good friend of ours. I saw him almost every day. Krystal left that night, and I heard her come home in the early morning and go to bed. That was when I found the money in her purse. So it was the next day."

"Are you sure?"

"Yeah. Why do you care?"

"Well, I have a confession to make."

"Spill."

"One of the reasons I wanted to talk to you is because I wanted to get some information on Krystal."

"Like what? Everyone knows about her drug use and criminal charges."

"That's true. But I am investigating Julito's murder."

"I thought they found the guy."

"Well… sort of. The guy pleaded guilty to the crime but claims that someone else killed Julito."

"Do you honestly think Krystal did?" Crystal asked.

"No. But Krystal arrived on the scene immediately after the shooting. The money from the crime was never found. Roughly $3,000. But get this: boxes of rolled coins were stolen as well."

Crystal's eyes opened wide. "You think that the money she threw at me was the money from the bodega?"

"It makes sense. Who keeps boxes of rolled coins unless you're a store owner? A roll or two of quarters, I can understand for wash day.

But a box of quarters makes no sense. Riddle me this: What kinds of rolled coins did she throw at you?"

"It was definitely quarters, dimes, and nickels."

"Any pennies or half dollars?"

"No. Why?" Crystal asked.

"Because a box of pennies was left in the safe at the bodega."

"So, what do you think happened?"

"I think she saw the dead body and the open safe and decided to take the money and then blamed it on my client. The money was never found, but your story sounds like Krystal took the money."

"What do you want me to do?"

"Would you testify for my client? He confessed to killing Julito, but we believe that we can prove he is innocent. He needs your help."

"Who's your client?"

"Carlos Vega. Do you know him?"

"No. Not at all."

"Will you help him?" Leon asked.

"I guess. I mean, all I can do is tell the story I just told you."

"Great. I appreciate it."

"Leon… have you seen Krystal lately?"

"No. I may go see her before the trial, but I have no idea how she's doing. Why do you ask?"

"Just hearing this makes me feel sad for her. I hope she's not involved with Julito's murder."

As they stood up to leave, Crystal hugged Leon and held tight to him. She was clearly upset about Krystal with a K. Leon held her tight. "I'm sorry," he said. "I know that you did the best you could for her. Take it from another drug addict. You can try to help an addict, but they have to want your help. Krystal only wanted your help to get her next high. She needs to hit rock bottom, maybe even more than once, before she will really want anyone's help."

A tear ran down her cheek. Leon wiped her tear and gave her another hug. "It was good seeing you again. I'm so proud of you for sticking with school and becoming a nurse. You seem very happy, and I think that's great."

Leon walked her to her car and watched her drive off.

CHAPTER 55

It was the last Saturday in spring. Steve and Jenny decided to pack breakfast and hike the Devil's Den, a popular trail north of Weston, Connecticut. They brought Buddy and hiked to the top of a hill. The sun was rising beyond the mountains, several miles away. Steve laid out the blanket for the three of them, while Jenny opened the mixed fresh fruit and bagels with cream cheese. Buddy had already eaten breakfast before they left, but that didn't stop him from begging for some fresh fruit.

Jenny and Steve sat next to each other and watched the sunrise. Buddy curled up in Jenny's lap to take a quick nap. Steve was never a fan of yoga, meditation, aromatherapy, or just getting in touch with your feminine side, but he had to admit there was something relaxing about watching the sunrise one day a week. This weekly exercise put his problems into perspective and allowed him to refocus.

"So… what's stressing you today? Trial still getting you down?" Jenny asked.

"Yeah. I've got the trial on my mind, but I'm handling it better."

"How'd you do that?"

"I focused on the things that I can do—and I'm getting them done. I still think about the fact that I know he is innocent, and odds are that I'm not gonna be able to get him out, but I try not to focus on that. I make sure that he has no false hopes of winning this trial and going home."

"What's stressing you out then?"

"Same thing. The future. The end of the contract is approaching. Not sure what my options will be and what I am going to do."

"Well… what are your priorities?"

"You and Buddy."

"Meaning what?"

"You two are my family. I don't want to be without you."

Jenny smiled. "Well, if you need to relocate, that's actually doable. With technology, I can run my business from anywhere. Now that you have helped me learn how to delegate, I can manage people from another state and come back here once a month to check up on everyone. I could expand to another state. Buddy and I are on board with relocation if that's needed."

They kissed, and Steve wrapped his arms around her, while Buddy stayed put in her lap. "I appreciate that, but I don't want to put a strain on your business."

"Well, you are the business savant. You would know if it would be a strain. Will it be a strain on the business?"

"I don't think so. You've been successful so far in delegating your responsibilities to others. You were supervising these people, and then you promoted people to supervise for you, so now you only need to supervise three people. At this rate, by the end of the summer, you will have someone supervise those three people for you. That will leave you free to focus on guiding the company in any direction you want to take it."

"So, the business is doing well. Buddy and I support you in whatever you do, as long as you make time for us so we can still be a family."

"You know this has been a hell of a year. A year ago, I was focused on getting a high-paying job, where I would willingly work eighteen-hour days, seven days a week. Now that I've met you, I don't want that anymore. I still want to work in business and law, but I don't want to be a slave to it."

"Well, I'm always hiring."

Steve said, "It's not a bad idea. I enjoy helping you with the business. It's possible to offer services to large law firms to manage their billing and document management. We would need a few computer tech experts in the field to guide us on this, but it's worth looking into. I can probably try to sell Big Frank on the idea, and he can tell all his connections at other law firms."

"That's a heck of an idea. I never thought of that."

"I just don't know what all of my options are at this point, and it's starting to make me anxious. Am I getting an offer from the firm that I'm not sure I want? Am I getting no offer and no phone call made on my behalf? Is Big Frank gonna allow Sam to develop a criminal practice and make me a partner? It's driving me nuts."

"I know. Just remember that you don't have to take any of these offers if you don't want to. *Our* business is doing great. You have no law school debt to pay off. Our expenses are extremely low since we moved in together. You are in a position where you can do what you want to do and not have to take a job that you don't want."

"I guess it boils down to figuring out what I want."

"So, what do you want?" Jenny asked.

"That's the problem," said Steve. "I don't know."

CHAPTER 56

"Okay," Sam called. "Give me the update."

"Brain trust assemble!" Steve yelled out in the office. Leon and Roxy slowly walked into the conference room, like it was early Saturday morning after a raging Friday night frat party. Sadly, it was nine on Monday morning, and it was time to get back to work. Both Leon and Roxy were sipping their Starbucks coffee that Sam had bought on his way into work. It was a Monday ritual for Sam to bring in coffee for the crew and get an update on all the cases that were going to trial; while Sam managed the office and the case load, it was Steve's responsibility to report the status of the cases back to Big Frank. Everyone appreciated the Monday morning coffee.

"What's the word on Vega?" Sam asked.

"We know who the real killer is; we just have to prove it," Steve explained.

"What else is new? Any progress on proving it?"

"Turns out that Krystal with a K was lying. She did steal the money from the safe. We have a witness who saw her with a large amount of money and rolled coins." Leon explained.

"That's great news. We still need to place the real killer at the crime."

Roxy chimed in, "Leon and I did a canvas of the neighborhood, and we found a witness who saw someone running down the alley. He fits the description of Mike Munoz."

Steve looked puzzled. "How did you do that? The cops did a thorough canvas of the street on the day of the crime and found no one. How did you do a canvas years later and found an actual eyewitness?"

"Cops are not perfect," Roxy smiled. "Once I had my lady jazz working on Detective Bynes, I did a follow-up phone call with him. He told me that since the killer ran out the front door, they only questioned people who lived along the street in front of the bodega. Since the theory is that the killer ran out of the back door and into the alley, Leon and I decided to canvas the apartments behind the alley."

"And you found an actual witness?"

"Yeah. His name is Rudy. He was a college student at UCONN at the time. Rudy was living on campus but came home that night for his sister's birthday. He got up early the next morning for an eight o'clock class. He heard some shots. He looked out his bedroom window and saw a man running down the alley. It was a tall Hispanic man. I showed him a picture of Mike Munoz. He said he was not sure if that was the guy."

"Not rock solid," Sam said, "but it helps. What are you working on, Steve?"

"Well, I have three other trials over the next two weeks. Aside from that, I'm preparing for the Vega trial. Carlos wants to work together on the trial prep. He knows the trial file as well as I do; he wants to help me draft the questions."

"Are you serious?" Sam asked.

"Yup. It's what he wants. I'm going to draft a set of questions for each witness. He'll give me his input. We'll see how it goes."

"You do understand that you're responsible for giving him the best trial possible, even if it means *not* doing what he wants?"

"Sure do. I also know that I didn't corner the market on ideas. I am more than happy to listen to what he has to say. He understands that I have the final say as to trial strategy."

"As long as we're clear. Some clients think that *they* tell *us* what issues to raise at trial and how to raise them. If you go by that logic, then you can be grieved or sued for malpractice for doing what they want instead of doing what is best for their case."

JOHNNY ROAST BEEF

CHAPTER 57

Mike Munoz was the chief of the Colombian Lords. He was initiated when he was in middle school, after he participated in killing a rival drug dealer who was causing trouble for the Lords. Once Mike took part in a murder, the Lords had leverage over him, and if he ever turned against them, they could implicate him as a participant in a murder. The initiation also showed loyalty to the gang.

Mike worked his way quickly through the ranks. He started out selling drugs on the street corner, a position many newbies work for years or until they accrue so many convictions that they end up spending a decade in prison as a persistent felon. To avoid getting busted on the street corner, Mike started delivering the drugs directly to his clients. By the time he reached high school, his client list was so long that he had several newbies working for him. Mike eventually mastered the art of delegating his responsibilities to others, so that he only needed to follow up on a few of his assistants. Mike built a small drug empire in Hartford, which came with the responsibility of collecting debts from delinquent clients. Eventually, Mike expanded his business skills into burglary and prostitution.

Mike's true rise to power came when he was able to launder the money from his illegal enterprises through legitimate businesses. Mike's relatives ran small businesses that barely turned a profit.

Mike became a business partner in all of these small businesses and used the proceeds of his illegal activities to fund his relatives' legitimate businesses. He even paid taxes. The other high-ranking members of the Lords saw the writing on the wall. They knew that Mike had the perfect demeanor to run the Lords and make it a profitable organization.

The Lords started to consume more small businesses, usually through relative connections, but sometimes through intimidation and fear. The bodega eventually became a source for money laundering after Julito's death. Julito's wife, Carmen, made Mike a partner in the bodega, and the bodega's profits suddenly increased by 40 percent. Mike worked with a criminal lawyer who advised him on how to make the Colombian Lords appear to be a legitimate business. The lawyer had an accountant on his staff who would maintain the books for all the businesses so that they could withstand an audit from the IRS. Also, the higher-level members of the gang received paychecks from these businesses as employees on their payroll.

Mike was at work when he received a call from Carmen. She needed him to come home. Mike and Carmen knew not to talk about Mike's work over the phone, so when she said she needed him to come home, it was because something had happened. Mike hurried home.

Carmen saw Mike pull up in the driveway. As Mike ran into the house, Carmen put their child, Anna, into the playroom.

"What happened?" Mike asked.

"Some guy named Leon came to the door and gave me this." Carmen handed a document to Mike. He read it a couple of times.

"It looks like you've been summoned to court to testify."

"Yeah. I understand that. My question is, why? Does this have something to do with your business?" She asked.

"It says this is about Carlos Vega. Who's that?" Mike asked.

"He's the guy who got convicted for killing Julito," Carmen replied.

"What?"

"Yeah. He's a party to the case. I have to testify at trial. Why? What am I supposed to testify about? Do you think they are trying to pin the murder on me?" Carmen asked.

"I don't know. I don't even know what the case is about."

"Mike, I'm scared. I don't want to go do this. I don't want to testify. I don't want to say something that I shouldn't say. I don't want to answer a bunch of questions. What do I do? I'm really scared here, Mike. I need you to tell me what to do. I want you to get me out of this."

"Let me call the lawyer. Maybe he can tell us what's going on, and what we can do." Mike walked over to Carmen and held her close. She began to cry. "Don't worry, sweetie," he whispered. "I'll get you out of this. Don't even worry about it. I'll take care of everything."

It was lunchtime, and Mike made lunch for the family. After lunch, he played with Anna for a while. Mike held his girls tight and then left to meet his lawyer.

CHAPTER 58

Dave Pruett was Mike Munoz's criminal lawyer. He was not a criminal lawyer. He was a *criminal* lawyer. He went to college in hopes of signing on with the Drug Enforcement Agency. His dream was to be an undercover agent and arrest drug dealers. After college, he was recruited by the DEA. Dave worked hard for the agency for several years and was a great agent. Unfortunately, he never moved up in the ranks. He remained a field agent while his peers were being promoted to high-paying jobs in Washington, D.C. Dave thought his hard work would pay off with a promotion, but he came to realize that his peers had high-level friendships and political affiliations. It was too late for Dave to start generating these relationships, and he refused to "ass kiss" his way to the top.

Fortunately, Dave was able to turn lemons into lemonade. He went to law school at night while he worked as an agent in the field during the day. Dave was developing his future clients from the drug dealers he arrested, so that he could start his own practice when he got out of law school.

When Dave left the DEA, he immediately had over 100 clients. Dave knew how to run a major drug ring without getting caught by the DEA. Most of his clients were the drug dealers he arrested when he was an agent. While Dave would represent drug dealers in court, the majority of his practice came from money laundering and educating his clients on money laundering. Dave taught his clients how to be organized and avoid the pitfalls and traps of money laundering. The majority of Dave's practice was illegal and unethical, but it was protected by lawyer/client confidentiality, meaning the conversations he had with his client regarding money laundering could not be used against him in a criminal case.

Mike Munoz was Dave's client and student. In fact, Mike was a very good student. Mike arrived at Dave's office, and the secretary walked him to Dave's conference room. Dave arrived a few moments later.

"Hi, Mike. I reviewed the subpoena that Carmen received, and I did some research on the case."

"Okay. So, what's going on?"

"Carmen was subpoenaed to testify in a case about the murder of Julito Hernaiz."

"What is the state going to ask her?"

"The subpoena is not from the state; it's from the defendant, Mr. Carlos Vega."

"What does he want her to testify about?"

"This is a habeas case. It's a lawsuit by Mr. Vega claiming that his lawyer erred, and he deserves a new trial. These cases almost never win. The defendants are represented by young and inexperienced attorneys. In fact, the lawyer in this case has only practiced for about a year. In the petition, they claim that you murdered Julito and that Vega was pressured into taking the deal. Now he wants out of the deal and to be recharged with the crime so that he can claim you are the killer and not him."

"So do you think I should take care of this?"

"No."

"Are you kidding me? This guy is saying I murdered Julito several years ago, and you say I should do nothing?"

"Look. These kinds of cases go on every day. People say the stupidest things to get a court to overturn their conviction. Maybe one case in two or three years is overturned and brought for a retrial. I've seen the witness list. The only witness who can potentially place you at the scene is Krystal with a K, and nobody will believe her. My advice is to do nothing. I'll coach Carmen on how to testify to the point where she feels confident."

"This is bullshit. I can have my guys take care of all of this in an afternoon."

"Mike. Listen to me. There is no way he will win this case. The guy admitted that he killed Julito. He will never overcome this. Let the trial happen. They'll ask Carmen some questions. She will be fine. Vega will lose the case and stay in jail. Nobody will think anything of it. If you do something to these witnesses, that could lead to an investigation, which could potentially reopen interest in the murder of Julito. More harm than good will happen if you try to stop this trial."

"I don't want Carmen to go through this."

"I've testified dozens of times. She just needs to be prepared. She'll be fine."

"This subpoena has both of us upset. This needs to stop now. What can you do to stop it?"

"If you try to stop it legally, then you'll raise suspicion about the murder. People will wonder what you are really hiding. What if this lawyer and his client go to the press and begin to talk about what really happened that night? If you let the case take its course, you'll be able to put all of this behind you."

Mike thought about it for a moment. "I guess you're right."

"This case is not a big deal. It's not going to get any press. Nobody is gonna know about it. There is no chance for him to win. Have Carmen call me and set up an appointment to prepare her to testify. She'll do great."

"Thanks for your time, Dave." They both got up, and Dave walked Mike to the office door.

Mike got in his car but did not start it. He sat and thought about what he should do. Maybe Dave was right, and he should let the whole thing slide. But that didn't sit well with him. No other Colombian Lord would take this shit from anyone. It was time to make his presence known. It was time to show Carlos Vega how he did things in his town.

Mike pulled out his phone and called some of his soldiers.

CHAPTER 59

Carlos was consulting with Hooch, Ice, Crazy-K, and the Blade regarding the approach he should take with Carmen.

"You gotta be delicate with her. If you go in there and act all gangster and shit, the judge is gonna get pissed at you and shut you down. The judge will want to punish you for harassing the victim's wife," explained Ice.

"Couldn't be any more wrong," said Blade. "You need to be aggressive. This lady had her husband murdered so that she could marry his killer and have his love child. You need to put her on display as the cold-hearted bitch that she really is."

"I actually agree with Blade on this one," said Crazy-K. "The judge isn't going to give you credibility anyway because you already confessed. You might as well get the most information out of her that you can and take this habeas to federal court."

"So, what's the wonder lawyer gonna do?" asked Hooch.

Carlos cleared his throat. "He said that he is going to try to walk a fine line with her. First, he wants to be delicate and get her to agree to some facts at the beginning and then show some documentation that will crush her credibility. Then he'll switch gears and start to get firm with her."

"What do you mean by 'firm'?" asked Blade.

"Firm, as in halfway between aggressive and nice. He doesn't want to tear her apart, but he wants to be tough enough to get the facts out."

"Is that what you want?" asked Ice.

Carlos explained, "Look, everyone knows that questioning a witness on the stand almost never goes the way that you planned. You may plan to go aggressive or be nice, but you have to be prepared to adjust to a different approach to get the information you want into evidence. So, I agree that taking the middle road may be the best way to adjust back and forth if needed."

"Let's go, ladies! Back to your cells!" the prison guards yelled.

Carlos and Hooch walked back to their cell. The cell door slammed behind them. Carlos noticed a newspaper lying on his bed. It was folded up and wrapped with a rubber band, like the newspaper boy had driven by and gently placed it on his pillow.

"What's that?" Carlos asked Hooch.

"It looks like you have a message. Better go read it."

Carlos grabbed it, took off the rubber band, and opened the paper. It was the New York Times. Neither Carlos nor Hooch read this paper, so it was clearly a message. Carlos noticed that certain words were circled in red ink within the different articles. Nothing was cut out of the paper, nor was there any message handwritten on the paper.

Carlos laid the paper out on his desk and began to look at the circled words. Hooch looked over his shoulder. "I guess the circled words are a message to you. I'll write them down," said Hooch. Carlos and Hooch scoured the entire newspaper, looking for all circled words. They double-checked to make sure they didn't miss anything. The circled words made the following message:

Carlos stop the trial immediately otherwise you and your witnesses will be dead before the case begins. Don't do anything stupid Colombia Lord.

"Probably couldn't find the word 'Lords' in the newspaper, so he had to settle for 'Lord,'" Hooch said.

"Looks like Julito's wife was served with a subpoena."

"What are you gonna do?" Hooch asked. "You might be able to go into protective custody."

"The reality is, I doubt I would be any safer in protective custody. The Lords can get you anywhere in prison. Any guard or inmate can be bribed. I thought this could happen. It's just shocking to see that my fears become reality."

CHAPTER 60

Steve was up and at 'em early on Monday morning. He showered, kissed Jenny and Buddy goodbye, hit the bagel shop on his way in, and made it to work by seven. Steve was pumped and ready to plow through a bunch of paperwork so that he could spend the rest of his day preparing for trial. Steve pulled into his usual parking spot. He grabbed his briefcase and stepped out of the car. As he walked across the parking lot, he noticed the word "Lordz" spray-painted several times.

Steve stopped in his tracks and looked around at the damage. His heart sank to his stomach. Steve had received threats before from potential witnesses or opposing parties, but that was as far as it had gone. The Vega case suddenly became real to him. Everyone's life was in jeopardy: His, Jenny's, Buddy's, Carlos's, and all the witnesses.

Steve walked to the front door. LORDZ was painted across the front door and on the sidewalk. Mike Munoz wanted to send a message. Steve opened the door and went to his office. The message light on his phone was lit; he had a message. It could not have been Carlos because Carlos could not have made a legal call after hours. Maybe it was a threat from the Colombian Lords. Steve set down his briefcase and picked up the phone. He took a deep breath and pressed the play button. It was Carlos's mom. She had received a call from Carlos last night. He asked her to call him.

Steve returned Mrs. Vega's call. She explained that Carlos had received a threat while he was in jail. The Colombian Lords told Carlos to stop the trial, or he and the witnesses would be dead. Steve assured her that everything would be okay.

Steve took a deep breath and considered his options.

"What the hell's going on here?"

Steve looked down the hall and saw Sam walking toward his office. "Looks like the decorating committee showed up," Sam laughed. "I guess Carmen Hernaiz-Munoz got her subpoena?" Sam asked.

"Looks that way. They threatened Carlos in prison as well. If we don't withdraw the case, then Carlos and his witnesses die."

"Is this your first threat?" Sam inquired.

"No. But it is the first time that someone has begun to follow through with one. What are we supposed to do in this situation?"

"Well... we can go to the court and ask for help. We can call the cops. I think a lot of that is pointless. Mike Munoz will claim ignorance, and there will be no charges brought against him. He will threaten people to try and scare them off, but my bet is that he won't actually follow through."

"What can we do?" asked Steve.

"I know it sounds weird, but let's call Big Frank and see what he thinks."

Big Frank arrived in the parking lot within the hour. Steve looked out his office window, which overlooked the rear parking lot, and watched as Big Frank got out of his Mercedes and looked at the writing on the building and the parking lot. Steve thought to himself, within a moment, Big Frank will come barging through the building and vent his anger. But that was not the case.

Big Frank opened the front door and went upstairs to the offices. He poked his head in Steve's office. "Get Sam, and we can all talk in the conference room."

Steve brought Sam to the conference room, where Big Frank had already made himself comfortable. Sam said, "Did you see that the decoration committee came by?"

Big Frank ignored the sarcasm. "What's going on here? Why are you being threatened?"

"It's a case that I have," said Steve. Steve then explained the theory of his case: that Mike Munoz, the leader of the Colombian Lords, is in fact the killer of Julito Hernaiz. These threats came about because of the pending trial and subpoenas that were served, probably because the victim's wife was served.

Big Frank took it all in, and then he thought about it for a moment. "Okay. I'll take care of it." Big Frank stood up and was about to leave.

"What exactly does that mean?" asked Steve.

"It means that this Munoz guy is trying to scare you with threats. I'll make the situation safe. Everyone and their families are safe. Just keep focusing on your work. Don't worry about this. Did you tell the witnesses about any of this?"

"No."

"Don't. Call them in a few days and review the testimony with them. Assure your client that he and his family are safe."

"Frank, what exactly are you gonna do?" Sam asked.

Big Frank turned toward Sam and Steve. "Sam. Steve. I will do what I always do. I'll do what I've done for decades. I'll protect my employees. I'll protect my employees' families. I'll protect our clients. I'll protect our witnesses and their families. Nobody threatens this firm. Nobody."

"Frank, you're dealing with serious organized crime," Sam explained.

Big Frank chuckled.

"I'm gonna call someone about the graffiti," Sam said.

"No," said Big Frank. "I'll take care of it. Just go ahead with business as usual."

Big Frank walked out of the building and drove off back to the office.

Sam looked at Steve. "Do you feel better now?"

Steve thought about it for a moment and said, "Yeah. Actually, I do. When Big Frank says he's going to take care of it, I believe him. In the meantime, I'll go see Carlos and tell him that we will have protection."

CHAPTER 61

Rico and Spider joined the Colombian Lords a few years ago. They were eager to move up in the organization. Mike saw their enthusiasm as an opportunity to throw them a bone. He ordered them to scare witnesses from testifying in the Vega case. Dave Pruett gave Mike a copy of the Vega case file, including the witness list. Mike then got the home and work addresses of the witnesses. Mike also provided additional information, such as whether they owned a gun or lived alone, and what car they drove.

Crystal with a C was the first on the list because she did not own a gun and she lived alone. Rico and Spider wandered through the hospital where Crystal worked, looking to see which department she worked in and whether there was a good place to corner her and threaten her. The Crystal with a C file came with a picture of her, which happened to be taken from her Facebook page. They finally located her in the emergency department, but people began to be suspicious of them, and they left. They would have to do a home invasion.

On their way to Crystal's, Rico stopped off at Giuseppe's Pizza and picked up a large pie with everything on it. Rico drove to Crystal's apartment and dropped Spider off. Spider carried the large pizza, posing as a deliveryman. The entrance to the building was through a locked door. Spider pushed all the buttons on the intercom system, and, like always, somebody buzzed the door and let him in. He examined the lock on the door. Spider noted that the lock brand for the entry door was Goliath. Spider and Rico had a lock kit in the trunk of their car, which they used for breaking into different houses, tools of the trade for work as part of the Lords. Spider had a ring of assorted pass keys, including a Goliath pass key. The front door would not be a concern.

Spider walked up the flight of stairs to apartment 235. The apartment door was perfect. It was located on the corner and was not in direct view of the peepholes from other doors. Also, the bolt lock and the bottom lock were Goliath locks. The contractor must have gotten a deal on Goliath locks and put them on all the doors. Spider knocked on the door and waited for someone to answer in order to create the illusion of delivering a pizza.

Spider walked back to the car and reported all the information to Rico. They drove around to the corner of the building so they could see when Crystal came home. They took out their set of Goliath pass keys and a set of bolt cutters in case she had a door chain for added security. They ate the pizza and talked for several hours until they saw Crystal's light go on at ten. They continued to monitor the lights in her windows. Eventually, several lights went out except one. At about one in the morning, the last light turned off. Rico and Spider waited an extra forty-five minutes to make sure Crystal was asleep.

Spider took the lead, and Rico served as lookout. Spider carried the pass keys, and Rico carried the bolt cutters. Spider got out of the car and walked toward the front of the building. Rico followed him, looking behind them as they walked. Spider approached the front door and began to work the pass keys to get into the building.

"Police. Hold it right there."

Spider turned around and saw a large man in a business suit holding a gun on him. "You're not a cop," Spider said.

The officer opened his blazer, revealing a badge hooked onto his belt. “I’m Detective Lojuidice. Burglary. Turn around and place your hands above your head.”

Spider sighed. He knew the drill. He assumed the position, and the detective cuffed him. Lojuidice grabbed Spider’s arm and guided him to a four-door sedan that was double-parked. Lojuidice placed Spider in the back of the sedan, where Rico was sitting.

Spider stared off into the distance. All he could think about was how angry Mike would be when he found out.

CHAPTER 62

Spider and Rico were taken to a poorly lit building in Hartford.

"Hey, this isn't the police station," Spider argued.

The detective reached into his pants pocket, pulled out a set of keys, and opened the door. Spider and Rico were guided through an office and then through a door in a warehouse. The warehouse was empty except for a few folding chairs and a couple of card tables.

Spider became angry and shouted, "Why the fuck are we here? This isn't the police station?"

Spider and Rico were still cuffed. They were seated in the folding chairs. The detectives remained silent.

"Answer me!" Spider yelled.

Lojuidice walked over to Spider and Rico. "Are you hungry? Do you want something to eat?"

Rico yelled, "Fuck you, pig. When am I gonna be read my rights? When do I get my phone call?"

"I need one of you to be the messenger, and the other one to be the example." Lojuidice looked at Rico. "Which one do you want to be?"

"Fuck you, pig. I'm not doing shit. I want my lawyer," Rico yelled.

Lojuidice smiled and began to chuckle.

"Fuck you. What's so funny?" asked Rico.

"Well, first of all, I am smiling at your stupidity. I thought you would have figured out by now that we aren't cops and this isn't a police station. You see, when we caught you at the apartment building, we arrested you like the cops would so we could avoid any suspicion. Second, you made my job easier because you've chosen to be the example."

"What?"

"My name is Johnny Lojuidice. People call me Johnny Roast Beef. This is my pal, Jimmy Peppers."

"What a stupid fuckin' name."

"You wanna know how I got my name?"

"I don't fucking care. We're Colombian Lords. If you fuck with us, there will be nothing left of you except for a grease stain. So let us go, and maybe I can convince Mike Munoz to let you live."

"Well, Rico, you're gonna care," said Johnny Roast Beef with a smile.

"How did you know my name?"

"I know all about you and your buddy Spider. I know that you were attempting to break into the apartment of Crystal Carlisle to scare her away from testifying at a trial. I know that the two of you sell drugs in your spare time for the Lords. At night, the two of you do some low-end burglary jobs. You still live with your mom. She doesn't know that you're in a gang. She thinks that you work in Julito's old bodega, and you got the paycheck to prove it. Unfortunately, she doesn't know that the bodega is just one of many small businesses that are used as a front to launder the Colombian Lords' drug business."

"Who the fuck *are* you?"

"I'm Johnny Roast Beef. They call me Johnny Roast Beef because I'm an artist. In my career, I've beaten thousands of people. Some of them, I've beaten to death. I don't hit with bats, crowbars, or jack handles. I just beat them with my fists. I'm an artist because I have studied how to beat someone. I know how to inflict the greatest amount of pain without killing someone. I can make anyone talk. Do you know how hard it is to break someone's femur by punching it? Most people have to kick it or use a hammer. But I can break your femur with just one punch. Anyway, I always save the face for last. It's sort of my calling card, if you will. You see, I inflict a ton of pain by breaking bones in your body and causing internal bleeding, but I always finish by punching you in the face so many times that you start to resemble a slice of roast beef. Hence, the name Johnny Roast Beef. Eventually, guys used to challenge me by buying a roast beef sandwich and taking out a slice to see if I could match the face to the slice of beef. I became very good at it. It took decades to master beating people to a pulp. Today, people don't bother mastering the art; they just shoot someone when they get pissed. It's sad. You see, when I give a beating, I instill fear and respect into my victim. They will never cross me. They will do whatever I say. The person you shoot, well… they just die. What's the value in that? You can't exercise dominion or control over someone who's dead."

"Well, Mr. Roast Beef, if anything happens to us, you and Mr. Peppers are dead, and so is your entire family. The Colombian Lords won't stand for it. We run this town."

"Do you know what the most valuable thing in the world is? It's information. Right now, you are going through life with inaccurate information. You and Spider spend your days selling eight balls because I allow you to. Mike Munoz and the Colombian Lords move the drugs in Hartford that I provide. Every drug you sell, every item you steal, every dollar you make from every prostitute you control happens because I allow it to happen. The Lojuidice family owns all of New England, and I own all of Connecticut. You and the Lords are nothing more than tenants on my property. If I ever want to evict you, I can. Mike Munoz and the Lords have power because I allow you to have power. I think that is some critical information that you don't have."

Rico and Spider sat quietly for a while. "I'll tell you anything you want to know," Rico said.

Johnny Roast Beef considered Rico's offer as he put on extra-extra-large latex gloves over his enormous hands. He stood over Rico and snapped the gloves after he rolled them onto his hands. "They say that you spend ten years of your life mastering your craft, ten years of your life practicing your craft, and another ten years teaching your craft. Today is your lucky day cause I'm gonna teach you my craft. Remember that thing I said about the femur?"

"Yeah," Rico said nervously. Johnny punched Rico in the leg, causing the bone to break through the skin. Rico began to scream in pain.

"See, Rico, it takes a lot of skill to do that." Johnny then punched Rico repeatedly in the ribs, first on the right side and then on the left. "Now the key to inflicting a lot of pain is to break ribs. Do you know why?"

Rico couldn't answer as he was having trouble breathing from all the broken ribs and internal bleeding.

Johnny continued, "You'll feel the pain from the broken ribs for months. You won't be able to sleep because of pressure on your ribs. Also, you're probably bleeding internally; you might have even punctured a lung. Don't worry, you still have time to get to a hospital." Johnny took the cuffs off Rico. "Now, give me your hand. I wanna show you something special." Johnny placed Rico's hand flat on the table. Johnny then punched the top of Rico's hand with his fist.

The pain was so excruciating that Rico began to scream at the top of his lungs with a pitch that didn't sound human.

"Catch your breath. You know what's cool about your hand. They will x-ray it at the hospital. Ask them how many bones in your hand are broken. They will tell you twelve. You see, I know I broke twelve bones in your hand because I am that good at this. Now, it's roast beef time."

Johnny proceeded to punch Rico in the face again and again. Johnny then said, "If you punch someone in the eyes several times, it quickly creates swelling and blood flow throughout the face, giving it that reddish-pink look. And now for the finishing touch." Johnny gave Rico a right hook across the nose, causing his nose to bleed all over his face.

Rico was sobbing from the pain while trying to breathe.

Johnny looked at him with a smile. "Well… I hope you learned a lot today. You don't have to thank me. That look of gratitude on your face is thanks enough."

Johnny turned to Spider. "Now… as for you."

"I'll tell you anything you want to know," Spider pleaded.

"I don't want information from you. I already know everything about you." He

unlocked Spider's handcuffs. "You are the messenger, and he is the example." Johnny Roast Beef handed Spider a large yellow envelope. "Here is the message that I want you to give Mike Munoz. If anything happens to Carlos Vega, any of the witnesses in the case, the law firm in the case, or anyone's families, then I will hunt down every Colombian Lord, including Mike Munoz, and make them look like Rico. I will take away your drug territory and give it to the fucking Irish. If you think I'm kidding, then just try me. In case you forget, I wrote my message down and put it in this envelope with some supporting documentation. Now, you can decide whether to take Rico to the hospital, but you will not lose this envelope because your life depends on it."

Spider helped Rico stand up and helped him walk across the room.

"I had my boys bring your car over here. It's parked outside. Go out the driveway and turn left onto Lilac. In about a mile and a half, turn right onto Orchard. Hartford Hospital will be on your right. Rico still has about an hour before he bleeds out. Ask if Dr. Kovich is on duty. He's familiar with my work."

CHAPTER 63

Mike Munoz had an emergency meeting with his attorney, Dave Pruett, at six a.m. Dave had received a text message in the middle of the night saying he had to meet Mike as soon as possible. Because Dave was in the middle of a trial, this was the only time he could meet.

Dave opened his office and sat at his desk, drinking coffee and reviewing e-mails. A few moments after six, Mike opened the door and walked in.

"We're all alone, Mike. Come on into my office." Dave stood up, greeted Mike, and invited him to have a seat. "Okay. I don't have a lot of time, because I'm on trial across town this morning. What's going on?"

"Remember how we talked about the Vega case and Carmen's subpoena."

"Uh-huh. That was two days ago. I still remember that conversation."

"Well, I decided to apply some pressure on Vega and some of the witnesses."

"You mean after I told you not to?"

"Yeah."

"Okay… did something happen?"

"I sent Rico and Spider out to put a scare into some witnesses, but I guess they got caught."

"You mean they were arrested? Tell me where they are being held, and I can arrange a bail hearing, possibly this morning."

"They're not under arrest."

"What happened?" Dave asked curiously.

"I got a call a few hours ago from Spider. They got caught by some guys who posed as police officers. They were taken to a warehouse, and Rico was beaten within an inch of his life."

"What happened to Spider?"

"Nothing. They did nothing to Spider, but they told him to get Rico to a hospital immediately or he would die from internal bleeding—and they were right. They also warned me not to mess with the Vega trial, the witnesses, the attorneys, or anyone's family. If I messed with them, they would kill every member of the Lords and our families."

"Do you believe them?"

"Ordinarily, I would find these people and kill them, but there's more."

"What else?" Dave inquired.

"They gave Spider an envelope. In the envelope was a list of every single member of the Colombian Lords, along with their names, addresses, social security numbers, names and addresses of family members, as well as the names and addresses of everyone's children and where their children go to school. They also had bank account numbers."

"Are you sure these people weren't cops?"

"They weren't cops. It was Johnny Roast Beef's crew."

"Johnny Roast Beef? What did you do to piss off Johnny?"

"I don't know. All I know is if I move forward, then he'll execute all of us and give my territory to the Irish gang. If I do what he asks, he may still be pissed off at me and kill us all anyway for whatever it is that made him mad in the first place. I don't know what to do."

"How's Rico?"

"He has a lot of broken bones, internal bleeding, and he will be in a lot of pain for several months, but he should be fully recovered in about six months."

"Yeah. That's classic Johnny. Did he do the hand thing?" Dave asked.

"Yeah," Mike replied softly.

"Was he right about the broken bones in his hand?"

"Yeah. He said he broke twelve bones in Rico's hand, and he was accurate."

"Do you want my advice?" Dave asked.

"Yes. You know Johnny better than I do. You know how I can make this right with him," Mike said.

"If I give you advice, will you take it this time?" Dave asked, with an I told you so implication.

"Yes," said Mike sarcastically, like a teenager being asked if they did their homework.

"If you want to make this right with Johnny, you have to start by fixing what you have done. Any threats you made will be given an apology."

"I can do that."

"Then, if I were you, I would personally give Johnny a gift and apologize for any misunderstanding."

"What kind of gift do I get for the man who has beaten thousands of people until they were unconscious? Does he want a punching bag, karate lessons, a chainsaw? Maybe a hooker or some drugs?"

"You may not think so, but Johnny is actually a family man. He will consider the drugs or the hooker as an insult to his values; that could just make him angrier."

"Then what?"

"Well... Johnny's a businessman. Make him an offer that will make him happy."

"Like what?" Mike asked.

"Bring him a gift basket."

"Like a muffin basket or a fruit basket?"

"No. Like a money basket. Give him at least $100,000 in cash as a gift to make amends."

"A hundred grand?!" Mike yelled angrily.

"Do you think $1,000 is a lot of money to Johnny Roast Beef? He and his family make millions of dollars every month. A thousand bucks is an insult. Show him you're serious. You may want to consider giving him a larger portion of your profits, so he knows that you are sorry and still want to work with him."

"What's the alternative?" Mike asked.

"The alternative is that you go to war with the entire Lojuidice network. You don't have the manpower to win that fight."

"But maybe I could survive it and set up elsewhere."

"Johnny doesn't work that way. Do you remember the El Lobo gang?"

"Yeah. A few years ago, they had a bunch of Puerto Rican kids in their crew."

"They had a gang of about forty or fifty people. The entire crew disappeared in one weekend. Bodies turn up here and there occasionally, but they were never heard from again. You ended up taking their territory."

"I remember that now."

"Johnny's crew is sophisticated and organized better than anyone else. He can make things like that happen. He could easily make the Lords disappear in a day. I think he has made that pretty clear. My advice is this: Don't push it. Do what Johnny says. You're in no position to challenge him."

"I hate being told what to do."

Dave looked Mike in the eyes. "Suck it up. You can't win this. Don't do it for you; do it for your family."

"What about the trial?"

"Like I said before. The trial is going nowhere. I'll prepare Carmen to testify. Nothing is going to happen from the trial. Just let it go forward, and it will fail on its own."

CHAPTER 64

"So how do we protect the new guy?" Blade asked.

"He can go into protective custody," explained Ice.

"Pass," said Carlos. "I don't want to be in a cell with a bunch of sex offenders. I'd rather be shanked in the yard than hang out with a bunch of pedophiles jacking off to Sesame Street."

"Well, he's in the cell twenty-two hours a day. He gets out of the cell for two hours a day to come here to the yard. Most murders happen in the yard," said Hooch.

"That's true. The Lords killed a guy here in the yard about a year ago. I think it's because murdering someone in the cell will be recorded on the video camera in every cell. The yard is harder to monitor. It's easier to kill someone and not get caught out here," advised Blade.

"Then it sounds like I need to stay in the cell until the trial is done."

"What about showers?" Hooch said. "We only get one shower a week, and you will start to stink pretty quick. I don't want to smell that."

"Do what everyone else does, just bird bath in your cell," said Ice.

"What?"

"You know. Just throw water over you from the sink in your cell and shower on the floor of your cell. Let the water run out of the cell. The guards will get pissed, but a lot of people do it," said Ice.

"Well… I gotta do what I got a do."

"What is your lawyer gonna do about it?" asked Blade.

"I don't know. He just said he'll take care of it."

"There's nothing he can do. You have to take care of yourself," said Blade.

"Let's go, bitches. Back to your cells," shouted one of the guards. Recreation time was over. Hooch and Carlos walked back to their cell. Carlos walked quickly, looking for other inmates who might try to kill him. Carlos and Hooch entered their cell and closed the door behind them.

Carlos looked up at his bunk and noticed an envelope on his pillow. It had to be another threat. He picked up the envelope and held it for a moment. Carlos was scared, but he knew that he had to open it. He slowly opened the envelope and saw that there was a greeting card inside. Hooch was staring over Carlos's shoulder. The front of the card said, "I'm Sorry" and had a drawing of a cat holding his paws out and shrugging his shoulders, as if he made a stupid mistake. Carlos opened the card and inside was a handwritten message. "Please continue with the trial. No one will be hurt. Sorry, M2".

"Who's M2?" Carlos asked.

"Must be Mike Munoz," Hooch stated.

"Why would he get me an apology greeting card?"

"Probably because Hickory Farms doesn't make an 'I'm sorry I threatened to kill you' cheese pack. This was the next best thing. I think that your lawyer kept his word and actually got you protected."

"Do you think it's some sort of a trick?"

Hooch held out his hands and shrugged his shoulders, like the cat in the card. "Beats me."

CHAPTER 65

It was Wednesday morning, and Steve was on the go. He made it to the gym early, came home, showered, grabbed a bagel, kissed Jenny and Buddy goodbye, and drove to work. Steve made the drive across town in just under twenty minutes and pulled into the rear parking lot of the building. When he arrived, four vans were parked in the back of the lot. Eight people wearing white coveralls were working on the building. Two were power washing the parking lot to remove the 'Lordz' graffiti. The other six were painters, and they were repainting the building to its original color. Apparently, gardeners had come earlier in the morning because fresh sod and petunias were planted in front of the building. The outside of the building was getting a facelift, and it looked good.

Big Frank had brought a crew of people in to fix the damage caused by the Lords; Steve wondered how long it would be before the Lords struck again.

Steve walked into the building, up the stairs, and then into his office. He hung up his blazer and rolled up his sleeves. He was going to spend the day focusing on the Vega trial, which was coming up in a few weeks. Roxy walked into the office. "Good morning, Roxy. How are you?"

"Any better, and it would be a sin," Roxy said. She handed Steve a message. "Your client Carlos Vega called. Said he received an apology last night from whoever threatened him."

"What?"

"That's what he said. He got a greeting card that apologized and told him to please go ahead with the trial."

"Okay. Thanks, Roxy."

"You bet, sweetie."

Steve walked over to Sam's office. "What's going on?"

Sam was on the computer. "Same old stuff. What's up with you?"

"No, I mean, what's going on? There's an army of people suddenly making the place look beautiful when it has clearly gone a few decades in disrepair. Carlos tells me that he suddenly received an apology from Mike Munoz, head of the Colombian Lords and the guy that I plan on blaming for the murder of Julito Hernaiz. It's a drastic change from what happened on Monday."

"Yup. Frank said he would take care of it. Looks like he did."

"How?"

"Well… Frank works in the corporate world and represents multi-national corporations and Fortune 500 companies. That's not any different than being a Mafia lawyer. Think about it. Every major corporation has a security department that helps the corporation protect its best interests. These security departments can strong-arm and pressure people to do things they don't want to do. Is that any different than what the Mafia does? In fact, many crime families have earned enough money to convert their illegal family business into legitimate family businesses; they then invest their money in major corporations and sit on the boards of several corporations. It's common knowledge that Frank has a close relationship with thousands of major investors, including Mafia crime families. It wouldn't shock me if he called one of these 'business associates' to fix our 'business problem.'"

Steve was stunned. "Frank has Mafia connections?"

"Well, I would think that if you work in Frank's world, it's impossible to reach his level of success and not have Mafia connections. Besides, working for a major corporation is not that different from criminal law."

Steve was always a fan of the classic comedy, *I Love Lucy*. He would occasionally break out classic lines from Ricky Ricardo. Steve looked at Sam and said, "S'plain Lucy."

"You and I have both represented drug dealers who killed another drug dealer in a fight about who can sell on a particular street corner. It's pretty clear-cut that this is murder. In the corporate world, it's common for major corporations to kill people and call it a business decision. For example, car manufacturers choose not to recall a car rather than install a safety device that would fix a flaw in the car's design. They decided that it's cheaper to pay out in a lawsuit than to pay for the factory recall. Some call that a cost/benefit analysis and a business decision; others would call it murder. Here's another one. Pharmaceutical companies make painkillers that are abused, and their products end up killing thousands of people and causing an epidemic. It's discovered that each pill could have a protective coating installed that would not allow it to be abused, but this would affect sales, so they decide not to use it. This is a business decision that results in killing thousands of people. The point I'm making is that me, you, and Frank all work with criminals; just with Frank, it's less clear-cut than in our cases."

"So, you think Frank had one of his connections have a discussion with Mike Munoz?"

"I don't know what Frank did, but yeah, I think that's what happened. Frank knows the entire Lojuidice family. They're major business investors and sit on the board of dozens of corporations. They own large amounts of property throughout New England. It's possible that one of them knows Mike Munoz or has a business relationship with him. They probably convinced him to stop the threats and repair the damage." Steve was trying to wrap his mind around the whole thing. “Look,” said Sam. “Don’t read too much into this. You’re safe. Your family is safe. Your client is safe. The witnesses are safe. Just focus on giving Carlos the best trial you can.”

Steve sighed. “You’re right. Thank you. I’m gonna get back to work.”

THE TRIAL

CHAPTER 66

Steve stared out the window in the legal visiting room, waiting for Carlos. Trial started in a couple of days, and he wanted to get Carlos ready to testify. Carlos walked into the room and shook Steve's hand, and then he hugged him.

"You okay there, pal?" Steve asked.

"I'm just grateful that you resolved the threats. How did you do it?"

"Apparently, I know a guy who can resolve the whole situation. Look, you don't need to know how it got taken care of, but just that it is taken care of. Today, I want to review your testimony. During the trial, I will call you as a witness. You'll testify and tell your story. At trial, I am going to ask you questions that are going to be open-ended questions. Things like "tell me what happened," "and then what did you do," and "what happened next. These are questions that prompt you to tell your story. The state is going to ask leading questions that suggest a yes or no answer. For example, 'Isn't it true you pled guilty to murdering Julito?' They will try to control your answers by getting you to say 'yes' or 'no'. Do you understand the difference?"

"Yeah. I went through this with Bob Maghee."

"Okay. Good. So let's go through your story once and make sure you are covering everything. We're not going to keep reviewing it because I don't want it to sound rehearsed. After that, we will go through some cross-examination."

"Sounds good." Carlos retold his story of what happened that day, from waiting to see Julito to getting arrested in the alley. Carlos came across as honest and told his story well. Clearly, he had done this before.

Steve moved his chair so that he was directly facing Carlos. "Let's go through some cross-examination," Steve said. "I will now ask questions that the prosecutor is likely to ask you. Isn't it true that you pleaded guilty to killing Julito Hernaiz?"

"Well, you see what happened is..."

"Yes or no, Mr. Vega?"

"Again, what happened is that I…"

"Sounds like you don't understand the question, so I'm going to repeat it and talk real slow so that you can comprehend it. Isn't it true that you pleaded guilty to killing Julito Hernaiz?"

"You don't need to repeat it…"

"It's really a yes or no question, can't you answer it?"

"Well, it's not a yes or no answer."

"Actually, it is. Did you plead guilty to killing Julito Hernaiz? Your Honor, I ask that you order the witness to give a yes or no answer."

"Yes. This sucks."

"Yes, it does. They will try very hard to force you to give a yes-or-no answer. Just remember that if you make a mistake in your answer, I can go back and have you straighten it out."

"Okay. The question you will be asked is why you are coming to the court after all these years and asking to take back your guilty plea? You need to have an answer for that."

"No problem."

"Also, the state's attorneys will have a copy of the transcript from when you pled, and they will ask you if you were lying when you admitted to killing Julito. If you agree that you lied during the plea, then you have to explain why you are not lying now."

"That's gonna be tricky."

"Yeah. You need to navigate that as best you can. Is that what Jimmy J told you to say if you wanted to take the deal?"

"That was the idea; I had to say I killed Julito to avoid a trial."

"Okay, then let's go with that because that's the truth."

"Alright."

"There are a few more things I want to go over with you about testifying. Never lie. I can't put you on the stand to testify if I believe you'll lie. If you lie, odds are that you will get caught, and your testimony will do nothing but hurt your case."

"No problem. I don't plan to lie. What else?"

"When you testify, you have all the time in the world. Listen to the question. Pause for a moment and then answer the question, but only the question. What I mean is, don't feel rushed. You have plenty of time to tell your story. Take all the time that you want to tell your story. Just make sure you cover the whole story. If you forget something, I will try to lead you back to the part of the story that you missed. You'll be nervous and want to speak fast; don't do that. Take your time.

"Got it."

"The other stuff I said applies mostly to cross-examination by the state. Listen to their question, pause, and then answer the whole question, but nothing more. You'll be tempted to answer before she finishes asking you the question. Don't immediately answer. Listen to the question and understand what she is asking, then pause for a moment. Pausing gives me the opportunity to object. If you answer the question right away, I may not be able to object in time, so give me the chance to object."

"That makes a lot of sense."

"And lastly, answer the question, but don't answer more than that. An example of that is once I had a client who was asked if he worked at the same place as the victim. My client said, "Yes. And boy was that tough." He should have just said yes, but he added more than what the question asked. The state then asked, "Why was it tough?" My client answered, "Because I had to work with the victim. I couldn't stand her. She was bitch." As you can imagine, this didn't help his case. So, listen to the question. Make sure you understand it. If you don't understand the question, then say you don't. Do you understand?"

"Absolutely."

"Remember, if you don't know the answer, then say you don't know. Don't guess, unless they ask you to guess, which I will object to. Also, if you forget something, that's okay. Any questions?"

"No. I think I'm ready."

"Okay. I'll see you on Monday." Steve and Carlos stood up, shook hands, and said their goodbyes.

CHAPTER 67

Steve met Attorney Garcon at court. They exchanged pleasantries and agreed about which documents would go into evidence. Judge Kopp, a former federal prosecutor, would be the judge and jury of Carlos's case. Steve had already tried ten cases before Judge Kopp; she was a tough audience and had never overturned a conviction in her three years at habeas court. Also, she had a reputation amongst the lawyers for being unprepared for trials, as she would not review any of the briefs summarizing the case before trial. Steve would have to explain the facts of the case in the first few witnesses so the judge could follow along. She rarely wrote her own decisions and had a clerk read the transcripts, review the exhibits, and write the decision for her.

Judge Kopp came out and reviewed a few preliminary matters with the parties. The courtroom was empty except for the potential witnesses, including Roxy. Steve called Detective Bynes as his first witness. Bynes came up to the stand, was sworn in, and took a seat.

"Good morning, Detective Bynes," Steve said. Steve positioned himself so that Bynes had a clear view of Roxy and her lady jazz. Roxy would also be there to testify if he changed his story.

"Good morning," Bynes said.

"Do you recall the case of State v. Carlos Vega?"

"Yes."

"What do you recall about the case?"

"The victim, Julito Hernaiz, was shot in the back of the head. The safe was open. The money was missing from it, including rolled coins."

"How much money was stolen?"

"A few thousand dollars in bills and some boxes of rolled coin."

"Did you ever find the money?"

"No."

"Did you ever find the murder weapon?"

"No."

"What else do you recall?"

"I interviewed a witness who said she saw Mr. Vega leaving the store with a sack of money and a gun shortly after she heard gunshots. The witness found the defendant in a mugshot book."

"What did you do next?"

"I met with the state's attorney, and she advised me to draft an arrest warrant to see if the judge will sign it."

"Did the judge sign it?"

"Yes."

"What happened next?"

"We found the perp in an alley and arrested him. I attempted to speak with him and hear his side of the story, but he lawyered up instead of talking to me."

"Did the case go to trial?"

"No. He pleaded to a lesser charge of manslaughter."

"Let's talk about your witness. Who was your witness in this case?"

"Krystal Wiznet."

"Do you know Krystal Wiznet?"

"Yes."

"How did you know her?"

Attorney Garcon jumped to her feet. "Objection. This is not relevant. He is trying to elicit whether the witness, who never testified in this case, had a criminal record. It has no bearing on this case."

"I'll allow it," said Kopp.

Bynes explained, "Krystal has a string of convictions for drug possession, prostitution, and some low-end crimes. This would have made her credibility questionable, so I was concerned that the judge may not sign the warrant."

"Okay. Did you have any other witnesses who placed Mr. Vega at the scene of the crime?"

"No."

"Did you look for witnesses?"

"Yes. We did a canvass of the area to see if anyone heard the gunshots or saw anything unusual."

"So, you did a canvass. Did you canvass the entire area?"

Steve caught Roxy's smile after the question was asked. "No. Based on the statement that the perpetrator ran out the front door, we canvassed all the apartments along the street in front of the bodega."

"So, you didn't canvass the apartments behind the bodega?"

"No."

"Did anyone look for DNA or fingerprints at the crime scene?"

"Yes. Of course."

"Were there any DNA or fingerprints of Mr. Vega found at the scene of the crime?"

"No. Nothing placed him at the crime scene except for Krystal's statement.

"No further questions."

Jackie Garcon got up and approached the podium. "Detective Bynes, is it your testimony that a judge found probable cause to arrest Mr. Vega and signed the warrant?"

"Yes."

"So, a judge found that there was enough evidence to charge Mr. Vega with the murder of Julito Hernaiz?"

"Yes."

"And Mr. Vega pled guilty to killing Mr. Hernaiz?"

"Yes, he did."

"No further questions, Your Honor."

CHAPTER 68

Krystal Wiznet was sworn in and ready to testify. Steve whispered to Carlos to put his hands in his lap. "Good morning, Ms. Wiznet."

Krystal looked at Steve and smiled, "Good morning."

"Do you recall the day that Julito Hernaiz died?"

"Yes. That was a terrible day. I remember it like it was yesterday."

"Where were you that day?"

"I was coming home from work, looking to get a cup of coffee and a donut at the bodega when I ..."

"Okay, let me stop you right there. Where were you working at the time?"

"Objection. What's the relevance?" asked Garcon.

"I was following up on her statement."

Judge Kopp looked at Steve, "Sidebar."

The judge asked Steve, "Counsel, are you trying to get Krystal to admit she was working as a prostitute?"

"Yes," said Steve.

"I'm not going to allow it. It's not relevant if she was a prostitute at this point in her testimony," whispered Kopp.

Everyone went back to their positions. Steve continued, "Okay, so you were going to the bodega. What happened next?"

"I heard gunshots."

"What did you do?"

"I stopped in my tracks, then I walked quickly to the bodega, when all of a sudden this man holding a gun and a sack of money came running out of the store and knocked me down."

"And who was this man?"

"Carlos Vega."

"Do you see Carlos Vega in the courtroom today?"

Krystal pointed at him and said, "Right there."

"Okay, so you say you see Mr. Vega run away from the bodega. How good a look at him did you have? I mean, it was pretty quick… right? He opens the door to the bodega and runs directly into you, knocking you down, and then keeps on running."

"I got a good look at his face."

"How did you get a good look at his face if he immediately knocked you down and then all you could see was the back of his head?"

"I saw that it was him when he knocked me down."

"Okay, let me show a copy of the statement that you gave the police." Steve handed her Exhibit A. "This is your written statement to the police, isn't it?"

"Yes."

"And it says that you recognized his hand tattoo?"

"Yes. I remember that I noticed the tattoo on his hand of an eagle."

"Which hand was that on?" Steve asked.

"His right hand."

"The one that he held the gun with?" Steve asked, verifying.

"Yeah," she confirmed.

"Okay, so in the short amount of time that you saw his face, you were able to see the gun, the bag of money, the tattoo of an eagle on his right hand as well… right?"

"Uhm, yeah."

"Is it fair to say that you focused your attention heavily on the gun and the tattoo on Mr. Vega's hand?"

"I noticed both."

"Yeah, but you really noticed the tattoo, because you knew that it was an eagle?"

"Yes, I knew it was an eagle."

"It wasn't a pigeon, was it?"

"No."

"It wasn't a sparrow?"

"No."

"Wasn't a cardinal?"

"No."

"It was an eagle?'

"Yes."

"Fair to say that you spent enough time looking at the tattoo to determine what kind of a bird it was?"

"Sure."

"Now you knew Mr. Vega before you saw him on this day, right?"

"Yes. I knew him from the neighborhood."

"How did you know him?"

"I saw him at parties from time to time."

"Did you know if he had a tattoo back then?"

"He did."

"So, you remember his tattoo from back then?"

"Yes."

"And because you remember his tattoo back then, you were able to determine that the tattoo you saw on the right hand of the person who came out of the bodega was the same tattoo that belonged to Mr. Vega, right?"

"Well… the tattoo helped me identify Mr. Vega."

"Okay. And the tattoo was on the right hand, isn't that what you told the police?"

"Yes."

"At this point, I would ask my client to hold up his hands and show the court his tattoo." Carlos complied and held up his hands for the court to see that the tattoo of an eagle was on Carlos's left hand.

"I ask the court to take judicial notice that Mr. Vega has an eagle tattoo on his left hand and no tattoo on his right hand."

Steve looked back at Krystal. "Ma'am, is it fair to say that your statement to the police is inaccurate?"

"Well, I guess I was confused which hand it was on."

"So that means your statement was not accurate?"

"Yes."

"You also signed a written statement a few years later, didn't you?"

"Yes, but it was signed under duress."

Steve showed Krystal her other statement that she gave to Mark Hutch. "Is this the statement that you signed under duress?"

"Yes."

"In this statement, you told Mr. Hutch that you did not see Mr. Vega with a gun or a bag of money, and that you, in fact, stole the money from the bodega."

"Under duress."

"You made this statement under duress."

"Yes."

"Okay, so this statement is not true?"

"No, it is not."

"And the statement you gave to the police *is* true? "

"Yes."

"I mean, except for the part about the tattoo on the right hand… right?"

"Yes."

"And you didn't take the cash from the safe and the rolled coin?"

"No. Totally not true."

"Okay, and you previously testified that you knew Carlos because you used to get high together?"

"That's what I said."

"Did you have a drug problem?"

Attorney Garcon objected, "Objection, this is not relevant."

"I will allow it," barked Kopp.

"Yes."

"Do you still have a drug problem?"

"I will always be an addict. Right now, I have been sober for a few weeks."

"Were you high when you gave your statement to the police on the day Julito died?"

"No, I was not."

"Nothing further, Your Honor."

"Attorney Garcon, do you have any questions?" asked Judge Kopp.

"Just a follow-up question. Ms. Wiznet, it's your testimony that you saw Mr. Vega leaving the bodega with a gun and money after you heard shots fired?"

"Yes. That statement is accurate. It is still my testimony."

"Nothing further."

CHAPTER 69

Crystal Carlisle was called to the stand and sworn in. Leon sat in the audience in case her story changed.

Steve began. "Good morning, Miss Carlisle."

"Good morning."

"Do you know Krystal Wiznet?"

"Yes. She was my roommate for a while."

"Did you know Julito Hernaiz?"

"Yes. We weren't close, but I used to see him every day when I would buy coffee from his store. He was a nice guy. We would chat, but I wouldn't say we were close friends."

"Okay. Do you recall the day he died?"

"I remember that day."

"Was Krystal your roommate at that time?"

"Yes."

"Did you get into an argument with her around that period of time?"

"Yes. She had not paid her portion of the rent for several months, and I was paying all the bills. I was getting frustrated with her. I thought maybe she was holding out on me and using her money for drugs. She couldn't pay her bills, and I was going to school and working full-time to make ends meet. I had bailed her out of jail a few times when she got caught stealing from department stores. Eventually, my jewelry and money started disappearing from the house. I tried several times to get her into rehab."

"What happened next?"

"I was struggling to pay the rent that month. I was afraid we were going to be evicted, so I thought I would go through her purse to see if she had any money to pay the rent. When I opened her purse, I found almost $2,000 in cash. I realized she was playing me for a fool. This was the last straw. We were gonna have it out, right then and there. I walked into her room and woke her up. She was mad that I woke her up and started yelling at me. I told her that I had spent a fortune on her: Bailing her out of jail, covering her rent for the better part of a year, paying some of her bills. I couldn't stand it anymore. I told her that I found the thousands of dollars in her purse."

"And then what happened?"

"She stood there and began to cry, and then she got mad. She grabbed her purse and then threw her wad of money at me. She said, 'If you want my money, then here it is.' She stormed into her room and came out with some boxes. I asked what she was doing, and she said, 'I'm paying you back for all the terrible things I did to you.' She then began throwing rolled coins at me. Hundreds of dollars of rolled coins."

"Was she still your roommate after that?"

"No. I threw her out after that incident. I packed up all her stuff and put it on the front porch. I told her to take her stuff and leave. She did. I never saw her until today."

"And this was after Julito died?"

"Yes. It was a few days after he died."

"I have no further questions, Your Honor."

Kopp looked over to Attorney Garcon. "Any questions for the witness?"

Jackie Garcon thought for a moment. Clearly, she was stunned. She had so much confidence that this case was a slam dunk that she hadn't asked her investigator to interview Crystal with a 'C'. "No, Your Honor, but I reserve the right to recall this witness in my case."

"Okay," said the judge. "Let's keep it going. Next witness."

Steve called the coroner and Art from forensics as his last witnesses for the morning. The coroner testified that Julito died from a gunshot wound to the back of the head. There was a large amount of blood loss, and the crime scene had blood splatter all over it. The killer fired the gun from a range of an inch or less from the victim's head. The coroner could not say for sure whether the shooter would have received blood splatter from the shooter; while it was possible that the shooter had no blood on him or her, he could not say for sure.

Art Fretel from forensics testified that he determined that someone stole boxes of coins from the safe after the shooting. This was based on the blood splatter in the safe and the shape of a box visible in it. Art got empty coin boxes from the bank that Julito used and determined that a box of quarters, dimes, and nickels was in the safe before the shooting and removed after the shooting.

It was 12:30, and the court concluded for the morning until 2 p.m. Steve and Carlos spoke in a small room on the side of the courtroom, which was designed for attorneys to talk with their incarcerated clients. "How do you think we're doing?" Carlos asked.

"Not bad. So far so good," Steve replied. "We got Crystal with a C's testimony in, which discredits Krystal with a 'K'. That shows that she was a weak witness and a possible suspect for killing Julito."

"What's next?"

"I'm gonna meet with Jimmy J and Bob Maghee over the lunch break and talk to them about their testimony."

CHAPTER 70

Steve walked across the street from the courthouse to the Thirsty Attorney Pub, a small restaurant and bar where defense attorneys and public defenders sat around and commiserated about their career choice.

Steve walked through the front door and saw Jimmy J and Bob Maghee sitting in a corner booth. He approached the booth, shook hands with them, and then took a seat. “Thanks for doing this, guys. I appreciate it. Do you remember the case?”

Jim nodded his head yes. Bob said, “How could I forget that case? It was such a disaster, with my investigator having a relationship with the witness. What a cluster-fuck.”

Bob said, “Look. Before we discuss this case, I just want to know if you are looking for me to fall on my sword.” The theory in a habeas case is that the defense attorney has to admit to making a mistake in order to get his client a new trial. This is a myth. In Steve’s experience, most defense attorneys are offended when a habeas is raised against them; they feel insulted even to suggest that they might have made a mistake. That is why most defense attorneys turn against the client and do what they can to support the state. Some of the more seasoned and less egotistical attorneys were not threatened by this and would help if they felt the situation called for it. Steve was attempting to see if he could convince these attorneys to take a bullet for Carlos.

"Here's the deal with this case. I talked to the FBI's confidential informant in the Colombian Lords about it. The informant said that a member of the Lords murdered the bodega owner because he was having an affair with the owner's wife. He truly is innocent."

Bob and Jimmy were silent and thought about what Steve had said. "Are you able to prove this?" Bob asked.

"The informant's statement is hearsay. It's inadmissible. But I did present evidence that Krystal was the person who stole the money from the safe. I am trying to prove that the wife of the bodega owner was pregnant with the true killer's child and had the code to get into the bodega. We also found a witness who will state he saw a man running away from the bodega who fits the description of the killer."

"Is that going to be enough?" Jimmy asked.

"Probably not, but it's the best I have. I know he is innocent, and it is nearly impossible to prove it at this point. That's why I'm asking for your help."

"Clearly, the biggest problem is that he took the plea and admitted guilt," explained Bob. "How are you gonna explain that?"

"That he was pressured to take the deal and that he did not have a complete investigation. Our further investigation shows that Krystal stole the money from the safe and implicated Carlos to cover it up. That's where you all come in. Will you guys help me with this? I understand if you won't, but I hope you will."

Jimmy looked at Bob. "I'll help you out."

"Me too," Bob said.

Steve smiled. "Thank you."

CHAPTER 71

Jimmy J was sworn in and took the stand. Steve stood in front of the podium and began. "Do you know the defendant in this matter?"

"Yes. I used to represent him."

"What case did you represent him on?"

"The murder case of Julito Hernaiz. He was charged with murder."

"Do you recall the case?"

"Yes. Julito owned a bodega on the southside of Hartford. He was found shot in the back of the head by the store safe, which was left open. The money was removed from the safe. A witness said she saw the defendant run out of the bodega carrying a bag of money and a gun."

"Okay. Did you get some discovery from the state?"

"Yes. They provided me with some police reports and autopsy reports, but they kept the name and information about the witness from me."

"What did you do about this?"

"I filed a motion to produce the information, and the court agreed that the state had to reveal the name and contact information of this witness to me or not use the witness in the trial. The state then told me who the witness was."

"Who was the confidential witness?"

"Krystal Wiznet."

"Were you familiar with Ms. Wiznet?"

"Yes."

"How were you familiar with her?"

Attorney Garcon stood up. "Objection, Your Honor. Counsel is trying to elicit irrelevant information about Ms. Wiznet to embarrass and discredit her character. This is irrelevant and inadmissible."

"Counsel, what are you doing here?" asked Judge Kopp.

"Your Honor, this information is relevant because it goes to the witness's ability to discredit Ms. Wiznet at trial."

"I'll give you some latitude, Counsel. Be careful."

"Thank you, Your Honor." Steve turned back to face Jimmy J. "If this case had gone to trial, do you think you would be able to discredit Ms. Wiznet's testimony?"

"Possibly. I could have tried to introduce information regarding her substance abuse or the fact that she has testified many times on behalf of the state to implicate defendants in a crime."

"Would this have discredited Ms. Wiznet's testimony at trial?"

"I can't say for sure. It's possible that a jury would have believed her, even if I had used information to discredit her."

"Okay. Did you do any further investigation into the matter?"

"No."

"Why not?"

"We were given an offer to plead to a lesser charge for less time. Carlos decided to take the offer."

"Do you think that you should have done an investigation before he took the plea?"

"Absolutely. I dropped the ball on that. Before he took the offer, I should have found out more about Krystal Wiznet."

"If you had known that Krystal stole the money from the safe, would it have affected your advice on whether to take the offer?"

"Yes. It would completely discredit Krystal's statement. She simply could have implicated Mr. Vega to cover up the fact that she stole the money from the safe. It potentially could have made her the killer, and I would have built a defense around claiming she was more likely to be the killer. Krystal had a motive to kill Julito, and Carlos did not."

"I have nothing further, Your Honor."

Attorney Garcon got up and asked, "Did I hear you right?"

"I beg your pardon," Jimmy replied.

"Are you putting on the record that you committed malpractice?"

Jimmy thought for a moment. "I can't say if what I did amounts to malpractice, but I definitely made a mistake in this case, and it impacted his decision on whether to accept the offer or not."

"But you had no way of knowing at that time if there was any evidence that Ms. Wiznet took the money from the safe, right?"

"I would have known if I had an investigator do the proper investigation."

"But didn't your client tell you that he wanted to take the deal?"

"Yes, he did."

"So, the investigation is irrelevant because he wanted the deal?"

"No. I should have insisted on the investigation, but I didn't."

"Is it true that you testified that the jury may have believed Krystal, even if you discredited her testimony?"

"No."

"You didn't testify to that?"

"No. You're taking it out of context."

"Please clarify for me."

"Sure. What I said was that if I had been able to submit evidence of Krystal's drug use or history as a career witness for the prosecution, then I may have been able to discredit her to the point where a jury would not believe her. Of course, there is still a chance the jury would believe her and convict Mr. Vega. On the other hand, if I had evidence that she stole the money from the safe, her testimony would have been discredited as an attempt to cover up her own crime. In fact, the case would probably be dismissed under those circumstances."

"No further questions."

CHAPTER 72

Bob Maghee was called to the stand next. He raised his right hand and was sworn in to testify.

"Attorney Maghee, thank you for coming in today."

"You're welcome."

"Do you know Mr. Vega?"

"Sure do."

"How do you know him?"

"I represented him on his first habeas case."

"How did that go?"

"How good could it have gone? I'm here testifying in his second habeas case." The courtroom had a good laugh.

"I take it that you lost."

"Yes."

"What happened?"

"Well, my investigator got a statement from Krystal, the state's only witness, confessing to taking the money from the safe and that she saw Carlos at the scene of the crime, but he did not have a gun and was not carrying money."

"I called Krystal as a witness to see if her testimony would go like her statement to the police or her statement to the investigator."

"How did it go?"

"She testified like the statement she gave to the police and not like the statement she gave to my investigator."

"What did you do from there?"

"I showed her the statement she gave to my investigator. She agreed she had signed it but said it was not true. She claimed that she signed it because my investigator offered her $1,000 to sign the statement and have sex with him."

"Were you shocked by this?"

"Yes."

"What did you do next?"

"I spoke with my investigator over the break and explained what Krystal said and that I needed him to testify against her."

"What did your investigator say?"

"Objection, Your Honor," yelled Attorney Garcon. "That's classic hearsay."

"Sustained. Counsel, rephrase the question," said Judge Kopp.

"Sure. You spoke with your investigator about what Krystal had said at trial. Based on what he told you about his relationship with Krystal, did you have him testify at trial?"

"No."

"Before the trial, were you aware that your investigator had a relationship with Krystal?"

"No."

"If you knew, would you have used a different investigator?"

"Absolutely."

"Did this incident impact the outcome of your trial?"

"Yes. The basis of our claim was that if the original attorney had conducted a proper investigation of Krystal, they would have found that she stole the money from the safe and that her credibility would have been impeached. I failed as Mr. Vega's attorney because I should have asked my investigator whether he had any relationship with Krystal Wiznit before he obtained her statement. If I had hired a different investigator, we would have been able to impeach Krystal. It's my mistake, and I take full responsibility."

"I have no more questions, Your Honor."

"Well, I do," said Jackie Garcon. "So, we can agree that you committed malpractice?" Clearly, she was angry that the former attorneys were not helping her case, so she decided to pressure them into submission.

Bob thought about his answer for a moment. "It wasn't my intention to commit malpractice, but yes, I made a mistake, and I am prepared to pay the consequences."

"Let's just be clear here. Are you specifically saying that you committed malpractice and that the defendant, Mr. Vega, should sue you for malpractice?"

Bob was getting mad that Attorney Garcon would suggest this. "Yes. Absolutely."

Jessica stood quietly for a moment, thinking of a response to Bob's admission of guilt. She realized that she had bullied him into admitting malpractice on the record, which would clearly help the defendant. She had let her anger get the best of her. She dared Bob to admit to malpractice, and he did. Odds are the defendant would not sue, but his admission on the record damaged her case. "No further questions."

Judge Kopp looked up at the clock. "We have time for one more witness. Who do you have?"

"Rosalita Vega."

CHAPTER 73

Carlos's mom was in her late fifties. She walked slowly to the witness stand. She raised her right hand and was sworn in.

"Good afternoon, Mrs. Vega."

"Good afternoon."

"Ma'am, do you know why you're here?"

"You want me to testify about my son, Carlos Vega."

"Exactly. Do you remember when Carlos was charged with killing Julito Hernaiz?"

"Yes."

"Did you talk to Carlos at that time?"

"Carlos and I were not close at that time."

"Why not?"

"About two years before that, we had a falling out. Carlos had a drug problem, and it had gotten worse. He was taking things from the house and selling them. Eventually, he took my wedding ring and hawked it to get high."

"Did you ever confront him about that?"

"Yes. He admitted it. He never denied that he would steal to get high. Carlos was a slave to his addiction. He left my house and moved onto the street. I hadn't heard from him in over a year. I heard on the news that he was charged with killing Julito, and I went to see him in jail."

"When did you see him?'

"Right before he pled guilty."

"What was your conversation about?"

"I wanted to clear the air. We talked about what happened."

"Okay, and when you say what happened, what are you talking about?"

"What I mean is we talked about him leaving and how we both wanted to have a relationship with each other. We both knew that we were unhappy with not seeing each other over the past two years. We both knew that his addiction hurt our relationship."

"Did you talk to him about the offer that was made?"

"Yes."

"What did you say?"

"Carlos told me that he wanted to take the case to trial, even though he got an offer for twenty-five years. I told him that I wanted him to take the deal so I could have a chance of seeing him walk out of jail in my lifetime."

"Did you pressure him to take the deal?"

Mrs. Vega sat quietly for a moment. "I wanted what was in his best interest."

"Okay. So, you thought having him take the twenty-five-year deal was in his best interest?"

"Yes."

"So aside from suggesting that you wanted him to take the deal, did you do or say anything else to get him to take the deal?" Mrs. Vega was quiet. "Do you need a minute to answer the question, ma'am?"

Mrs. Vega began to cry. "It's hard to put into words, but I did pressure him into taking the offer."

"How? How did you do this?"

"When I saw him in jail, he was sober. I could tell that he had been clean for a while and was the old Carlos that I used to know. I knew that he was feeling terrible for what he did to me. He knew that my wedding ring was the only thing of value that I had and cared about. I knew that if I asked him to take the offer, he would do it because he felt as if he owed me. So, I pressured him, and he did what I asked."

"I see. Do you regret doing this?"

"I always believed that Carlos was innocent, but I didn't want him to take the chance of going to jail for the rest of his life. As time went on and he explained that there was very little evidence against him and that the only witness had actually stolen the money from the safe, I began to believe that I had done my son a great injustice. And now, I feel the guilt of keeping him incarcerated by denying him his chance to be free. I feel terrible, and I only hope that he will forgive me."

"No further questions."

"Any cross-examination?" the judge asked Attorney Garcon.

"Sure. Mrs. Vega, you talked to your son about taking the offer, correct?"

"Yes, I did."

"Did you threaten him in order to take the deal?"

"No."

"Did you offer him money?"

"No. I didn't have any money."

"Did you tell him you wouldn't love him anymore?"

"Of course not."

"Did you say that the only way to rekindle your relationship was to take the offer?"

"No."

"So, essentially, you gave him your two cents?"

"No. I definitely applied some pressure on him."

"Yeah, but he had to make the decision for himself, right?"

"I guess, but I helped guide him to that decision."

"But it was his decision to make, right?"

"Yes. If I could have made it for him, I would have taken the deal on his behalf."

"Nothing further."

Judge Kopp looked at the clock on the wall and said, "That's it for today. Let's reconvene tomorrow at ten o'clock." The judge stood up and walked into her chambers. Carlos and Steve went into the room next to the courtroom, where they could talk.

"So how do you think it went?" Steve asked.

"Good. Much better than my last trial. I was a little surprised by my mom's testimony. I didn't think she was going to say that she laid a lot of guilt on me."

"That was a little surprising. She was very convincing. One thing I wanted to talk to you about is Jimmy J and Bob. They both went out on a limb for you today. They believe in your innocence and essentially put themselves in a position where they admitted to committing malpractice. I can only ask that you not take advantage of them; don't raise a malpractice claim against them. The only reason they did that was because I know them, and they agreed to put themselves in that position to give you a chance for a new trial. If you raise a claim for malpractice against them, you're basically kicking them in the balls for doing you a favor."

"I get that. They don't have to worry. Please let them know that I know what they did for me, and I am very grateful."

"You got it. I'll see you tomorrow." Steve walked out of the visiting room and back into the courtroom, where he grabbed his bag. Attorney Garcon was waiting for him.

"Are you parked in the parking structure?" she asked him.

"Yup. Going my way?"

"Sure." They began to walk towards the parking lot.

"Steve, what's the deal with these lawyers?"

"What do you mean?"

"This whole falling on the sword thing. Why are they doing it?"

"Because he's innocent."

"You believe that?"

"No. I know that."

"I know I'm gonna hate this question, but how do you know he's innocent?"

"If I tell you everything, will you give him a new trial?'

"No."

"Okay, well, if I tell you everything, will you *consider* giving him a new trial?"

"No. You know I can't."

"Why not? Aren't we supposed to be here to make sure that justice happens? Are you saying that if I can prove to you that he's innocent, you won't grant him a new trial?

"It's not how it works. The court has to grant it."

"No. You can agree with my client's petition, and the court will have to grant it."

"I can't do that."

"So, it's a 'you have to talk to your boss' type of thing?"

"I just can't do it."

"Okay, well, let me ask you this... what can I do today to get a new trial for my client? What do you need from me?"

"Steve, the only way for that to happen is to have the court rule in your favor. There's nothing I can do."

"Okay, then why are you interested in knowing why I'm busting my ass on this case and why his prior attorneys are putting themselves out on a limb for this guy?"

"Just curious, I guess."

"So, if I show all my evidence and let you meet with confidential informants who implicate someone else in the murder, are you going to be able to live with yourself, knowing you denied an innocent man a new trial?"

"Well, there's nothing I can do, but I see your point. See you tomorrow." Jackie walked to her car and drove off.

CHAPTER 74

It was the second day of trial. Steve got up early and went to the gym. He worked out on the elliptical trainer while reviewing his questions for Carmen Hernaiz. He showered, grabbed a bagel and coffee, and drove to court.

Steve met Carlos in the visiting room, next to the courtroom. "How we doing, big guy?" Steve asked.

"Not bad. I'm tired from these back-to-back court dates of waking up at three in the morning and returning to my cell at eleven or twelve at night."

"This should be the last day."

"What's in store for us today?"

"Well, we have Carmen Hernaiz first, and then we have the witness who saw a guy who looks like Mike Munoz."

"Am I gonna testify?"

"You don't have to, but you should in order to explain why you felt coerced into taking the deal and that you would not have taken the deal if they had done a proper investigation."

"Okay, let's get started."

Steve went out to the courtroom and set up his notes, files, and case law on the desk, along with his notepads. Judge Kopp came out. "Any preliminary matters we need to discuss?" She asked.

"Nothing from me," Steve stated.

"Me neither," said Jackie Garcon.

"Then call your next witness," said the judge.

"The defendant calls Carmen Hernaiz." Steve looked to the back of the courtroom. An attractive young Hispanic woman stood up and walked toward the witness stand.

"I brought my attorney with me," she announced to the court.

"Okay," said the judge. "Who represents you?"

A man stood up from the back of the court. "David Pruett, Your Honor. I represent Mrs. Hernaiz."

"Okay," said the judge. "How are you representing her today?"

"I am here to make sure that her rights are not violated."

"What rights do you think will be violated, Counsel?"

"Well, her right against self-incrimination."

Judge Kopp looked at Steve. "Counsel, do you plan on asking this witness about her participation in a crime?"

Steve looked at the judge and said, "I am going to ask some questions about the victim. If the witness's counsel feels this will involve a Fifth Amendment right, then let's be on the safe side and read the witness her Fifth Amendment rights."

"Very well," said the judge, and she read the witness her rights, explaining that Carmen did not have to answer any questions that could convict her of a crime. The witness was then sworn in. "Whenever you're ready, Counsel."

"Good morning, Mrs. Hernaiz."

"Good morning, sir."

"I wanted to ask you some questions about your late husband, Julito Hernaiz."

"Go ahead."

"Mr. Hernaiz owned the Corner Bodega?"

"Yes, he did."

"Did he work in it?"

"Yes."

"When did he work there?"

"Almost every day."

"How long would he work each day?"

"It varied."

"Can you clarify that for me?"

"No."

"Why not?" Steve thought to himself that she was being decisively vague and giving as short an answer as possible.

"His hours varied every day."

"Okay. Did he always open the store?"

"Usually."

"Was there an alarm system in the building?"

"Yes."

"Did you have the code to disable the system?"

"I don't recall."

"You don't know if you had the code."

"That's right."

"Okay, so after his death, did you open the store for anyone? I mean, the bodega is still open, so someone had to open it. Did you open it?"

"Yes, I opened it."

"So, you had the code or were able to get it?"

"Apparently."

"So, that's a yes?"

"Yes."

"So, you had access to the code to get into the bodega?"

"Yes."

Steve thought for a moment. He was getting mad, and Carmen was taking advantage of the situation. Fuck it, he thought to himself. Let's just rip the band-aid off. "Okay, shifting gears here. You were pregnant at the time of Julito's death?"

"Yes."

"I am showing you a copy of your child's birth certificate. Is this accurate?" Steve handed Carmen the birth certificate for her daughter.

"I don't see why this is important."

"Well, I didn't ask you that, did I? Let me repeat the question for you. I'm going to use some simple words for you to understand. Is this a copy of your daughter's birth certificate?

"I guess so."

"You've never seen a copy of your child's birth certificate?"

"Yes, I have."

"It says Julito is the father. Is that true?"

Carmen was appalled. She sat there with her mouth open in amazement. "Of course, he was the father. We tried for so long to have a child, and then we finally got pregnant. And then your client murdered him." She began to cry.

Steve moved quickly and showed no sympathy. He handed her Exhibit R, a copy of the autopsy report. "Ma'am, I am handing you a document. It's your late husband's autopsy report. Please turn to page 35 and read the last paragraph."

Carmen opened the document and read the last paragraph. "Testicular scar from a vasectomy. Medical records indicate the subject had a vasectomy five years ago."

"The autopsy and your former husband's medical records indicate he had a vasectomy five years before he was killed. Doesn't that make it impossible for him to be the father of your only daughter?"

"I don't know."

"How is it that you claim he was trying to have children with you when, in fact, he didn't want to have children, and he got a vasectomy?"

"That's his daughter."

"You are aware that perjury is a felony in this state and lying on the stand is perjury?"

"He's the father of my child."

"Isn't it true the father of your child is Mike Munoz?"

"No."

"In fact, Julito would have known that you cheated on him with Mike Munoz if he found out you were pregnant?"

"No," Carmen said with anger.

"In fact, you were so scared that you had Mike Munoz murder your husband?"

"Objection," Jackie yelled. "There's no evidence of this. He's badgering the witness."

Judge Kopp looked at Steve. "Sustained. Watch it, Counsel."

"You gave Mike Munoz the code so that he could murder your husband for you?"

Dave Pruett yelled, "Don't answer that. Plead the Fifth."

"Objection, Your Honor," yelled Jackie. "Badgering."

"Sustained."

"Now you're married to Mike Munoz?"

"Yes."

"Didn't you collect a lot of money from a life insurance policy you had for Julito?"

"He took out the policy, not me."

"And now you and his murderer share income from the life insurance and from the corner bodega?"

"Objection again, Your Honor."

Judge Kopp looked at Steve. "Enough, Counsel. Do you have any other questions for the witness that don't include calling her a murderer?'

"One last thing." Steve took Exhibit G, a mugshot of Mike Munoz. Steve approached the witness without asking the court's permission. "Is this a picture of your current husband?"

"I don't know."

"Doesn't it say his name on the plaque that he is holding? This is your current husband, Mike Munoz, isn't it?"

"Yes."

"Nothing further. I think I've made my point."

Judge Kopp looked at Jackie. "Any questions?"

"No."

Carmen walked away from the stand, crying. Dave Pruett met her in the middle of the courtroom and put his arm around her, trying to comfort her. Carmen pushed him away. "Thanks for letting me get crucified up there. You were no help at all. I'm gonna tell Mike about this." Carmen walked off.

Steve watched the judge. She heard Carmen's comments.

CHAPTER 75

"The defendant calls Rudy Garcia." A tall, thin Hispanic man walked up and took the witness stand; he was sworn in. "Good morning, Mr. Garcia."

"Good morning."

"Thank you for coming in today. We greatly appreciate it."

"You're welcome."

"Where do you currently live?"

"I live at 135 Howard Avenue in Hartford."

"How long have you lived there?"

"About fifteen years."

"Is that an apartment?"

"Yes. I'm on the first floor."

"Okay, and where are you in terms of the corner bodega?"

"I am about a half block south."

"Do you remember the day that Julito Hernaiz died?"

"Yes."

"Where were you that day?"

"I came home from school the day before for my sister's birthday. I stayed the night, but I left early in the morning to catch my eight o'clock class."

"Where were you going to school?"

"University of Connecticut, at the main campus in Storrs."

"How long does it take you to get to campus?"

"About a half hour, with no traffic. I needed to leave around seven in the morning to make my eight o'clock class."

"What do you remember about the day that Julito died?"

"I was up early in the morning, around five thirty. I showered and was getting ready for school. I heard two shots fired. I was in the bedroom, and I looked out the rear window to see what was going on."

"Did you see anything?"

"At first, I didn't, but I kept looking."

"Where were you looking?"

"I was looking out the rear window of the bedroom, which overlooks the alley that runs between my street and Ivy Street, which is the street that the corner bodega is on."

"Okay, so you're looking in the alley. What happened next?"

"I see a man running down the alley from the direction of the bodega."

"What did he look like?"

"He was a tall man with a strong build. Hispanic man. Black hair. He was wearing dark clothing."

"What time was this?"

"It was just about two minutes after the gunshots; around six."

"Mr. Garcia, I am showing you Exhibit G, which is a photograph. Does this look like the man you saw in the alley?"

"It might be. I can't say for sure."

"Let me ask you this. Did the man in the alley look like my client, Mr. Vega, who is seated next to me?"

"Not even close. Your client is too small to be the guy in the alley."

"Did you ever tell the police what you saw?"

"No. I was away at school for a couple of weeks. When I came back home, I heard the news. I heard they arrested somebody. I didn't know who.'

"Do you know if police ever came to your door and asked if anyone saw anything unusual?"

"No. That never happened."

"Nothing further."

Jackie stood up. "Good morning, Mr. Garcia. I only have a few questions. Did the man in the alley have a gun?"

"I didn't see one."

"Was he carrying money?"

"Not that I could tell."

"Did you ever go to the police with this information?"

"No. I didn't think they wanted any new information. I heard that they already arrested somebody."

"So, you do not know if the person that you saw in the alley killed Julito, do you?"

"No. I don't know."

"Thank you. Nothing further."

CHAPTER 76

Steve leaned over and whispered to Carlos, "Are you going to testify?'

"Yeah."

"Remember what I told you about taking your time and listening?"

"Yeah."

"Okay, let's do it," he whispered. "Defendant calls the defendant to the stand." Carlos was sworn in and then sat down. "Mr. Vega, why are you here today?"

"I filed a habeas petition requesting to withdraw my plea and take my case to trial."

"And why do you want to do that?'

"Because I believe that I was pressured to take the plea offer, and I believe that my original lawyer did not do an adequate investigation into my case. If he had done an adequate investigation, he would have discovered evidence that Krystal Wiznet actually stole the money from the safe, and she would have been impeached by this evidence."

"Okay. Let's peel that onion. Tell us why you were pressured into taking the deal."

"I was guilted into it by my mom. The only way I could take the deal was to plead guilty. I was never given an alternative to a guilty plea, such as a nolo contendre plea, where I would accept the offer but not admit guilt to killing Julito. So, my only choices were to try the case and risk lifetime incarceration or plead guilty when I am innocent. I feel like there was really no choice."

"What do you mean that you were guilted into taking the deal by your mom?"

"I was in jail, and I had an offer. My lawyer was going to come to the prison and review all the evidence and my options with me. Mom showed up all of a sudden. I hadn't seen her in almost two years. She knew I was feeling guilty about how I left. She told me that she wanted to see me get out of jail and didn't want me to try the case. I felt guilty, and she knew it. She wanted me to take the offer so that she could see me walk out of jail in her lifetime. I felt like taking this deal was the only way I could make it up to her."

"Okay. Let's talk more specifically about a better investigation. What do you think an adequate investigation would have found?"

"I believe that a thorough investigation would have shown that Krystal stole the money from the safe. This would have discredited her statement that she saw me leave the bodega with a gun and a bag of money. It takes away any reason I would have to kill Julito. Julito was my friend. I had no reason to kill him. Police said that I killed him for the money so I could use it to buy drugs. Krystal stealing the money takes away that motive."

"Are you aware that if the court grants your request, you will be recharged with murder and you will have to try this case?"

"Yes."

"Do you understand that if you lose that trial, you will probably be sentenced to life in prison?"

"I understand. I am still asking the court to grant my petition. I want the opportunity to get my freedom back."

"I have nothing further, Your Honor."

Jackie Garcon sat in her chair for a moment, trying to restrain herself. When it came to inmates testifying in their cases, she loved to cross-examine them. It was like a feeding frenzy, and she was the biggest shark in the water. She slowly walked to the podium and laid out her notes, then took her time organizing them. The plan was to build tension in the inmate and increase the witness's already nervous anxiety. She has done this for years, and it always worked. "Good morning, Mr. Vega," she said, like the spider to the fly.

"Good morning," Carlos replied.

"Let's talk about how your mom guilted you into taking the plea." Jackie held up her fingers to make air quotes when she said the word guilted.

"Alright," said Carlos passively.

"Your mom guilted you into taking the deal?"

"Yes."

"Wasn't it your decision?"

"If I wanted to make up for what I did to my mother, I had to take the deal."

"Yes or no, it was your decision to take the deal?"

"I decided to please my mother."

"Yes or no?"

"Yes, I pleased my mother."

"Your Honor, I want a yes or no answer."

"Can you give her a yes or no answer?" Asked the judge.

"I did. I said yes."

Jackie looked at Carlos. "You pleaded guilty to killing Julito Hernaiz, correct?"

"I said what I had to say to take the deal."

"Yes or no, did you plead guilty to killing Julito Hernaiz?"

"I took the deal. It's in the transcript, which is in evidence."

"Your Honor, can you instruct the witness to answer yes or no, please?"

The judge looked over at Carlos and said, "Are you able to answer yes or no?"

"Sure. Yes, I took the deal. My answer includes the word yes."

"So, now you are saying you didn't kill Julito Hernaiz?"

"I never admitted to killing Julito. I just did what the state wanted me to do to take their deal. There was never an option of saying I want the deal even though I didn't kill Julito, so I took the only option offered."

"So, you admitted to killing Julito?"

"I said what the state told me to say to take the deal. I would have pleaded guilty to the Kennedy assassination if it had gotten me the deal. I said whatever the state told me to say to take the deal."

"Nothing further, Your Honor."

Judge Kopp looked at Steve. "Closing arguments, or do you want to take a break and collect your thoughts?"

"Actually," Steve said, "I would rather waive closing arguments and write a post-trial brief."

"Jackie, what do you want to do?" asked the judge.

"Whatever's clever," she replied.

"Briefs it is. How much time do you need?"

Steve and Jackie looked at each other. "How about two weeks?" Jackie asked.

"That's fine with me," Steve said.

The trial was complete. Steve talked with Carlos in the visiting room. "Carlos, what questions do you have?"

"Do you think we won?"

"I don't want to give you any false hope. Odds are overwhelmingly against you. You didn't get the judge I was hoping for. I will write a detailed brief outlining your entire case, and I will review it with you before I file it. Again, I don't want to get your hopes up."

"Carlos looked down. I know the odds. I am still hopeful."

Steve stood up and said, "I will see you in a little over a week with a draft of the brief."

"Sounds good. Thanks for all your help, Steve."

Steve smiled. "My pleasure."

END OF CONTRACT

CHAPTER 77

Summer was coming to an end. Steve had a meeting scheduled for the end of the week with Big Frank. He was finally going to learn about his options. In the meantime, Steve was spending the week preparing the final set of reports and giving Big Frank all the final updates on all the cases.

When all was said and done, Steve and Sam had completed a combined 107 trials in one year. All cases were up to date. All the paperwork was filed. In short, Steve and Sam had righted the ship, and they were back in the good graces of the public defender's office. Steve had done everything Big Frank asked of him; now it was time to see if Big Frank would keep his end of the bargain.

Steve had no more scheduled trials as he was unsure whether he would still be practicing habeas law after the end of the week. He filed his brief for the Vega case over a month ago and had been waiting for a decision ever since. He replayed the trial over and over in his head. Steve prepared himself for the worst outcome, but the question was how he would handle the inevitable when it came. And then it came.

"Steve," yelled Roxy from across the hall.

"What's up, lady?"

"It's here."

Steve knew she meant the court had faxed the decision in Carlos's case. He went downstairs to Roxy's desk. "You got it?" Steve asked.

"Yeah… it's right here," Roxy said.

"Did you read it?"

"No, but I saw that it's only three pages, so I kinda already know. I'm sorry. It's a tough break."

Steve took the decision and went into his office and closed the door. He took a deep breath and read the decision. Then he read it again, and again, and again. Steve never got over the fact that he and the firm would put in a lot of time into a trial, and the court would reduce months of work into a three-page decision that merely listed why Carlos wanted a new trial and that he did not meet the standard to get one. Of course, they would mention that Steve did not present any "credible" evidence to convince them to give Carlos a new trial.

He had to tell Carlos right away. And he needed to get the paperwork started on an appeal. Carlos wasn't like any other client. They had become friends. They had worked closely together. Aside from talking about the case, they talked to each other about their lives. They were both momma's boys; they were raised by single women who supported them in all that they did. It was odd how Carlos and Steve started on a similar path in life, though Carlos went in a different direction. Carlos could see in Steve how things could have been if he had not gotten involved in drugs. Steve saw in Carlos the reality that criminals are not that different from the rest of society. Perhaps if he had different friends or more stress as a teenager, he would be just like Carlos.

Steve sat and stared out the window and gathered his thoughts. He spent another twenty minutes getting himself prepared to devastate Carlos.

CHAPTER 78

Steve gathered his paperwork and walked across the street. He waited with the non-lawyers who were waiting to see their loved ones in jail. Steve sat silently in the corner waiting to be called.

"Vega," shouted one of the guards.

"Right here," Steve said. The guard guided Steve through the maze of corridors and locked doors until they reached legal visiting room number six. Steve walked into the room and waited for Carlos.

He looked through the window of the door, watching inmates walk by; Steve couldn't play his usual game of guess the client, as he already knew what Carlos looked like. So he just stared out the window, replaying in his head how he would approach this. Give him the bad news, let him read the decision, tell him about his options, and then say goodbye.

Carlos entered the room. "The decision came down?"

Steve said, "Have a seat. I got the decision just a few minutes ago, and I came over." Steve slid him the decision.

"It's bad?"

"Yeah. Go ahead and read the decision, and then we will talk about it."

Carlos read the decision, and then he read it again. "This sucks."

"My thoughts exactly. She does mention all the claims you are making but says that we didn't meet the standard. Doesn't really mention the facts we presented, except that she states that she did not find our witnesses credible."

"Why would she do that?"

"Well, she knows that you will appeal her decision."

"Yeah. That's how the game is played."

"So, she bases her decision on the facts that she finds. While we believe Crystal with a C, she will say that Krystal with a K was more believable. The appellate court will not question why she believes Krystal with a K more than Crystal with a C, because they did not watch her testify. Her decision is probably not going to be questioned by the appellate court."

"So, it's gonna be hard to appeal her decision?"

"It will be hard but not impossible. Professor Kent is my old law school professor. He is the best appellate attorney in the state. I asked him to take your case, and he agreed. He and his law students will review your case and give you the best appeal possible. All you have to do is sign the paperwork that I filled out, and he will begin to work on your appeal."

"Thank you. I appreciate that. What else can I do?"

"You know the drill. I'm sure Hooch, Ice, and Blade have given you the options. You can file your third habeas, you can file a sentence modification, or you can request a pardon. You might be able to file a motion for a new trial. They are all long shots. Why don't you do the appeal, and if that doesn't work out, I will be happy to try doing a sentence modification for you?"

Carlos signed the papers for the appeal, and then he stood up. Steve stood and shook his hand. Carlos hugged Steve, and then he began to cry. "You're gonna be okay, Carlos. You're gonna make it out of here. Just don't give up." Carlos composed himself and went back to his cell.

CHAPTER 79

Steve walked back to his office. He stared out the window again until he heard a knock on the door. "Come on in," Steve said.

Sam walked into the office, closed the door, and took a seat. "I heard about the Vega case. I'm sorry. Did you talk to him already?"

"Yes. He signed the appeal paperwork. I got Professor Kent to take the appeal on his behalf. He and his students will work on it and give Carlos the best appeal possible."

"Very good. How are you taking it?"

"I've had better days."

"What do you have on your plate?"

"Nothing. I finished all the reports and updates and e-mailed them to Big Frank. My case load is complete. All my files are closed out."

"When's your meeting with Big Frank?"

"Lunch on Friday, my choice."

"Typical Frank. One last thing you need to do."

"What's left?"

"Take time for yourself. You didn't take a day off this year. Use your vacation time. Why don't you go home and just think about everything? Spend a couple of days with Jenny. Go to Block Island. Then come back and meet with Big Frank."

"That sounds good. Maybe I will."

"Just do me one favor."

"What's that?"

"Think about the offer I made you. I know it's not as glamorous as anything Frank will offer. But you may realize that it fits you."

CHAPTER 80

Jenny and Steve ordered two bowls of clam chowder from Charlie at Charlie's on the Pier in Newport, Rhode Island. It was Thursday evening, and they had been on vacation since Sunday night. Steve had never been here, but Jenny told him that the cliff walk along the beach was a beautiful hike. How could Steve and Buddy resist? They had a great few days in Rhode Island, and Steve was in the moment. He did not spend his time with Jenny brooding over the Vega trial or what type of offer he would receive from Big Frank. Instead, he enjoyed his time with Jenny.

Steve and Jenny were watching the sunset while eating clam chowder on the Newport pier. The meeting with Big Frank was tomorrow. Jenny reached out and held Steve's hand and said, "Okay. I have not asked about anything work-related the past few days, but I thought you would want to talk about it. So if you want, we can talk about it. You know I'm a good listener."

"You're not a good listener. You're a great listener."

Jenny smiled. "Thank you. Now, do you want to talk? If not, that's okay, too."

"I feel like I am finally at peace with the whole thing. It feels good. The past few days have been magic." Buddy jumped up into Steve's lap. Steve held Buddy against his chest, and Buddy put his head on

Steve's shoulder and curled his neck against Steve's neck. This was Buddy's patented head hug. It was Buddy's way of saying he loved you.

"Well, you have several opportunities that you can take, including a partnership with a special firm headed by a sexy former athlete and a canine extraordinaire."

"Regardless of my decision, I plan on making that a permanent partnership."

Jenny chuckled for a moment and gave a nervous smile.

Steve pulled Buddy off him and placed him on top of the picnic table where they had set up their dinner. Steve held Jenny's hand in his hand. He got down on one knee. "No matter what decision I make tomorrow, I know that it's gonna be okay because I have you. You are the cornerstone of my life, and I want you in my life forever. I love you, and I want to spend the rest of my life with you. Will you marry me?" Steve then pulled out a box with a ring. It was a smaller diamond, because Jenny didn't like large jewelry.

Jenny didn't hesitate. "Yes." She threw her arms around him and kissed him. Buddy wanted in, and it became a group hug.

They stayed one more night at the hotel and then drove back to Hartford early in the morning.

CHAPTER 81

"Well, kid, I gotta say that this is a first. I've never done a business lunch at the Taco Factory. Most of the associates make me take them to some fancy French restaurant or spend $200 on raw fish at some sushi joint. I have to say, this is different," said Big Frank.

Steve explained, "Well, now you are on my turf. You see that picture on the wall behind you?" Frank took a look at it. "That is a picture of Eugenio Delgado. He invented Colombian coffee. Do you feel humbled?"

Big Frank started laughing his usual belly laugh. "You got balls, kid. You really do."

Steve laughed, too. Steve and Big Frank talked small talk and enjoyed their tacos. It was a new tradition at the firm to not talk business at lunch until after the meal was over.

The waitress came and cleared the table, and then she brought coffee. Big Frank looked at Steve and began his deal-making process. "So, kid, you had a hell of a year. You did everything I asked you to do. I was impressed that you completed a total of sixty-two trials this year. I don't know anyone who did sixty-two trials in one year. You have serious trial skills now."

"Thank you. That means a lot to me, especially coming from you."

"Well, kid, you've earned it. I am offering you the job of second-year associate, working in our mergers and acquisitions department. Based on the work that you have done this year, we decided to make you a second year. You will work mostly with Don Myers and his team. I may need you from time to time to do some litigation. Since you have so much experience, you can provide some help to the litigation department with depositions and maybe even some trials. Your starting salary will be $300,000 a year. You get your choice of health care plans. Your car choices are still BMW or Mercedes, but they are the lower-end models. Also, because you will be a second-year associate, we will pay for your fees to one country club of your choice. The country club comes with an obligation to attend at least half of the annual functions and mixers to develop business relationships to promote the firm." Big Frank opened his briefcase and pulled out the large envelope containing his benefits package. "You get three weeks of paid vacation and five sick days."

"What are my obligations?"

"We expect at least 2,000 billable hours every year. Of course, we're not gonna punish you if you do more." Big Frank let out another chuckle. "I like that part. So, what do you say, Steve? I'm giving you everything you asked for a year ago and more. I'm paying you like a second year, so it's like you had the job last year. I have a contract in here. All you have to do is review it and sign. What do you say, kid?"

"What else you got?"

Big Frank was stunned. "I'm not giving you more money; we have a pay scale that I can't deviate from. I can possibly consider a signing bonus, but it won't be much. That's the best I can do."

"No, I'm talking about the golden ticket."

"What?"

"A year ago, you told me that you were Willie Wonka and were willing to make a call on my behalf to anywhere I wanted. I want to hear more about that."

"Are you actually turning down a job with the firm?"

"You know, if you had offered half of this a year ago, I would have jumped at it. I would still be there today, devoting my life to the firm and producing more work than anyone else. Today, I have no interest."

"So, what happened? What made you go all soft and runny inside?"

"Well, this year was a serious eye-opener for me. A year ago, I wanted to be you—Big Frank Rockingham, the attorney and businessman. I wanted to be the guy who had the power conference room. I wanted to be you, the guy who knows everyone in corporate America, the guy who everyone listens to for legal and business advice. When I had to put that dream on hold and focus on the habeas contract, I ended up developing a life of my own. My identity wasn't Steve Lansford, the attorney and businessman. It was just Steve Lansford, regular guy with a hobby, a girlfriend, a dog, and job. So, when the habeas contract ended, it was time to return to being Steve Lansford, the attorney and businessman. But the problem is that I am not just Steve the attorney, I'm also Steve the regular guy. You see, no matter how much I want to be you, I can't be you because I'm still Steve Lansford, regular guy. And I like that. I know for a fact that I can't work for the firm and be Steve Lansford, regular guy. You and I both know that the job won't allow for that."

"I'm not gonna pressure you, kid."

"You can try. It's not gonna work."

"Is there anything I can do to talk you out of this?"

"No. I think I'm set in my position."

"Well then, what do you want me to do?"

"I want my phone call."

CHAPTER 82

Steve sat in the waiting room of the prison. It had been a week since Big Frank made the phone call on his behalf. He sat in the corner and thought about the life ahead of him, and he smiled.

"Vega," called out the prison guard. Steve was escorted through the maze of corridors and locked doors until he was told to wait in visiting room six.

Steve waited for a while. It was eight in the morning, which is usually before most inmates wake up. Carlos was no exception. Steve looked through the window in the door of visiting room six and saw Carlos walking slowly as he was trying to shake the sleep off and prepare for a legal conversation that he wasn't aware he was going to have.

Carlos walked into the room, and Steve stood up and greeted him. "Hi Steve, I didn't know we were going to meet. What's going on?"

"Hey, Carlos. I have something I need to explain to you. I need you to focus."

"Uhm… okay." Carlos sat down and faced Steve.

"Carlos, this is a weird conversation, but I'm going to explain it as best I can."

"Alright."

"A year ago, I was hired by a firm to do habeas work. If I did a good job for a year, the firm would do one of two things. They would either give me a job in the firm or they would make a phone call on my behalf to get me a job wherever I wanted. It was a great offer."

"Congrats, Steve. It's a hell of an offer. What did you take?"

"I took the phone call."

"How'd it go?" Carlos asked.

"Well, my boss knows everyone in the business world and the legal world. So he can make a lot of things happen. He's a pretty powerful guy."

"Oh yeah."

"Yeah. He's the reason Mike Munoz apologized and backed off."

"Wow."

"Anyway. Instead of having him call about a job for me, I had him make a call to the governor on your behalf. My boss got him to agree to give you a pardon."

Carlos sat in disbelief. He was stunned. Then he became angry. "Are you fucking with me?"

"No. It's true. The governor called the commissioner of the Department of Corrections last night and told him about the pardon. The documents have been signed, and the prison administration is processing you right now. You are supposed to be released tomorrow at five a.m." Steve handed him an envelope. "Here is a copy of the paperwork. It's legitimate. It's not a joke. You're not being punk'd."

Carlos began to cry. He held onto Steve and continued to cry. "So, what do I do now?"

"It's up to you, but I would call your mom and tell her to pick you up tomorrow. When you get back, your cell block counselor will tell you what I told you. You have the rest of the day to say goodbye to your friends and pack your stuff.

"Steve, how can I thank you for this?"

"You already did. I told you that you would make it out of here."

EPILOGUE

"What is it with you guys and this taco place? Is this where you have all your business meetings?" Big Frank asked Steve and Sam. This was his second trip to the Taco Factory in less than a month.

"It's a big deal for us," explained Sam.

Big Frank cleared his throat. "Okay. I'm here. Why am I listening to you and the boy wonder?"

"We have some ideas about the firm," explained Sam.

"This should be fun," Frank said sarcastically.

"Steve and I are forming a partnership."

"Are you saying that you are leaving the firm?"

"We have a series of contracts to take criminal cases through the public defender's office. We will handle criminal trials, appeals, and habeas corpus cases. Since we straightened out the contract last year, they love our productivity. We were also able to get a contract representing criminal defendants in federal court. Steve and I believe that we can build a firm on these contracts and then begin to get private cases. On the side, we would like to do car accidents and personal injury work."

"Are you going to shut down your Rockingham & Meyers Office and fire the staff?"

Steve spoke up. "We have two plans. The first plan is to maintain a relationship with your firm. Rockingham & Myers would provide us with this building rent-free. Our firm would pay for property taxes on the building. Rockingham & Meyers would pay for a modest remodel of the inside of the building. In return, the profits of this firm would be split equally between Sam, the firm, and me. Each would receive a third."

"What's this costing me?"

"Well," Steve explained, "the firm paid off the building about twenty years ago, and our firm would pay for the property taxes going forward. We would ask that your firm pay for a modest advertising budget. We'll pay for the salaries of Leon and Roxy."

"When do you think you will be profitable?"

"The contracts are already in place, and we will start work on them tomorrow. We should have income by the end of the month. Money should be flowing well the month after that. We've arranged for malpractice insurance in our own names. We are ready to go."

"What if I say no?"

"Well, that is plan B. We have a smaller office down the road lined up. We can be out of the building in a few weeks. We will build our practice on the contracts that we already have and eventually build up an advertising budget. The only real problem is that Leon will have to move out of the building's apartment in the process."

Sam cleared his throat. "As you like to say… Roll the dice and move your mice. Time to make a decision."

"I'm gonna need a moment," Big Frank said.

Steve said, "You have until you finish your taco platter to give us an answer."

"You stole my move, kid." Big Frank finished his tacos. For a guy who complained about the food, Frank finished his taco platter without a crumb on the plate. He wiped his mouth on his napkin and said, "You gotta deal. Have a tentative agreement to me by the end of the week."

"You got it," said Sam.

"I think this will work out well," Big Frank said. "You guys will run the firm. You hire who you want. You manage the employees, the accounts, and the contracts. We will help you out financially if you need help. You will give us a third of the profits."

"Sounds great," said Steve.

Big Frank reached out and shook Steve and Sam's hands. "I always thought you two worked well together. I am very proud of both of you. I truly mean that. Now, let's make some money."

www.ingramcontent.com/pod-product-compliance
Lightning Source LLC
LaVergne TN
LVHW052223200926
848481LV00001B/195
* 9 7 9 8 9 9 4 7 7 4 3 0 4 *